SKY HIGH LIVING
CONTEMPORARY HIGH-RISE APARTMENT AND MIXED-USE BUILDINGS

Published in Australia in 2002 by
The Images Publishing Group Pty Ltd
ACN 059 734 431
6 Bastow Place, Mulgrave, Victoria 3170, Australia
Telephone (61 3) 9561 5544 Facsimile (61 3) 9561 4860
E-mail: books@images.com.au
Website: www.imagespublishinggroup.com

Binder, Georges.
Sky high living: contemporary high-rise apartment and mixed-use buildings.

Bibliography.
Includes index.
ISBN 1 86470 094 7.

1. High-rise apartment buildings. 2. Tall buildings.
3. Skyscrapers. 4. Multipurpose buildings.
5. Joint occupancy of buildings. I. Title.

720.4

Coordinating Editor: Eliza Hope
Designed by The Graphic Image Studio Pty Ltd, Mulgrave, Australia
Film separations by Digital Imaging Group Pty Ltd (DIG), Port Melbourne, Australia
Printed by Everbest Printing Co. Ltd. in Hong Kong/China.

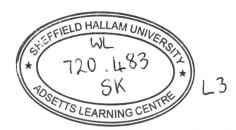

CONTENTS

CONTENTS CONTINUED

PREFACE
by Donald J. Trump

New York City always has been and will continue to be the quintessential home of sky-high living. High-rise residential towers embody the best of who we are and who we want to be.

Ever since the pyramids, humans have wanted to build to the sky. In New York City, however, the essence of sky-high living isn't about simply building to the sky—it is about inhabiting the sky. Like my latest project, Trump World Tower designed by Costas Kondylis & Partners, we build "mansions in the sky" as glass boxes suspended above the clouds and the congested metropolis below.

As the birthplace of high-rise residential design, New York City always has been and will remain the world's leader in cultivating the finest high-rise residential properties in the world.

An entirely market-driven phenomenon, the concept of high-rise residential living is being reinvented every day on a highly competitive and accelerated basis around the globe. The ability of a project's design to both "satisfy and sell" in direct response to the cultural, social, and economic conditions of any city at any given time, is the key to success for that high-rise residential property around the globe.

Whether in New York City or Hong Kong, the essential economic longevity of each project is ensured by building quality living units that represent good real estate value to the developer building it as well as to those choosing to live in it. Universal concerns of high-rise residential design addressed by developers and their architects throughout the world include placing a premium on inhabitants' access to light, view, and air.

The true variation in the global map of high-rise residential design occurs in the emphasis that is placed on the image of the building and the definition of lifestyle that it promises. Due to recent economic growth and demographic trends, Beijing, Hong Kong, Shanghai, and Singapore are building high-rise residential buildings at a more rapid rate than any other city in the world. The tall buildings in Asia, however, are still seen largely as a sensible solution for sustaining high-density development in a rapidly urbanized area. In the mature United States' high-rise residential market, however, properties such as Trump World Tower in New York City are seen as nothing less than a hallmark of 21st-century high-rise residential design, style, and luxury.

As the quality of high-rise residential living has become increasingly sophisticated, so has the marketing know-how associated with the development of each project. In New York City, the design of the typical high-rise residential project is so finely tuned to meet the needs and the aspirations of its target buyers, that developers have—at most—a six-month window of opportunity to get their product to market and sell.

Subsequently, today's developers are constantly seeking new marketing strategies to effectively position their projects in the marketplace. In New York City, two fundamental questions above and beyond the cachet of location, steer the development of the luxury residential market: namely, what creates value in real estate? And, what can be offered to justify a "luxury" price for an apartment? The three factors most commonly used to position a property in today's marketplace are: name, apartment layouts, and amenities.

Whether it is Trump Place, Trump International Hotel and Tower or Trump World Tower, I have consciously branded the Trump name. Throughout the world, buyers know that the Trump name is synonymous with the best quality, design, service, and style that luxury high-rise living has to offer.

As a result of residents currently seeking a sense of stability and permanence in their choice of home, today's greatest luxury is space. Consistent with the trend toward large gracious apartments, the pre-war style of apartment layouts is considered the most desirable. In a market where family units are in peak demand, the average luxury apartment today ranges from 2500 square feet to 4500 square feet. Whether a contemporary expression of architecture like Trump World Tower or a more traditional one like 610 Park Avenue, the classic pre-war design with its implicit adherence to a hierarchy of spaces, elegant proportions, and quality detail is widely considered today's gold standard for high-rise luxury, residential living.

The bar is consistently being raised on new amenities offered by today's high-rise residential buildings. In addition to fully equipped spas, elegant gardens, and sophisticated communication technology, a key component of New York City's luxury residential market is the new concept of "service" that I introduced to the market at Trump International Hotel and Tower. Capitalizing on the mixed-use concept, I used Trump International Hotel and Tower to create a residential model in which the hotel services such as a 24-hour concierge, gourmet food preparation, and housekeeping were made available to full-time residents. Such premium services are now becoming a staple of the luxury residential lifestyle.

Like New York City, Asian cities have seen intense competition, both internally and amongst each other, in erecting sky-high buildings. Designing such buildings in the commercial realm has been particularly important as symbols of power and prestige. This phenomenon, however, has been less relevant to recent residential development where tall building living is simply a necessity to meet market demands.

As we stand at the beginning of the new millennium, the international landscape of high-rise residential design will continue to evolve in response to new developments in technology and our choice of lifestyles. Perhaps in no other city, however, has high-rise residential design left a more indelible mark either in its spirit or its built form than in New York City, where sky-high living has become synonymous with one of the greatest urban experiences of our time.

Donald J. Trump
The Trump Organization
New York City, NY, USA

1   The Trump World Tower, New York City, NY, USA (photograph architecturalphotography.com, courtesy Costas Kondylis & Partners LLP)
2   Trump International Hotel and Tower, New York City, NY, USA (photograph courtesy The Trump Organization)
3&4   New York City skyline seen from the Trump World Tower's penthouse level (photography Michael Martin, courtesy The Trump Organization)

INTRODUCTION
by Georges Binder

1 Ritz Tower (center left), Emery Roth and Thomas Hastings, 1926 and the Galleria (center right), David Kenneth Specter, 1974, New York City, NY, USA (photography Norman McGrath/courtesy David Kenneth Specter & Associates)
2 Century Apartments, New York City, NY, USA, Office of Irwin S. Chanin, 1931 (photography Georges Binder/courtesy Buildings & Data s.a.)
3 Water Tower Place (left), Loebl Schlossman Dart and Hackl with C.F. Murphy Associates, 1976; 860–880 Lake Shore Drive Apartments (center, foreground), Ludwig Mies van der Rohe, 1951 and John Hancock Center (center), Skidmore, Owings & Merrill, 1970, Chicago, IL, USA (photography Timothy Hursley/courtesy SOM)
4 University Plaza, New York City, NY, USA, I.M. Pei & Partners, 1966 (photography Cervan Robinson/courtesy Pei Cobb Freed & Partners)
5 860–870 United Nations Plaza, New York City, NY, USA, Harrison & Abramovitz, 1966 (photography Georges Binder/courtesy Buildings & Data s.a.)
6 Marina City, Chicago, IL, USA, Bertrand Goldberg Associates, 1964 (photography Marshall Gerometta)
7 Lake Point Tower, Chicago, IL, USA, George Schipporeit and John C. Heinrich with Graham, Anderson, Probst and White, 1968 (photography Georges Binder/courtesy Buildings & Data s.a.)
8 Centre International Rogier, Brussels, Belgium, Jacques Cuisinier, 1961/demolished 2001 (photography Remy Bauters/courtesy Mrs. Madeleine Smets-Hennekinne)
9 Tour Totem, Paris, France, Andrault-Parat Architectes, 1978 (photography Georges Binder/courtesy Buildings & Data s.a.)

The tall residential architectural market has dramatically changed in the past 10 years. We are now discovering more and more super-tall residential projects, as tall as 70 or 80 stories high in North America, Asia and Oceania, but more importantly, it is the overall scale of these projects that is now reaching levels seldom seen before, even considering commercial towers. In the near future, in a series of Chinese cities there is a chance that the idea of an individual skyscraper as an architectural sculptural object may be lost in favor of multi-tower clusters of high-rise buildings. Today, projects in Hong Kong very often include a series of 50-story buildings that can include as many as 10, 20, 30, or more similar towers, and be comprised of several thousand dwellings. Europe is the only place where there is a revival, such as in the Netherlands, of what we could call the classic modernist residential high-rise: a 25- to 35-story-high tall building. However, current plans for super-tall residential or mixed-use high-rises may eventually lead at to the construction of such buildings in Europe at the end of this decade. On the "Old Continent," super-tall projects have been planned for locations in the Netherlands, the United Kingdom, and even Sweden.

The early years

The Ritz Tower (1) might well be one of the first grand skyscrapers meant for "sky-high living" when completed on Park Avenue and 57th Street in New York City in 1926. The fact that the Ritz Tower was an apartment hotel and not a pure residential building allowed for a greater height by zoning apartment building regulations. The Ritz Tower designed by Emery Roth with associate architect Thomas Hastings rose indeed to 165 meters/540 feet with its 41 luxury stories. A few city blocks away, the Art Deco buildings located on Central Park West in New York City are probably among the most well known and most beloved residential tall buildings of the pre-war era: these include the San Remo (1929) by Emery Roth, the Eldorado (1930) by Margon & Holder with Emery Roth as associate architect, the Majestic (1930), and the Century Apartments (2) (1931) by the Office of Irwin S. Chanin. These buildings created a new kind of tall living quarters and, at the same time, they created a portion of the New York City skyline that remains virtually unchanged more than 70 years later. Simultaneously, projects were erected in other parts of the world; in Buenos Aires, the 110-meter/361-foot residential Kavanagh building designed by Sanchez, Lagos and de la Torre was built in 1936—the tallest building in South America. And in France, the Tour Peret in Amiens designed by Auguste Peret was built the following decade in 1949. Although construction ceased, the project was completed in 1960.

The contemporary early years: predominantly in Chicago and New York City, followed by a series of world cities

To see the first contemporary "glass" residential buildings we had to wait until 1951: the 26-story 860–880 Lake Shore Drive Apartments (3) in Chicago designed by Ludwig Mies van der Rohe set new standards for tall residential architecture and for architecture in general, whether commercial or residential buildings, or low- or high-rise buildings. One has to note that Mies van der Rohe had already completed his first high-rise building in 1949—the 21-story concrete Promontory Apartments in Chicago.

In 1952, Frank Lloyd Wright designed the 19-story Price Company Tower for Oklahoma's Bartlesville. The concrete building with cantilevered floors remains one the few examples of a tall building having "mixed-use floors" (one-quarter residential and three-quarters office) on almost every level.

Before becoming known for their glass office towers, I. M. Pei & Partners put their mark on several tall concrete residential buildings: Kips Bay Plaza (1962) and University Plaza (4) (1966) in New York City, Society Hill (1964) in Philadelphia, as well as Century City Apartments (1965) in Los Angeles. For most of these early projects, the talent of Pei was complemented by that of the real estate mogul William Zeckendorf. In 1966, 860–870 United Nations Plaza (5) designed by Harrison & Abramovitz brought the international style to residential high-rise architecture in New York City, right next to the United Nations Headquarters. While in 1974, the four towers of Waterside designed by Davis, Brody & Associates expressed an interesting urban use for the East River riverfront. The same firm completed the Harlem River Park Towers in 1975, following a similar concept along the Harlem River.

In 1964, Bertrand Goldberg Associates designed the unique Marina City (6), an early American multi-use project encompassing the two famous 64-story twin circular towers on the Chicago River. In 1968, George Schipporeit and John C. Heinrich designed what remains today one of the most arresting tall buildings of any kind: the 883-apartment Lake Point Tower (7). Originally designed to be part of a three-tower concept, the single tower continues to remain unique in all senses of the word. The 65-story concrete tower with its undulating bronze-colored insulating glass curtain wall still has a prominent position on the Chicago waterfront, facing Lake Michigan. A couple of years later, not far away, we saw the completion of the John Hancock Center (2) in 1970 designed by Bruce Graham and Fazlur Kahn of Skidmore, Owings & Merrill. It became the tallest mixed-use project in the world and featured the highest apartments on earth on the 92nd floor. More than 30 years later, these are still the highest residential units ever built. It has been often claimed that on a cloudy day, residents have to call the concierge down below to inquire about the weather as their own windows are obstructed by clouds. In this series of 1960s' Chicago icons, we must not forget to mention the firm Harry Weese & Associates and one of his famous Chicago projects, the twin 30-story Commonwealth Fullerton Apartments built in 1973. It is also to Harry Weese that we owe the United States Courthouse Annex in downtown Chicago, built in the same year, an elegant 27-story triangular jail, which is another kind of "sky-high living" … 1974 brought to New York City one of the first major high-rise buildings to break the pattern of the typical glass box-like roof of the time: the 55-story Galleria (1) designed by David Kenneth Specter. It was also one of the first mixed-use high-rise projects built in the city. The south-facing wintergarden rooms on the odd-numbered floors are only one of the numerous features of the Galleria's very special characteristics. The four-level, 1626-square-meter/17,500-square-foot penthouse apartment, a sort of "greenhouse in the clouds," gives the building a very special identity in the skyline. The penthouse is structured to allow for landscaped terraces and garden. The Galleria is the result of a successful conjunction of public and private interests: the early 70s was one of the worst times for the New York City office market considering the office glut at the time; there was a wish from the City administration to favor a better mix of uses in the central business area and eventually a zoning regulation allowed more built space—an FAR or floor area ratio of 18 instead of 15—in return for the creation of public spaces at ground level, allowing free public access to a covered atrium arcade linking 57th Street to 58th Street. All in all, Specter, his client Madison Equities, and the different levels of authorities involved allowed the creation of a timeless, sensitive urban project.

Before the above-mentioned mixed-use giants made their mark in the United States, a project was being planned in Brussels and was completed in 1961: the 30-story Centre International Rogier (8) designed by Jacques Cuisinier was the idea of A.-W. Smets, who created one of the most extensive mixed-use projects ever built. The building, demolished at the end of 2001, was one of Europe's tallest at the time of completion. It was comprised of apartments, offices, retail, theatres, an entertainment penthouse club lounge, as well as a covered bus station, a parking garage, and an exhibition center in a adjoining lower building. Also in Brussels, near the Expo 58's Atomium,

the Cité modèle is a coherent modernist high-rise residential ensemble mainly completed in 1966 on a 18-hectare/44-acre site. The orthogonal master plan was to be become a "model" for community housing. The project, which was to also include a series of individual houses, was designed by Renaat Braem, Victor Coolens, l'Equerre, René Panis, le Groupe Structures, and Jean Van Doosselaere. The Cité modèle epitomizes the "tower in the park" concept on the Belgian scene. The master plan was also to include a series of common equipment for the community, but its implementation was neglected while the ensemble was completed. Not far away, in Antwerp, a series of residential towers were planned to be completed from the mid-50s to the early 70s by architects such as Jul De Rover, Hugo Van Kuyck, and Léon Stynen. While in 1972, in between Brussels and Antwerp, in small town Boom, R. Braem, J. Van Camp, and P. Van de Velde designed what remains one of the most isolated high-rise buildings in Belgium, the 22-story concrete Kruiskenlei residential tower, with its curved corners, is indeed the only tall building in an otherwise low-rise environment.

In Germany in Stuttgart, Salute designed by Hans Scharoun in association with Wilhelm Frank was completed in 1963 and features an unconventional plan with angular balconies in the form of open-air rooms. Salute crowns a series of earlier projects completed in Germany: in Berlin, the 18-story Unité d'Habitation by Le Corbusier in 1958 (although not really a high-rise building in its typology) and a 16-story tower block in 1960 in the Hansa Quarter by Van den Broek en Bakema, with its split-levels and public sundeck. A couple of years later in Bremen, Alvar Aalto completed the 22-story Neue Vahr building, mainly comprised of single-room studios, each with its own loggia. All levels offer a south-side corner area meant for common use, but these were hardly used as such by the occupants as originally envisioned by the architect.

Other European projects were to follow. Every major city wanted to have its series of tall residential projects, however, these very often lacked design and urban qualities. Among these projects there is a series of towers in Paris in the Quartier d'Italie, and on the Front de Seine, near the Eiffel Tower and facing the Seine River, where one project is set apart: the very articulated Tour Totem (9) completed in 1978 by Andrault-Parat Architectes. Also in Paris, next to the La Défense district, the "Tours Nuages" (Clouds Towers) series designed in the 70s (1974–8) by Emile Aillaud comprises 1600 dwellings. The 18 low- and high-rise towers—of which two reach the height of 100 meters/

328 feet—feature an interesting use of concrete structure and plans, and the façades, with their freeform windows, are among the only ones in a tall building painted in an artistic manner all the way up to the roof. A park promenade was built around the towers. Not far away, Défense 2000, completed in 1974 and designed by Proux, Demones and Strot, is, with its 46 stories, France's tallest residential tower and no new residential project is expected to break this record in the near future. Elsewhere in France, the concrete 30-story Trois Tours designed by Anger, Puccinelli, Pivot and Junillou in Grenoble became an instant landmark when completed in 1966, with its unique plan made of two triangles linked by the service core, creating a unique geometric allure. But it is probably the 1952 12-story Unité d'Habitation in Marseilles—again not really a high-rise building—designed by Le Corbusier that set up a new inventive prototype for sky-high living, and a series tall buildings were to follow in the same city in the coming years: Le Sulfur City by Devin and Bentz in 1955 and Le Brasilia designed by Fernand Boukobza in 1967.

In Spain, Madrid has the 25-story organic-like Torres Blancas—famous for its rounded terraces—completed in 1971 by architect Javier Saens de Oiza. While London in the United Kingdom has the strange Trellick Tower designed in 1968 by Ernö Goldfinger and the three 38–40-story Barbican towers, eventually completed in 1972 and designed by Chamberlin, Powell & Bon. Glasgow produced numerous tower blocks in the 60s that didn't do

7

8

9

much for architecture. In that decade, Scotland was the place where public authorities were probably developing more housing projects than in any other European country. Not to be forgotten when talking about Europe, the 1958 28-story Torre Velasca designed by B.B.P.R. that brought to Milan in Italy partly cantilevered apartments sitting on top of the building office levels, high above the heart of the city. Also in Milan, the 30-story building located on Via Vittor Pisani is a pure modernist version of the mixed-use high-rise building designed in the early 60s by Soncini & Mattioni.

In Africa, in Léopoldville (now Kinshasa, Democratic Republic of Congo), architect Claude Laurens completed two identical 60-meter/197-foot towers in 1954, each with an outside vertical circulation core. The Sabena buildings, as they were known as, were meant to accommodate the staff of the Belgian airline that eventually went bankrupt in November 2001.

In Australia, Harry Seidler is the architect of the 1961 25-story Blues Point Tower (10) in North Sydney in one of Sydney Harbour's peninsulas, with the famous bridge in the background. Seidler studied a theoretical scheme for the site that included a series of similar towers complemented with lower buildings, but none of these were ever erected. More a slab block than a tall building, we should also mention the 1962 10-story Diamond Bay Apartments in Dover Heights, erected on high rock cliffs facing Sydney's Pacific Ocean front. The result created one of the most dramatic effects of contemporary architecture in a natural environment.

10

11

In Japan, the 308,702-square-meter/ 3,322,868-square-foot Ashiyahama Seaside Town (Hyogo Prefecture) completed in 1973 is an attempt by public authorities to create a new high-rise city comprised of a series of buildings of 14 to 29 stories, providing "aerial parks" as common areas.

This short summary of early contemporary residential tall buildings would not be complete without mentioning the South American Copan apartment building in São Paulo built in 1957. This undulating 32-story S-shaped building designed by Oscar Niemeyer still stands apart on the city skyline with its horizontal brise-soleil.

Today
The Americas

Today, active markets for residential tall buildings in the United States are still in Chicago and New York City, but also in the Miami area, while in Canada it is Vancouver, followed by Toronto, which tops all other markets in the country.

Chicago and New York City are booming when it comes to residential tall buildings. Despite the expectation that architects should be able to design any kind of building, it seems that some have found a niche in the specific area of tall buildings as there appears to be several firms specializing in this building type. In Chicago, DeStefano and Partners, Lucien Lagrange Architects, and Solomon Cordwell Buenz & Associates are major players, not to mention Skidmore, Owings & Merrill, the designer of several residential and mixed-use towers in the windy city, including the recent design for Donald J. Trump of an 86-story, 343-meter/1125-foot-high mixed-use project, which should eventually become the Trump Tower Chicago on the site of the seven-story Chicago Sun-Times building, a prime location on the Chicago River.

In New York City, in the first half of the twentieth century, Rosario Candela, James E.R. Carpenter, and Emery Roth are very famous, while in the second half of the century, they were followed by architects such as Robert L. Bien, Davis, Brody & Associates, Kelly & Gruzen, the Office of Philip Birnbaum, and Samuel Paul and Seymour Jarmul. In more recent times Costas Kondylis & Partners, Schuman Lichtenstein Claman Efron Architects, and Frank Williams & Associates are among those firms that are designing a high percentage of residential tall buildings in their overall architectural production.

In Canada, an already very active firm in the 60s, is Webb Zerafa Menkès Architects (now WZMH/Webb Zerafa Menkès Housden Partnership Architects), which has designed a

Miesian-style 32-story Le Cartier luxury condominium in Montreal. Today, firms such as Architects Alliance and Busby + Associates Architects have also entered the circle of residential building creators. Some architects have, to some extent, even specialized in designing "clusters" or coherent groups of residential high-rise buildings; particular note has to be taken here of James KM Cheng Architects in Vancouver. Cheng's Quayside Marina Neighborhood (11) (1998/2002), the Palisades, and the Residences on Georgia are interesting examples of such projects.

Since the early 80s with the iconic Atlantis (1982) and the Imperial (12) (1983) in Miami designed by Arquitectonica, the area has seen many new residential projects, and in most recent years, several very tall projects have been completed on Brickell, near downtown Miami, Miami Beach, and South Beach, where over-40-story towers have been allowed. This is to the disappointment of some as it is a major break in the low- to mid-rise skyline that has been familiar in the area for decades.

A revival for mixed-used projects

There is presently a revival of mixed-use projects in New York City, including the Park Imperial/ Random House and One Central Park/AOL Time Warner Center (13), both under construction in New York City and designed by Skidmore, Owings & Merrill (SOM). Another well-known New York City mixed-use building by SOM is the 1974 Olympic Tower, co-developed on Fifth Avenue by a family trust of Aristotle Onassis. The luxury mixed-used building was taken to even taller heights—in all the senses of the word—when Donald J. Trump put his mark on Fifth Avenue in 1983 with the completion of the 58-story Trump Tower designed by Der Scutt, Partner in Charge of Design at Swanke Hayden Connell Architects. A few years later in 1987, a few blocks away on 57th Street, another developer, Harry Macklowe, created a very dominant and yet elegant triangulated sharp-edged, dark-glassed 67-story mixed-use building: the Metropolitan Tower, which obviously bears the Macklowe's design touch and was signed by Schuman Lichtenstein Claman Efron Architects. Today, other real estate players such as Millennium Partners are also developing tall mixed-use projects—mainly residential/ hospitality—in several locations including Atlanta, Boston, Miami, New York City, and San Francisco, and are all designed by Gary Edward Handel + Associates in association with other firms. On its own, Chicago continues to regularly witness the construction of very tall mixed-use buildings such as the Park Tower in 2000 by Lucien Lagrange and Associates following the trend set up by iconic projects such as Marina City (6), John Hancock Center (3), and Water Tower Place (3).

Looking further south, we note in Panama a series of residential tall buildings in Panama City. While in 1996 in Argentina, modernist Mario Roberto Alvarez y Asociados designed the 50-story Torre Le Parc in Buenos Aires, which became the tallest building in the city until recently with the construction of Torres El Faro, designed by Arquitectos Dujovne - Hirsch y Asociados.

Europe

Few residential high-rise buildings have been built in the 80s in Europe and we had to wait until the early 90s to see a revival of the European residential tall building, and for the most part, this concerns mainly the Netherlands. In Amsterdam, Neutelings Riedijk Architecten designed the 20-story Ij-toren in 1998, famous for its carved-out sections, and in 1997 atelier PRO architekten completed the Watertower Entrepôt. While in Rotterdam, de Architecten Cie designed the 102-meter/335-foot Schielandtoren (14), which ended the perspective of a pedestrian-only retail street promenade in 1996, and Wiel Arets Architect & Associates designed the 102-meter/335-foot dark twin De Hoge Heren in 2001. Also in Rotterdam, we note the cruciform Hoge Maas designed by Benthem Crouwel Architekten in 2001, while in 2006 the much-talked-about De Rotterdam designed by the Office for Metropolitan Architecture (Rem Koolhaas) will eventually be completed. The 45-story, 135,000-square-meter/1,453,140 square-foot project—located in between office towers designed by Renzo Piano and Norman Foster—will be comprised of three multi-functional towers. In Tilburg, construction has started on Westpoint (15); when completed in 2004, the 47-story building designed by Van Aken Architektuur en Stedebouw will become, at 141.5 meters/464 feet, the tallest residential project in the Netherlands. Another project may override it in a few years in the race for the highest "sky-high living" project when the Parkhaven Toren (16) designed by Kohn Pedersen Fox Associates is eventually built. The 392-meter/1286-foot, 90-story mixed-use tower may actually become the tallest building in Europe. The usual outcry heard everywhere else in Europe when a new tall building project is being unveiled is generally not found in the Netherlands, probably, in part, because tall buildings in Europe are usually seen as being unable to cope with historic urban fabrics; however, in cities such as Rotterdam, there is very little historic urban fabric remaining because

of World War II destruction. Also, as is the case in American cities, tall building construction in the Netherlands also allows secondary cities to make their mark on the map.

In Spain, several moderately tall residential projects are now under construction in Barcelona at Diagonal Mar (17), a new project developed by Hines with local partners. Diagonal Mar is a mixed-use ensemble located within a 34-hectare/80-acre landscaped site. Part of the project, Illa de Llac, is comprised of two 22-story residential towers designed by Kaufman & Meeks and Bonet, Steegman and Tiana and was completed in 2002. In the future, another eight residential towers will complement the seafront ensemble, which will also comprise of offices, hotels, a convention center, as well as a 250-store shopping mall and a 14-hectare/35-acre public park already completed. In the resort town of Benidorm—a city full of ugly concrete residential tower blocks—the 41-story Neguri Gane, with somewhat a human skeleton allure, was completed in 2001 by Pérez-Guerras Arquitectos & Ingenieros and Urbano Igaralde Telletxea, and is now the second tallest building in the city.

In the United Kingdom, London may eventually witness the rebirth of the European residential tall building in the coming years as it is presently witnessing the rebirth of the commercial tall building. Several tall mixed-use and residential buildings are currently being considered by a series of architects, including Renzo Piano Building Workshop, whose 66-story mixed-use London Bridge Tower might introduce in the future super-tall (residential) architecture to the London skyline with an over 300-meter/1000-foot-high tower. Also in London, the 49-story, 180-meter/590-foot-high Vauxhall Tower, designed by Broadway Malyan for the St. George Wharf site, might become the country's tallest residential tower if eventually built.

Up North in Malmö in Sweden, a country with few tall buildings, construction of Turning Torso is in progress. The 54-story residential tower designed by Santiago Caltrava will be comprised of nine cubical units. The entire construction turns 90 degrees as it curves upward, which explains the project's name. Also in Malmö, the Scandinavian Tower, a 325-meter/1066-foot, 85-story mixed-use tower designed by Wingårdh Arkitektkontor, is also under consideration but not yet under construction.

On the Eastern side of Europe, Moscow in Russia is the only place where residential tall buildings have recently been completed while others are under construction.

10 Blues Point Tower, North Sydney, Australia, Harry Seidler, 1961 (photograph courtesy Harry Seidler & Associates)
11 Quayside Marina Neighborhood, Vancouver, BC, Canada, James KM Cheng Architects, 1998/2002 (photography James KM Cheng/courtesy James KM Cheng Architects)
12 The Imperial, Miami, FL, USA, Arquitectonica, 1983 (photography ©Y. Futagawa/Retoria, courtesy Arquitectonica)
13 One Central Park/AOL Time Warner Center, New York City, NY, USA, Skidmore, Owings & Merrill, 2003 (digital image Archimation/SOM/courtesy SOM)
14 Schielandtoren, Rotterdam, The Netherlands, de Architecten Cie., 1995 (photography Daria Scagliola and Stijn Brakkee/courtesy de Architecten Cie.)
15 Westpoint, Tilburg, The Netherlands, Van Aken Architektuur en Stedebouw, 2004 (rendering courtesy Van Aken Architektuur en Stedebouw)
16 Parkhaven Toren, Rotterdam, The Netherlands, Kohn Pedersen Fox Associates, under study (photograph courtesy KPF)
17 Diagonal Mar, Barcelona, Spain, 2002–2005 developed in partnership by Hines (photograph courtesy Hines)

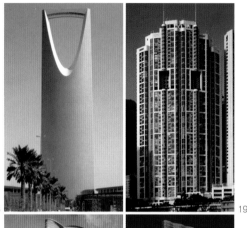
18

20

22

24

26

19

21

23

25

Middle-East

In the Middle-East, in Israel tall buildings are gradually becoming part of the daily life, and cities such as Dubai and Abu Dhabi (although the Abu Dhabi projects average no more than 18 to 20 stories) tend to see the residential tall building as a logical way to build residential projects today. In Riyadh in Saudi Arabia, a city with not many tall buildings, the extensive mixed-use 300-meter/984-foot-high Kingdom Centre (18) completed in 2002 by Ellerbe Becket and Omrania & Associates features some of the highest residences in the Middle-East, with apartments located more than 150 meters/492 feet high.

Asia and Oceania

Until 20 years ago, Asian residential tall buildings were mainly located in Hong Kong and lacked architectural design qualities—scale was an asset on its own—until the late 80s, which were eventually crowned by a series of projects, including the 1991 Queen's Garden (19) designed by P&T Group. Recently designed residential tall buildings are as tall and architecturally arresting as the commercial ones. The streamlined 73-story, 252.3-meter/-828-foot-high Highcliff (20) and the 69-story, 207-meter/679-foot-high Summit (21) designed by Dennis Lau & Ng Chun Man, the three towers forming the 74-story, 242-meter/794-foot-high HarbourSide designed by P&T Group, and other projects brought new kinds of iconic residential architecture to the Hong Kong skyline. Other projects under construction in Kowloon in Hong Kong will be taller than ever in terms of the number of levels: the three Victoria Towers designed by Rocco Design will reach 63 stories, while the tallest tower in the five-tower Sorrento project designed by Wong & Ouyang will reach 75 stories. Together with a planned 102-story, 480-meter/1575-foot-high Union Square office and hotel tower designed by Kohn Pedersen Fox Associates, some of the above-mentioned residential towers will create a coherent cluster of super-tall towers seldom seen anywhere else on earth. Actually, it will probably become the tallest residential ensemble ever built on such a large scale.

Today, mainland China is also the land of the tall residential building where individuals now have a wider access to private ownership. Shanghai's 1.6 million-square-meter/17,222,400-square-foot—and yes, that is 1.6 million—COSCO Brilliant City (22) is a huge residential project designed by East China Architectural Design Institute (ECADI), which indicates how large Chinese projects can be and how vast the Chinese needs are in terms of new residential construction. The project will be comprised of 11,000 apartments when fully completed in 2004. Other cities such as Beijing are now also favoring high-rise designs and the 150,000-square-meter/1,614,600-square-foot Sunshine 100 (23), with its bright colored façades, is designed by Denton Corker Marshall.

In Singapore, which also has a tradition of building tall, although with less density than in cities such as Hong Kong, we note several projects by Ong & Ong and DP Architects, while we could also mention the curvaceous four-leaf clover in the plan of the 34-story Draycott Tower by Timothy Seow completed in 1978, or the new 30-story twin Amaryllis Ville designed by P&T Group.

In the Philippines in Makati City in Metro Manila, the 52-story Pacific Plaza Towers designed by Arquitectonica created in 2001 is comprised of tall, undulating delights, while Architecture International made its modernist mark on several projects recently completed or under construction in Makati City and Manila: Glorietta 4, 1322 Roxas Boulevard, and One Legazpi Park. Skidmore, Owings & Merrill is also an active player in the area and their Rockwell Center (24) is a very coherent urban ensemble comprised of different buildings, forms, and heights. Each building is clearly designed and positioned on the landscaped site while taking into account the other buildings and their views. The 39-story Luna Gardens and the 46-story oval in the plan of Rizal Tower are the tallest residential buildings within the project.

In Japan today, there are several residential buildings that are even more impressive than in other countries, as in many cases they stand tall in a low-rise urban environment. For example, Kawaguchi City (Saitama Prefecture) where the 186-meter/610-foot-high, 55-story Elsa Tower 55 (25) designed in 1998 by Takenaka has become the country's tallest residential tower with 650 housing units. Elsa Tower evolves around a huge atrium comprised of several "sky pocket parks." More recently, Atago Green Hills (26) completed in 2001, brought a new kind of mixed-use development to the center of Tokyo. The 42-story project designed by Cesar Pelli & Associates is comprised of the 186-meter/610-foot-high Mori Tower, a square office building, and the 157-meter/515-foot-high Forest Tower, the residential building. They are nestled in a park-like environment as part of this ambitious urban ensemble. Mori Building Co. Ltd., the Atago Green Hills' developer, is also well known for being the developer of the 95-story Shanghai World Financial Center by architects Kohn Pedersen Fox Associates, which should eventually be completed in Shanghai in a few years.

In Seoul in South Korea, there is an emerging super-tall residential market with projects such as the 66-story Tower Palace I (27) designed by Samoo International Architects to be completed by the end 2002 and the 69-story Tower Palace III (28) designed by Skidmore, Owings & Merrill, which is currently in progress.

Finally, it is not possible to summarize a selection of Asian projects without mentioning Malaysia and a project such as the MBf Tower (29) (1993) in Penang designed by ecology-minded Ken Yeang from T. R. Hamzah & Yeang.

In Indonesia, we note the 35-story Four Seasons Towers designed by RTKL and the Golf Terraces designed by Development Design Group in Jakarta. While in Tangerang, the 52-story Amartapura Residential Palace twin towers designed by Richard Dalrymple Architect and PAI impose their strong presence on the site.

In Australia, Harry Seidler is the architect of the 1997 Horizon (30), which, in line with architectural and structural ideas drawn by the architect a couple of decades ago, also has a very "residential" flavor and iconic image. While Seidler's Cove will follow shortly, other Australian-based architects such as Nation Fender Katsalidis Architects have shown expertise in high-rise design with their 36-story Republic Tower (31) in Melbourne attracting lots of attention. This and other projects lead the now Fender Katsalidis Architects to be entrusted to design the next "tallest residential building in the world," the 91-story, 297-meter/975-foot-high Eureka Tower (32), also in Melbourne. Whilst in Surfers Paradise, Atelier SDG has designed Q1 (33), an 80-story, 320-meter/1050-foot-high condominium scheme that will be even taller than the Eureka Tower when completed in 2005. Not to forget the 75-story World Tower in Sydney by Crone Katsalidis Associates. Australia is also emerging as a country where the "sky-high living" seems to have become more and more part of the daily life in large cities.

Transformation and reuse of former commercial buildings

The residential tall building can also become a way to inject new life into an outdated commercial high-rise building. This process happened in Chicago and in New York City, among other locations: the former Bertrand Goldberg Associates' Astor Tower Hotel completed in Chicago in 1962 was transformed in 1996 by DeStefano and Partners and Donald Lee Sickler Associates into a residential tower. While in New York City, the former 1971 Gulf + Western office building was transformed by Costas Kondylis & Associates and Philip Johnson, Ritchie & Fiore Architects in 1997 into

a residential and hotel project to become the Trump International Hotel & Tower (34). In Dallas, a scheme by RTKL was studied for the transformation of the former Republic National Bank into a residential condominium. Originally designed by Harrison & Abramovitz, this aluminum-skin building was a well-known Dallas landmark when completed in 1954. Transformation of commercial buildings into residential or mixed-use buildings have also taken place in other locations of the world such as Sydney, where the former steel-framed, 21-story IBM building was transformed by Crone Associates into the 29-story Observatory Tower condominium.

27

28

29

30

18 Kingdom Centre, Riyadh, Saudi Arabia, Ellerbe Becket and Omrania & Associates, 2002 (photograph courtesy Omrania & Associates)
19 Queen's Garden, Hong Kong SAR, P.R. China, P&T Group, 1991 (photography P&T Photographic Department/courtesy P&T Group)
20 Highcliff, Hong Kong SAR, P.R. China, Dennis Lau & Ng Chun Man Architects & Engineers, 2002 (digital image courtesy Dennis Lau & Ng Chun Man)
21 The Summit, Hong Kong SAR, P.R. China, Dennis Lau & Ng Chun Man Architects & Engineers, 2002 (photography Frankie Wong & Michael Tse Photography, Hong Kong/courtesy Dennis Lau & Ng Chun Man)
22 COSCO Brilliant City, Shanghai, P.R. China, East China Architectural Design Institute (ECADI), 2001/2004 (photography Ni Yan/courtesy ECADI)
23 Sunshine 100, Beijing, P.R. China, DCM-Denton Corker Marshall, 2002/2003 (photography Georges Binder/courtesy Buildings & Data s.a.)
24 Rockwell Center, Makati City, Philippines, Skidmore, Owings & Merrill, 2000 (photography Steinkamp/Ballologg/courtesy SOM)
25 Elsa Tower 55, Kawaguchi City, Japan, Takenaka, 1998 (photography courtesy Takenaka)
26 Atago Green Hills – Mori and Forest Towers, Tokyo, Japan, Cesar Pelli & Associates, 2001 (photograph courtesy Mori Building Co. Ltd.)
27 Tower Palace I, Seoul, South Korea, Samoo International Architects, 2002 (photograph courtesy Samoo)
28 Tower Palace III, Seoul, South Korea, Skidmore, Owings & Merrill, 2004 (photography Steinkamp/Ballologg/courtesy SOM)
29 MBf Tower, Penang, Malaysia, T.R. Hamzah & Yeang, 1993 (photograph courtesy T.R. Hamzah & Yeang)
30 The Horizon, Sydney, Australia, Harry Seidler & Associates, 1997 (photography Eric Sierins/courtesy Harry Seidler & Associates)
31 Republic Tower, Melbourne, Australia, Nation Fender Katsalidis Architects, 1999 (photography John Gollings Photography/courtesy Fender Katsalidis Architects)
32 Eureka Tower, Melbourne, Australia, Fender Katsalidis Architects (digital image courtesy Fender Katsalidis Architects)
33 Q1, Surfers Paradise, Australia, Atelier SDG, 2005 (digital image courtesy Sunland Group)
34 Trump International Hotel & Tower, New York City, NY, USA, built in 1971, renovated in 1997 by Costas Kondylis & Associates and Philip Johnson, Ritchie & Fiore Architects (photograph courtesy Costas Kondylis & Partners)

31

32

33

34

Effect of daylighting and ventilation requirements upon tall building design in Hong Kong

Typical high-rise residential floor plans in Hong Kong—which can also be found in mainland China (bear in mind that China is allegedly the world's largest market for residential tall buildings)—differ widely from the rest of the other typical residential floor plans found elsewhere in the world. Indeed, Hong Kong's Building (Planning) Regulations (B(P)R), first enacted in 1956, stipulate the requirements for lighting and ventilation of different rooms found in residential buildings, namely those for habitation, preparation of food, and bathrooms and lavatories. Common staircases to multiple-occupant buildings also require natural lighting under the B(P)R.

Living rooms and bedrooms must meet the most stringent criteria and this typically affects the overall disposition and orientation of buildings.

Under the B(P)R, kitchens must face into "external air," that is, toward the outside of the building, while bathrooms must face into "open air," which can either be toward the outside or into a lightwell. The dimensions of lightwells for "open air" must increase with building height, rendering their use impractical for high-rise buildings and thus giving rise to the distinctive and highly articulated cellular "cruciform" and "trident" floor plans of most residential high-rise buildings in Hong Kong today.

Hotels, in the case of which reliable provision of adequate mechanical ventilation and lighting can be reasonably anticipated, have long enjoyed exemption from the natural lighting and ventilation requirements for bathrooms that apply to other building types. The requirements have also been commonly waived in the case of larger office buildings.

Since 1997, the Building Authority in Hong Kong has accepted proposals for new residential buildings that depart from the B(P)R by providing mechanical ventilation and artificial lighting to bathrooms and lavatories in lieu of natural lighting and ventilation. This relaxation of the B(P)R allowed by the government could have a significant effect upon plans, the variety of apartment layouts available, and upon the amount of external building envelope and concomitant long-term maintenance. So far, however, the freedom to dispense with natural lighting and ventilation to bathrooms and lavatories has not enjoyed a good response from the market and the majority of new housing being built in Hong Kong still conforms to the B(P)R.

The B(P)R have obviously induced a variety of diverse articulated (35) or cruciform plans with longer linear façades, while most of the typical floor plans in other parts of the world, such as North America (36), Europe (37), and Australia (38), are more compact-looking and often found in the more conventional shape such as square, rectangle, or circle. The worldwide residential tall building market has a strong Chinese base, and thus the "Hong Kong-type" residential tall building is probably the one that is being built the most today. The overwhelming majority of apartments in the Hong Kong territory are still provided through one type or another of cruciform tower block with eight apartments per floor in the private sector and to up to 16 per floor in the public-funded sector.

We should also note that in Hong Kong, typical usable floor area for privately developed projects is in the range of 50–60 square meters/538–646 feet for a two-bedroom unit and 60–75 square meters/646–807 feet for a three-bedroom unit.

Regarding the Building (Planning) Regulations, acknowledgement should be made to the information kindly provided by Alexander Lush, Associate at Dennis Lau & Ng Chun Man Architects & Engineers (H.K.) Ltd. in Hong Kong SAR.

Floor numbering

Eventually, there will be locations such as Hong Kong where many buildings will have floor numberings where there are no levels 4, 14, 24, 34, 44, 54, and so on, as these are unlucky numbers. The same may also apply to level 13, as for this is also considered unlucky for many North American high-rise buildings. And while the North American skyscraper starts the floor numbering with the ground level as level 1, we note that in Europe, the ground level is level 0. It means that level 1 in Europe is level 2 in North

35

35–38 The Hong Kong's Building (Planning) Regulations have obviously induced a variety of diverse articulated (35) or cruciform plans with longer façade linear while most of the typical floor plans in other parts of the world such as North America (36), Europe (37), and Australia (38) are more compact looking and often found in the more conventional shape such as square, rectangle, or circle.

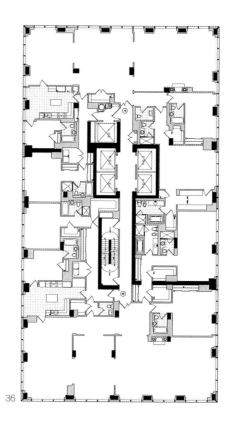

36

America. The mix of data from projects from around the world in a single publication can become a little confusing when compared, therefore discrepancies may occur in the numbering of levels as compared to other sources.

Conclusions

The residential tall building used to be an American and a Hong Kong product only and as tall as 20 to 40 stories high. It now tends to be as tall as the new commercial high-rise buildings and is now found in many other parts of the world. Fifty- to 60-story residential projects are now very common and 2001 even witnessed the completion of the new "world's tallest residential only building" to date in New York City: the 262-meter/860-foot, 72-story Trump World Tower designed by Costas Kondylis & Partners.

Booming cities in North America are Chicago, Miami/Miami Beach, and of course New York City. Also in New York City, we are now witnessing a revival for mixed-use high-rise projects previously mainly seen in Chicago. Other American cities are also introducing mixed-use tall buildings, while a few limited examples are located elsewhere in the world.

In some instances, the residential tall building has injected new life into an outdated commercial high-rise building. Such successful schemes have been completed in recent years in large cities including Chicago, Melbourne, New York City, and Sydney.

In Europe, the Netherlands easily beats the "Old Continent" in terms of residential tall buildings, and since the commercial tall building market is as active today in the region as it was in the 60s and the 70s, then one has to admit that the Netherlands is the only European country to really favor—both from a commercial and political standpoint—the "sky-high living" way of living. While a 30-story building is still considered very tall when it comes to residential buildings in Europe, the future might witness an emerging market for tall residential buildings in the United Kingdom—mainly in London—if the tall buildings currently being designed are eventually built.

The Middle-East favors more and more tall residential buildings in locations such as Abu Dhabi, Dubai, and Tel Aviv, just to name a few.

In Asia, Hong Kong continues to be the "sky-high living" Mecca, while major mainland Chinese cities are rapidly following the same approach. Slowly but surely, Hong Kong is reaching heights—60 or 70 stories are now common and 80-story projects are under construction—for living quarters previously only envisioned on such a large scale in science fiction novels and movies.

Finally, Australia, in locations such as Melbourne, Surfers Paradise and Sydney, has seen in recent years more and more residential tall buildings as a common way of living with the next world's tallest residential buildings already under construction.

A major difference between Asia and the rest of the world is the density introduced into the city by super-tall residential high-rise buildings. And if the FAR (floor area ratio) could be less important in many Hong Kong projects than it is in Chicago or New York City projects, the effect of so many projects being built simultaneously in an already very dense area is unmatched anywhere else. Unmatched anywhere else, but watch out, mainland China, in locations such as Beijing or Shanghai, will change tremendously in the years to come.

The much taller and more dramatic designs of the tall residential high-rise projects we now experience on a daily basis have, to some extent, caused the typical residential character and flavor of these buildings to disappear—for example, balconies are often no longer part of recent projects—in favor of a much more iconic-style of architecture, previously seen mainly in commercial tall buildings.

In terms of skyscrapers, or even in terms of architecture in general, the twentieth century was the century of the commercial skyscraper. The twenty-first century may well become the century of the residential skyscraper and "sky-high living" a way of life for many.

Georges Binder
Buildings & Data s.a.
Brussels, Belgium

37

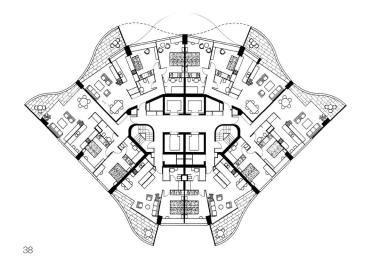

38

35   Olympic City, Hong Kong SAR, P.R. China, P&T Group, 2000 (plan courtesy P&T Group)
36   The Trump World Tower, New York City, USA, Costas Kondylis & Partners, 2001 (plan courtesy Costas Kondylis & Partners)
37   Weenatoren, Rotterdam, The Netherlands, Klunder Architecten, 1990 (plan courtesy Klunder Architecten)
38   Horizon, Sydney, Australia, Harry Seidler & Associates, 1997 (plan courtesy Harry Seidler & Associates)

CONTEMPORARY BUILDINGS
1960-1989

Centre International Rogier (also known as Tour Martini)

110 m/361 ft
30 stories
Offices, residential, theaters, retail,
penthouse Martini Club
1961 (demolished in 2001)

Brussels, Belgium
Jacques Cuisinier

Almost a decade before the completion of the multi-use John Hancock Center in Chicago, Brussels had its own high-rise multi-use project already completed in 1961: the Centre International Rogier (also known as Tour Martini). The 30-story concrete structure was comprised of 85 retail shops at ground level, two theatres, offices, 155 apartment units, an entertainment club as well as public garage, a covered bus station, and an exhibition center in a adjoining eight-story building at the back of the tower. The project, designed by Jacques Cuisinier and developed and built by A.-W. Smets from Lotimo s.a., was so innovative in terms of mixed-use intricacy, few high-rise projects in the world ever reached such a high number of purposes. Astonishing as it may sound, the project was financed by Lotimo s.a. without any bank loan, only by selling one floor at a time as they were completed, one by one.

The top three levels of the 110-meter/361-foot-high building, which are made of a steel structure, offered high-end meeting and gathering rooms known as the Martini Club. The Martini Club was reached by a 5.5-meter/18-foot per second elevator.

A Brussels 1960s' icon, the Centre International Rogier has lost its magic over the years and began to fade less than 20 years after its completion as the future of Brussels did not lie in high-rise residential mixed-use projects.

The project was the tallest building in Belgium when completed and one of the first to reach 30 levels in Europe. At the end of 2001, it became the tallest Belgian building ever to be demolished. Soon, a new high-rise office building will be erected in its place, as presently there is no market in Brussels for either residential or mixed-use tall buildings.

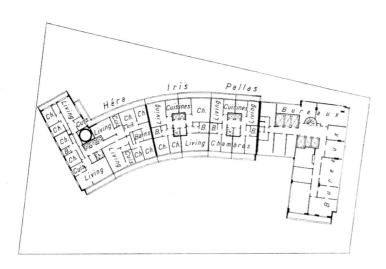

right   Main elevation seen from Place Rogier
top left   Construction site in March 1960 seen from the Botanical Garden
above   Typical floor plan
photography   Remy Bauters / courtesy Madeleine Smets-Hennekinne;
              La Technique des Travaux / courtesy G. Binder/Buildings & Data s.a.
              (Floor plan)

Astor Tower

91 m/300 ft
28 stories
Residential
1962/1996

Chicago, Illinois, USA

Bertrand Goldberg Associates (1962); DeStefano and Partners, Ltd. (1996); Donald Lee Sickler Associates (1996)

DeStefano and Partners, with associate architect Donald Lee Sickler Associates of Baltimore, Maryland, was selected by Astor Tower Condominium Association to design and implement an all-new exterior envelope for this 28-story, 91-meter/300-foot tower on Chicago's near north side. To replace the original 1962 single-glazed exterior wall system, DeStefano and Partners developed a new structural double-glazed steel wall section using low-e glass for exterior application in four-window sections. After erection, the existing non-performing wall was removed in pieces from the inside. Owners were never exposed to the elements, and the fully occupied tower was returned to as-new 1996 quality with only minimal disturbance.

Astor Tower was originally designed as a hotel by the late Bertrand Goldberg, and was constructed in the same period as Goldberg's more well-known Marina City. Because Astor Tower is now in the Astor Street landmark district, the DeStefano and Partners revitalization was subject to City of Chicago landmarks review and approval.

The new exterior, a minimalist envelope, which respects the modernist aesthetic of the original while providing state-of-the-art performance, comfort, and durability, received a 1997 *Distinguished Building Award* from the American Institute of Architects' Chicago Chapter.

above & top right   Astor Tower
photography   Hedrich-Blessing
right   Astor Tower before renovation
photography   Leslie Schwartz Photography

University Plaza

84 m/275.5 ft | New York, New York, USA
30 stories | I. M. Pei & Partners Architects and Planners
Residential
1966

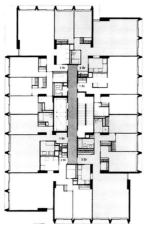

University Plaza consists of a 30-story residential complex comprising two towers for NYU graduate students/faculty, one middle-income co-op apartment tower, public sculpture court, and parking.

This three-tower project was undertaken to relieve NYU's housing shortage in its transition from commuter college to residential university. The city transferred the urban renewal site to the university provided that one third be reserved for Mitchell-Lama moderate-income cooperatives.

The sheer size of the 534-apartment project precluded integration with low-rise Greenwich Village, and thus tall, slender shafts were designed in counterpoint. Each has a pinwheel plan with solid sheer walls and skeletal grids extending out from a central core to break the tower masses into smaller, vertical elements. Interiors vary, but externally the towers are identical,

unified by architectural concrete that was poured in-place in reusable fiberglass forms to yield the greatest possibilities within the very low budget mandated. The resultant grids identify the "spatial packages" inside, the depth of a standard apartment defined by the sheer walls' 6.7-meter/22-foot expanse.

At ground level the towers are directional. NYU's two buildings lead onto a landscaped plaza while the co-ops open onto their own mews. Orientation notwithstanding, the towers collectively define a central urban space dominated by a sand-blasted concrete bust of Sylvette—Picasso's second major public work in the United States and the first of its kind in the western hemisphere. The sculpture's installation at NYU (atop the project's underground garage) serves the public, art and education alike.

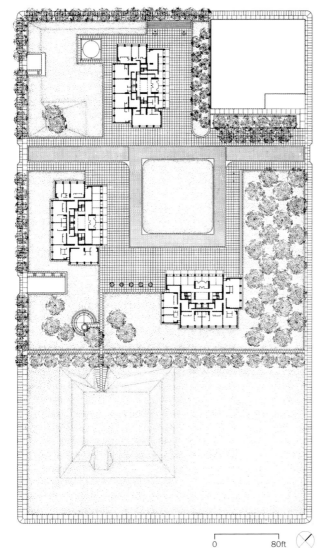

0   80ft

top left   Typical floor plan
above   Site plan
right   The towers were designed in counterpoint
to low-rise Greenwich Village, view to east
photography   Cervan Robinson

John Hancock Center

344 m/1127 ft | Chicago, Illinois, USA

100 stories | Skidmore, Owings & Merrill LLP

Retail, offices, residential, observatory

1970

The John Hancock Center is a 260,000-square-meter/ 2.8-million-square-foot multi-use complex and is the highest residential building in the world. The 100-story tower tapers from bottom to top to meet the different floor space requirements of various tenants. Commercial spaces, including 27,800 square meters/300,000 square feet of entrance lobbies, occupy the base of the tower. The complex also contains 75,400 square meters/812,00 square feet of office space and 711 apartment units, ranging from efficiencies to four-bedroom luxury residences. Additional facilities include restaurants, health clubs, retail facilities, a swimming pool, and ice-skating rink as well as a transmitter for Chicago's major radio and television stations.

The tower's exterior columns and spandrel beams create a steel tube that is reinforced by the clearly articulated diagonal members and structural floors that meet those diagonals and corner columns. No high-strength steel was used, allowing less than 30 pounds of steel to support each square foot of floor area. The total result is a simple and highly efficient system for a structure of this height.

top left   The tower is tapered from bottom to top in keeping with the programmatic requirements of the building. Structurally, the exterior members of the steel frame represent a stiffened tube.

photography   Timothy Hursley

above   "Sky" lobby on the transit floor between offices and apartments

photography   Hedrich-Blessing

right   Overall view from southeast

photography   Timothy Hursley

Galleria

155 m/510 ft
55 stories
Residential, offices, retail, health clubs, restaurants, public space
1974

New York, New York, USA
David Kenneth Specter

22

One of the first two buildings in New York City to take advantage of new "covered pedestrian space" incentive zoning legislation, which gave developers financial advantages in exchange for creating public space, this 55-story mixed-use structure was the tallest reinforced concrete building at the time of its completion.

The lower third of the building includes a public "street" connecting 57th and 58th streets, just east of Park Avenue, multiple parking levels, retail stores, an interior sidewalk café, 10 levels of office space, and a three-level health club with restaurants, private dining rooms, swimming pool, sundeck, and fitness center. The upper two-thirds of the building consists of 252 condominium apartments (whose typical floor plan was designed by architect Philip Birnbaum), a terraced tenant lounge space, three duplex units, and a quadruplex penthouse apartment also designed by David Kenneth Specter.

The commercial and residential entrance areas at or near street level are visually connected and both energize—during a significant part of the 24-hour cycle—the 30-meter/100-foot-high skylit atrium, which is the focus of the public "street" that passes through the site. The Galleria received the *Concrete Industry Board Award of Merit* and the *Design & Environment Award of Excellence*.

below   Skylit atrium
bottom left Typical residential floor plan with wintergardens on odd numbered floors (21–47)
below right Overall view from the southeast
photography Norman McGrath

Four Leaf Towers

134 m/439 ft
40 stories
Residential
1982

Houston, Texas, USA

Cesar Pelli & Associates Inc.; Albert C.Martin & Associates; Melton Henry/Architects

The two 40-story towers contain 400 residential units with four two-story penthouses. The twin towers are topped with truncated, pyramidal roofs that contain two-story penthouses with open corner terraces. The rich colors of the façade are interwoven to create a shiny, textural pattern. These reddish tints belong to the brick and terra cotta of the surrounding neighborhood. A formal garden with a lawn, shallow pools, paths, and flowering shrubs connects the two towers.

The curtain wall is tinted vision glass with three colors of ceramic glass supported by a fixed fluoropolymer painted aluminum frame. Each building has a flat-slab, reinforced concrete structural system.

Special features of the 3.8-hectare/9.3-acre site include a swimming pool, tennis courts, gymnasium, saunas, and landscaped gardens, with parking for 700 cars below grade and surface parking for another 70 cars.

below   Site plan
right   View looking east
bottom left   Typical penthouse floor plan
bottom right   Curtain wall details
photography   Balthazar Korab

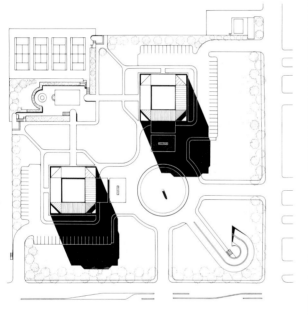

The Atlantis

53.94 m/177 ft
20 stories
Residential
1982

Miami, Florida, USA
Arquitectonica

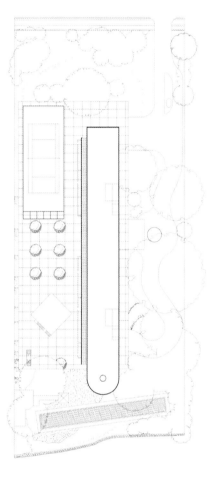

The Atlantis is a 96-unit condominium apartment building on Biscayne Bay south of downtown Miami. This building, more than any other, calls attention to the provocative, photographic nature of Arquitectonica's work. The Atlantis is a 20-story slab building with a 11-meter/37-foot-long cube cut out of the center to create the "sky court" for building residents. The sky court has three elements: a whirlpool, a red spiral staircase, and a palm tree, all set along the waving yellow wall.

The Atlantis is sited perpendicular to the waterfront so that it can easily be seen both from Brickell Avenue and from nearby Interstate-95. Its imagery is simple and powerful. On the south side of the building the glass wall is covered by a three-story blue masonry grid—a brise-soleil that hides cantilevered balconies.

The north face is covered in gray reflective glass punctuated by four yellow triangular balconies. The end of the building facing the bay is shaped as a nautical curve, creating living rooms with 180-degree panoramic views. On the other end, facing the city, a red masonry triangle on the rooftop conceals the mechanical equipment and provides an urban form.

The long, slender building—it is 91 meters/300 feet long but only 11 meters/37 feet wide—has just six apartments per floor and two elevator cores. The apartments at the base are two-story duplexes with double-high living rooms and private courtyards. The Atlantis won a *Progressive Architecture* award in 1980 and judge Frank Gehry praised it for its sculptural quality and surrealistic imagery.

left   Site plan
right   The end of the building facing the bay is shaped as a nautical curve, creating living rooms with 180-degree panoramic views
below The Atlantis is a 20-story slab building with a 11-meter/37-foot-long cube cut out of the center to create the "sky court" for building residents
photography Norman McGrath

Kanchanjunga Apartments

84 m/276 ft
27 stories
Residential
1983

Bombay, Maharashtra, India
Charles Correa Architects/Planners

In Bombay a building has to be oriented east–west to catch the prevailing sea breezes, and to open up the best views in the city: the Arabian Sea on one side and the harbor on the other. But these unfortunately are also the directions of the hot sun and the heavy monsoon rains. The old bungalows solved these problems by wrapping a protective layer of verandahs around the main living areas, thus providing the occupants with two lines of defence against the elements.

Kanchanjunga, an attempt to apply these principles to a high-rise building, is a condominium of 32 luxury apartments of four different types, varying from three to six bedrooms each. The interlocking of these variations is expressed externally by the shear end walls that hold up the cantilevers. The tower has a proportion of 1:4 (being 21 square meters/226 square feet and 84 meters/276 feet high). Its minimalist, unbroken surfaces are cut away to open up the double-height terrace gardens at the corners, thus revealing (through the interlocking form and color) some hint of the complex spatial organization of living spaces that lie within the tower.

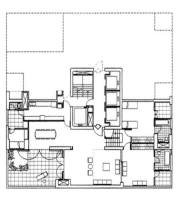

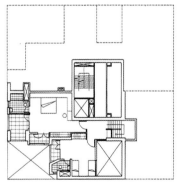

top left   Portion of façade facing Bombay Harbour to the east
photography   Charles Correa
above left   Four-bedroom unit: entrance level
above right   Four-bedroom unit: upper level
right   Terrace gardens in the sky
photography   Salil Simon

Trump Tower

202 m/664 ft
58 stories
Retail, commercial offices, residential
1983

New York, New York, USA

Swanke Hayden Connell Architects (Architect of Record);
Richard Seth Hayden, FAIA, RIBA (Principal in Charge of the Project);
Der Scutt (Partner in Charge of Architectural Design)

Trump Tower, a 58 story mixed-used building, located on Fifth Avenue and 56th Street in Manhattan, is frequently described as the world's most-talked-about address. At 202 meters/664 feet, Trump Tower was the tallest concrete building in New York City at the time of completion. The building is noted for its 263 luxury condominium apartments, its 13 stories of offices, and a monumental six-story, skylight-covered atrium around which 50 of the world's most luxurious shops are located.

Donald J. Trump mandated his desire for a unique and exciting building solution that would not only complement Fifth Avenue, but would provide a significant architectural statement of the urban fabric and skyline of New York.

The form of the building evolved from a direct response to the urban context of the site. Its plan respects the influences of neighboring structures. The northeast side of the tower is shaped to complement the former IBM Building adjacent to it. The sawtooth faceting of the tower mass denotes a residential

character of the building and provides two different views from every room of the condominiums—each with walls of floor-to-ceiling glass.

The exterior of the building is clad in a warm bronze reflective mirror glass. The fragmenting of the tower façade enhances the mass giving it strong vertical emphasis. The sculptured form also provides a dramatic architectonic cascading set of terraces, which can be landscaped for use by office tenants.

Trump Tower has approximately 9290 square meters/100,000 square feet of retail space; 14,864 square meters/160,000 square feet of commercial space; and a gross building area of 70,453 square meters/758,376 square feet. Built on a relatively small lot parcel of 0.3 hectares/0.8 acres of 3265 square meters/35,145 square feet, the 58-story building is the successful result of one of the most complex zoning packages ever undertaken in New York City.

below   Retail atrium
photography   Jamie Ardiles-Arce
bottom left   Lobby level/1 floor plan
bottom right   Exterior

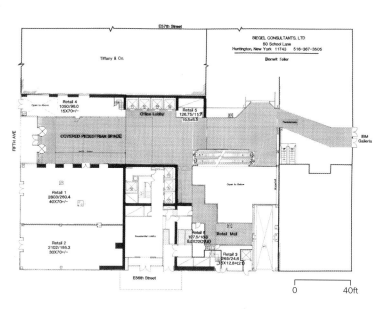

388 Market Street

114 m/375 ft | San Francisco, California, USA
26 stories | Skidmore, Owings & Merrill LLP
Residential, commercial offices, retail
1985

Programming for 388 Market Street called for a mixed-use development containing 8454 square meters/91,000 square feet of housing, 883 square meters/9500 square feet of retail space, 2694 square meters/29,000 square feet of parking, and 22,714 square meters/244,500 square feet of office space. The 1672-square-meter/18,000-square-foot site is the smallest of the triangular blocks created by the 36-degree intersection of two street grids in the heart of San Francisco's financial district. The building generated by this unusual and prominent site takes on a shape reminiscent of Market Street's traditional "flat-iron" buildings. The plan form of the tower literally expresses the pivotal position the building occupies in the city grid, while at the same time making reference to its much larger neighbor, the cylindrical 101 California Street building.

Executed in polished Imperial red granite and clear glass, the building is sculpted in a manner that expresses its geometric components (circle and triangle) as well as its functional components (retail, office, and housing). Utilizing the entire triangular site, the lowest two floors are designed for retail shops. Together, these floors form a 12-meter/40-foot-high formal base that is in scale with the width of Market Street and that aligns with the bases of three historic buildings facing the site from the opposite side of the street. A two-story public gallery bisects the base to connect Pine and Market Streets and serves as separate lobbies for office, housing, garage, and retail spaces.

top left   Ground-floor lobby east
above   Rounded southern corner at Market and Front streets
right   South-facing view at the intersection of Pine and market streets
photography   Jane Lidz

Tung Wang Palace

65 m/213 ft
18/19 stories
Residential
1985

Taipei, Taiwan

C.Y. Lee & Partners

The plan of this project is to provide residences for mainly medium- and high-income earners. The major challenge in the design was to create both a traditional and modern "Chinese Urban Compound Residence" in an urban center. In the past, it was assumed Chinese architecture could only develop in a horizontal manner rather than in a vertical manner. This building, with an L-shape, attempts to break this assumption, and to set up a high-rise residential building façade with a Chinese character and, by means of a varying roof skyline, to add some fun to the urban landscape.

According to such a concept, in the building façade and space arrangement, Chinese-style architecture idioms are adopted as much as possible; including red tile, red brick, cross application

of corridor and pagoda, aerial garden, and the large Chinese-style garden on the first floor. It is hoped that in the mobilization line and façade arrangement, the intent of a Chinese "recreation" garden is created, facilitating every angle in each space to be perceptive and fun. More importantly, an attempt was made to produce a city index with great Chinese architecture idioms within the city.

The roof is formed by an interactive composition of corridors and pagodas based on the rise and fall of the mountain ridges in Chinese landscape paintings, which adds unexpected fun to the skyline in the city. A roof garden for each household further provides joy to each residence and creates a sense of a garden platform.

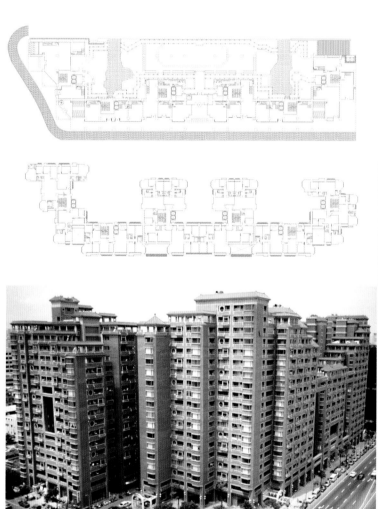

top left   Ground floor plan
middle left   Typical floor plan
above   Corner view from major 2 street
right   Building façade

100 United Nations Plaza Tower

176 m/578 ft
55 stories
Commercial, residential
1986

New York, New York, USA

Der Scutt Architect (Design Architect) Schuman, Lichtenstein, Claman & Efron (Architect of Record—base building)

100 United Nations Plaza Tower is located in an international landmark environment and is a distinctive residential condominium.

The tall tower overlooks the formal gardens and the flags of the nations. Breathtaking views of the East River and Beekman Place, also to the east, enhance the vista from all the easterly apartments. To the west, the glorious New York skyline of midtown Manhattan is unequalled in its exciting profile. The elegant drive-in port cochere entrance to the lobby adjoins a multilevel 929-square-meter/10,000-square-foot landscaped garden.

The tower's architecture is special and distinctively different. The tall slender proportions of the building are reminiscent of the United Nations Tower itself. The south façade includes an added amenity of elegant triangular balconies, which contribute to the residential spirit of the building. The large windows give the building's external appearance a sense of order while maximizing the views for the occupants. Full-width terraces provide an environment for sunlight and shade.

Perhaps the most remarkable characteristic of the 100 United Nations Plaza Tower's architecture is the distinctive top. A pyramid of terraced penthouses crowns the building. The architectural form creates a special kind of vitality for a rich living experience. The shape gives the building an immediate symbolic, identifiable image. The penthouse residence is at once artful and classic. For those choosing to live high in the sky, an exhilarating experience flourishes with the architectonic invention. These penthouse apartments realize considerable added sales revenues to the project developer.

The lobby was designed with rich materials including fabric, bronze, marble, and wood. Furnishings in the contemporary classic mode welcome the residents with splendor.

The project was a successful collaboration between Der Scutt Architect (the design architect) and Schuman, Lichtenstein, Claman & Efron, Architects (the base building architect of record).

below | Exterior—two views
photography | Der Scutt
below right | Color rendering (exterior)
photography | Richard Baehr
bottom left | Typical floor plan

Olympia Centre

219 m/720 ft
63 stories
Residential, offices, retail
1986

Chicago, Illinois, USA

Skidmore, Owings & Merrill LLP

Olympia Centre is a major multi-use addition to Chicago's Magnificent Mile. Sixty-three stories and 219 meters/720 feet high, the 132,000-square-meter/1,420,000-square-foot building includes 204 luxury condominiums, 30,400 square meters/ 327,000 square feet of rental office space, a four-story Neiman Marcus Department Store, and a three-and-a-half-level basement parking garage. For the development, SOM provided architectural and engineering services as well as condominium and public interiors design.

The 5000-square-meter/53,338-square-foot site is located on the east side of Michigan Avenue between Superior Street and Chicago Avenue and wraps around the 777 Michigan Avenue Building. The site has approximately 37 meters/121 feet of frontage on Michigan Avenue, 72 meters/235 feet on Superior Street, and 54 meters/175 feet on Chicago Avenue.

The building's massing combines low-rise and high-rise portions with a major tower located on Chicago Avenue. By adopting this resolution, the building's design preserves the low-to-middle rise character of Michigan Avenue and Superior Street, reinforces the open space edge already existing along Chicago Avenue,

provides better views for the condominiums due to their location in the upper half of the tower, and allows the department store more freedom in structure and in layout.

A major feature of the tower design is the integration of clear-span office space with an economical condominium structure. This is accomplished by maintaining a constant width of core structure while reducing the lease-spans beyond the core in the office portion in a smoothly curved and continuous exterior slope to the narrower width appropriate to the condominiums above. The tower structure combines a reinforced concrete exterior tube with conventionally reinforced concrete flat-slab floors in the condominiums, and a joist-slab floor system in the office, department store, and parking garage portions. The low-rise structure is framed in steel above grade and concrete below. On the fifth level, a central mechanical room includes a combined refrigeration plant for all uses with separate central fan systems for the office and department store areas. The condominiums are conditioned by individual fan coil units located within each unit. The project is completely sprinklered, and the combination office and condominium service elevator has stops at all levels to function as a firefighter's elevator.

below & below left   204 condominium units take up the top 39 floors of the tower; condominium amenities, such as a lounge, party rooms and catering kitchen, swimming pool, locker rooms, exercise room, and a racquetball court, are provided at level 24

bottom right   The building's inventive massing combines low- and high-rise portions with a large tower to preserve the character of the street it fronts

photography   Hedrich-Blessing

The Park Belvedere

112.8 m/370 ft
35 stories
Residential, retail
1986

New York, New York, USA

Frank Williams & Partners, Architects

This 35-story residential tower rises at the corner of Columbus Avenue and 79th Street, opposite the Museum of Natural History and the museum's Theodore Roosevelt Park. The Park Belvedere has unobstructed views of Central Park because of its relationship with the low-rise Museum of Natural History as well as one of Manhattan's great residential streets, Central Park West. The Park Belvedere's silhouette has been designed to recall the romantic profiles of the Central Park West skyline, landmark towers such as The San Remo, The Beresford, The Century, and The Majaestic.

The building's 46-meter/150-foot granite and masonry street wall allows it to blend in with its 14-story neighbors. The architects designed a trellised setback at the first tower floor to help preserve the existing scale of the new building with existing buildings. Also, the tower is similar in height to the buildings along Central Park West. The rose-colored masonry tower incorporates punched windows and the corners of the entire building all have corner windows that open up magnificent views of the new Rose Museum, as well as unparalleled views of Central Park.

A variety of residences are provided within the building. There are 155 apartments housed within this tower: 75 80-square-meter/850-square-foot, three-bedroom apartments; 68 130-square-meter/1400-square-foot, two-bedroom apartments; and 12 149-square-meter/1600-square-foot, three-bedroom apartments. The smaller apartments are located at the base of the tower. Almost all of the apartments face south or east, toward Central Park. They all feature well-equipped kitchens, handsome cabinetry, washers and dryers, large picture windows, and walk-in closets. A series of setbacks at the penthouse levels provides each penthouse with a spacious wrap-around terrace. These apartments also feature 4-meter/12-foot ceilings and fireplaces.

The residential entrance is on West 79th Street, while Columbus Avenue has strong retail continuity. There is a community facility doctor's office on the far westerly edge of the West 79th Street frontage.

above   View of the residential tower, looking through the new Planetarium at the Museum of National History
right   Floor plan, upper level residences
bottom left   Floor plan, lower level residences
bottom right   The residential tower as it faces Central Park and overlooking the park behind American Museum of Natural History
photography   Robert Cameron/Cameron & Co.; Veronica Garaycochea-Williams; Wolfgang Hoyt/Esto; Mohamed Yakub

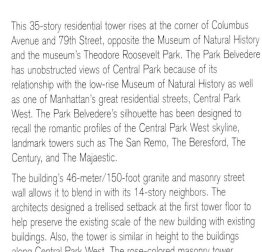

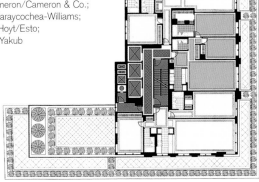

279 Central Park West

New York, New York, USA

Costas Kondylis & Partners LLP (formerly Costas Kondylis & Associates PC)

279 Central Park West is a 23-story mixed-use residential/community facility building containing residential stories with approximately 38 residential units, a professional unit on a portion of the ground floor, a school unit (part of the Waldon School) on a portion of the sub-cellar through fourth floors, and a garage unit in a portion of the sub-cellar of the building.

The building's arched Central Park West entranceway leads into a lobby of approximately 84 square meters/900 square feet.

Recreational areas consist of indoor and outdoor areas of approximately 121 square meters/1300 square feet located on a portion of the fifth floor and include a children's play area, an exercise area, and a landscaped outdoor recreation area.

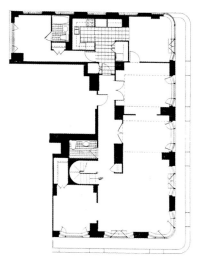

above   Three-quarter view
top left   View from street
left   Penthouse 3A (lower duplex) plan, 19th floor
photography Architecturalphotography.com

The Corinthian

166 m/546 ft

New York, New York, USA

55 stories

Der Scutt Architect (Design Architect); Michael Schimenti, P.C. (Production Architect)

Recreation/health club, commercial
offices, residential

1988

Der Scutt was commissioned in March 1985 to create the design concept for the mixed-use developments at the site of the old East Side Airlines Terminal building in New York.

The 55-story project is in excess of 92,900 square meters/ 1 million square feet, which includes 865 luxury condominiums and approximately 7432 square meters/80,000 square feet of commercial space.

A unique feature of the architectural concept is the semi-circular bay window in every living room, which provides for magnificent

panoramic views of the Manhattan skyline from inside the apartment while creating an unusual sculptural mass, which heightens the visual drama of the building. The Corinthian is an enormous structure and this sculptural effect diminishes the bulk visually.

The basic massing of the tower initially is curved so as to take advantage of views from various locations in the tower, and at the same time position the maximum number of apartments away from adjacent taller buildings.

below   Site plan
below right   Exterior
bottom left   Lobby
photography   © Peter Mauss/Esto.

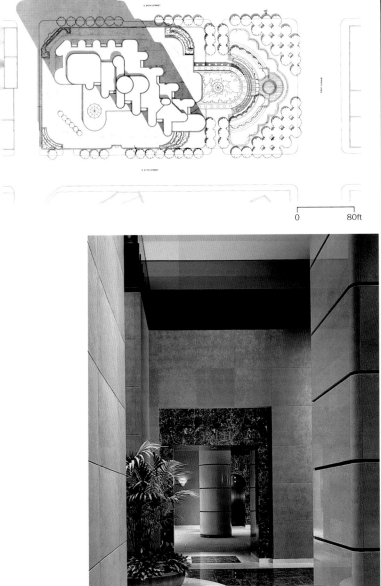

CitySpire

248 m/814 ft
72 stories
Residential, offices, retail
1989

New York, New York, USA

Murphy/Jahn, Inc. Architects

Situated at the northern edge of New York City's historical Broadway theater district, CitySpire is one of Manhattan's tallest and most prominent residential/mixed-use towers.

Envisioned as a return to the romantic image of the skyscraper, the formal concept of the CitySpire tower arose from both a concern for contextual appropriateness (that is, the adjacent theater and buildings lining Central Park) and a pragmatic solution to the exacting criterion of midtown Manhattan's zoning resolution.

Careful attention to scale and materials at the tower's base attempts to relate the 56th Street façade to its existing neighbor. Rising out of this contextually responsive base in a series of three setbacks is a stone-clad octagon shaft with lateral wings of glass projecting to the east and west. These wings ultimately terminate

at the 61st floor releasing a 24-meter/80-foot diameter omnidirectional tower with copper dome into the skyline.

The incremental transformation of the lower street wall into a central shaft with wings and finally a solitary tower was inspired by the stringent height and setback regulations described by the zoning ordinance. In this way, the architectural form not only attends to the issue of contextual decorum, but also respects the practical requirements of light and air to the urban environs.

But far beyond the prosaic rigors of economics and zoning compliance, the idea and image of the CitySpire tower embraces the very tradition of tall buildings by reintroducing the organization of base-middle-top—recognizable architectural forms—and the materials of traditional construction.

below   Typical floor plan, 46th–59th floors
below middle   Typical floor plan, 7th–23rd floors
bottom right   Street level
photography   Scott Frances/Esto
bottom left   View overlooking Central Park

0   40ft

Wonderland Villa

103 m/228 ft
35 stories
Residential, commercial
1989

Kwai Chung, Hong Kong SAR, People's Republic of China
Dennis Lau & Ng Chun Man Architects & Engineers (H.K.) Ltd
(formerly Ng Chun Man & Associates Architects & Engineers (H.K.) Ltd)

Wonderland Villas is a residential development aimed at the upper end of the market. The layout of the estate is predominantly linear, with blocks forming an undulating terrace that follows a ridgeline of the Golden Hill that ultimately extends to a summit in Kam Shan Country Park. The project is one of the most visible developments in Hong Kong and can be seen from Hong Kong Island, Lantau Island, and many points in the New Territories.

The project's isolation and its elevated position allow for good views in all directions. In the case of larger units within the complex, it has been possible to provide dual-aspect apartments that extend through the blocks.

below   Apartments on the lower floors are provided with substantial balconies
right   Swimming pool and cylindrical clubhouse
bottom right   The development follows the golden ridgeline
bottom left   The landscaped gardens
photography   Frankie Wong and Michael Tse Photography, Hong Kong

RECENT BUILDINGS
1990-2002

The Wilshire

104 m/340 ft
27 stories
Residential
1990

Los Angeles, California, USA
KMD; Richard Magee Associates

38

Echoing the residential skyscrapers of New York City's Central Park, the 27-story, 97-unit Wilshire luxury residential tower has a deeply pitched copper roof, numerous balconies, and a façade both rich and varied. These are just a few of the interior and exterior details that made this the most successful—and highest-earning—new building to come on the market in its era. Completed in 1990, with Richard Magee Associates as architect of record, The Wilshire incorporates a number of residential high-rise innovations, including individual elevator lobbies for all units and floor plans in which unit sizes vary at different levels of the building. These features, along with a private club and wine cellar, contribute to a 97 percent net-to-gross efficiency, lower construction costs, and faster sales.

Designed for a highly visible site on Wilshire Boulevard, the building makes extensive use of balconies and glass-enclosed conservatories on the lower levels to admit natural light and to take advantage of panoramic views stretching from Century City to Beverly Hills and Westwood.

Inside the Wilshire's entry gate is a formally landscaped, French-cobblestone-paved court, which leads to a two-story lobby finished in marble and polished granite with mahogany paneling. The lobby floor is honed, pale cream limestone surrounding an elaborately inlaid rosette of pink and gold marble. Valet parking is available in a three-level, below-grade garage. The lower two floors include two-story townhouses with large private gardens. A health club shares the first level and features a swimming pool, exercise facilities, weight room, party room, and an outdoor garden. Upper level units offer double-height living rooms with fireplaces in both the living room and master bedrooms. Two-story penthouses with large terraces occupy The Wilshire's top floors.

left   Duplex penthouse with a double-height
          balcony crowns The Wilshire
photography   Tim Street-Porter
above   Manicured garden areas provide semi-
          private outdoor access for residents
photography   KMD
opposite left   The Wilshire, one of Los Angeles' luxury
          addresses
photography   Brady Architectural Photography
opposite right   Central park-like view of Los Angeles
photography   Brady Architectural Photography

Trump Palace

190 m/623 ft
55 stories
Residential, retail
1990

New York, New York, USA

Frank Williams & Partners, Architects

This 55-story, 190-meter/623-foot tower was the tallest all-residential building in New York when it was completed. Trump Palace has a wonderful scale that is reinforced by a stepped architectural form that owes a great debt to the Chanin Building and Rockerfeller Center's GE Building. A base of low-rise shops and townhouses preserves the existing streetscape.

This site, formerly the site of the New York Foundling Hospital, is a 0.4-hectare/1-acre site between East 68th Street and East 69th Street on Third Avenue. Retail continuity is provided along Third Avenue, while a large, densely wooded public plaza opens along East 68th Street for the entire neighborhood to use as an open-space amenity.

A variety of ways to live are organized at this important site. Five-story townhouses are organized along the side streets with separate elevators, while the 55-story residential tower has its lobby entrance on East 69th Street. The tower accommodates 283 apartments, which range in size from 56 square meters/600 square feet to 372 square meters/4000 square feet. Most units feature three bedrooms, formal dining area, staff quarters,

and four-and-half bathrooms. This tower offers the top six floors as single penthouse floors. These apartments feature 9-meter/30-foot by 15-meter/50-foot living rooms with separate dining rooms.

The granite-base tower is a light-colored, highly patterned, rose brick and glass structure, with a glossy, dark trim at the street level. Balconies and sliding glass and casement bay windows are organized in horizontal and vertical bands. These details, combined with shallow setbacks, serve to add a residential scale to the tower. String courses that encircle the building help to accentuate the setbacks.

A separate, free-standing building on East 6th Street, which helps the complex tie into the city's existing fabric, accommodates an additional 45 apartments. Private gardens and recreation space are located between the 68th Street building and the 69th Street wing. A private roadway, which cuts through the Trump Palace, was also established.

Below-grade parking has entrances and exits on each of the narrow side streets of East 68th and East 69th streets.

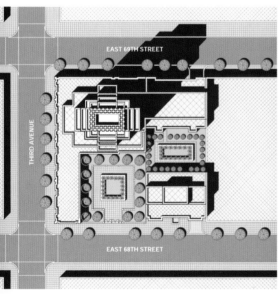

above — Site plan
middle — The Tower has a stepped architectural form, which gives a good scale to the Residential Tower
right — The Tower grows out of a base, which is in scale with the neighborhood
opposite left — The Residential Tower is shown in context with the Piere Hotel
opposite top right — Upper level residential Floor plan
opposite bottom right — The concierge reception desk has a rich mahogany wood contrasted with light marble floor
photography — Jock Pottle/Esto; Mohamed Yakub

Weena Apartment Tower

Rotterdam, The Netherlands

Hoogstad Architecten; Bureau voor Bouwkunde

Location

This is one of the Netherland's tallest apartment towers and was built in 1990 in the center of Rotterdam's inner city, between Hofplein and Central Station. Next to the metro line, this slim, 34-story tower continues on from the Lijnbaan shopping mall.

Between the tower and the Weena thoroughfare lies a pedestrian plaza with water feature and sculpture providing the tower with an excellent location on Weena. On the southwest corner of the tower is the head office of Unilever. This building is 46 meters/ 151 feet high and was also designed by Jan Hoogstad.

A pedestrian plaza with water feature and sculpture is to be built between the tower and the Weena thoroughfare, providing the tower with an excellent location on Weena. Construction has recently started on a new head office for Unilever in the southwest corner of the site. This building is to be around 46 meters/151 feet high and is also designed by Jan Hoogstad.

Design

The tower comprises 122 subsidized rental apartments and two luxury penthouses. At 103 meters/338 feet, this makes it the highest wholly residential tower in the Netherlands.

The structure of the tower is architecturally articulated by making the two northern dwellings and the two southern dwellings into two dark, slim volumes separated by a highly transparent, light slab. This slab projects out high above both residential volumes, and the upper section, which houses the elevation cleaning installations, and can be fully rotated. A preliminary study into the ideal structure for the towers resulted in a plan with four apartments per story, each one with a south-facing loggia. Each apartment has a panoramic view overlooking the plaza, Weena, and the inner city.

The three-story substructure houses the central hall, the technical spaces, and storage. From the third story upwards the building comprises 122 subsidized two–, three-, and four-bedroom rental apartments. The two penthouses are situated on the 33rd and 34th floors. On each floor, two of the four spacious apartment entrances face directly onto the lift area, the other two also have access, via their own hallway, to one of the two staircases.

Each apartment is equipped with spacious reception rooms and large panoramic windows. The apartments on the north side offer a reception room with an open-plan adjoining study room, a separate kitchen, and one or two bedrooms. All the apartments benefit from spacious south-facing loggias; the combination of traffic noise and high winds at great heights make loggias more suitable than balconies.

The floor plans of the apartments on the south side show some variations in depth due to the recesses in the south elevation.

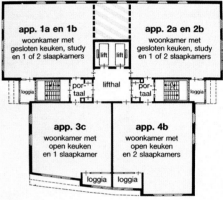

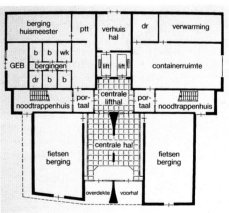

opposite left & right   View of the south façade of the apartment building. To emphasize the slimness of the tower, the façade is lightly staggered. By means of color this relief contrast gets extra attention.

left   The atrium generates the transition from interior to exterior. The predominantly white color combination and the glass tiles lead up to an impression of clearness and light.

above   Floor plans

photography   Sybolt Voeten

Weenatoren (The Weena Tower)

106 m/348 ft
34 stories
Offices, residential
1990

Rotterdam, The Netherlands
Klunder Architecten

44

The tall buildings that distinguish the Rotterdam horizon complete the reconstruction of the inner city that was destroyed completely by the bombing in 1940.

Built on an area of 30 meters/98 feet by 40 meters/131 feet and grazed by a large traffic boulevard in the heart of the city, the tower building was originally conceived for residential use only, as the urban zoning plan provided. However, a study on automobile traffic noise pollution led the architects to design a building with residential spaces on the higher floors only, and service activities on the floors closer to the Weena expressway. Thus the building's first 13 floors were reserved for offices.

The building organism's attachment to the ground brings out a number of the fundamental elements forming the design's guiding ideas:

A monumental two-story-high semicircular portico very well plays its role of filter between the outside public space and the interior private space, and establishes a relationship between the ground floor's two principal functional spaces: the entrance lobby for the 10,500 square meters/113,022 square feet of offices distributed over the lower 13 floors, and the entrance lobby for the 72 apartments lying in the remaining higher floors.

A central block (in which the elevators and emergency stairs serving the apartments and the offices are kept separate and distinct) leans toward the outside, compressing the porticoed space that thus expands into the office lobby. Two significantly present escalators, closing sandwiching a flight of stairs, lead to a mezzanine floor from which there is access to the elevators connecting the various offices floors.

Once the first two floors are passed, the building's median axis becomes the axis of symmetry both of the offices and of the apartments, which have two different typologies.

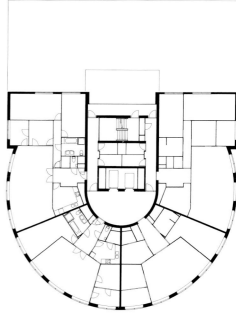

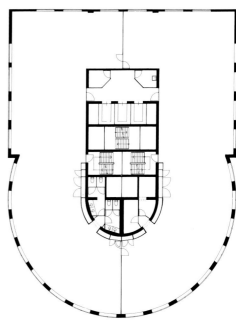

opposite left Entrance hall of offices
opposite right South façade, view from street level
left Southwest façade
top right Typical floor plan, apartments
above Typical floor plan, offices
photography Marcel van Kerckhoven

La Tour

87 m/285 ft
24 stories
Residential
1991

Westwood, Los Angeles, California, USA

Starkman Vidal Christensen (Design Architects);
Sheperd Nelson & Wheeler (Executive Architects)

The design challenge was to create an alternative to luxury housing in the Hills. High-rise apartments that could be a valid choice taking advantage of the breathtaking views and having the safety of a 24-hour-a-day concierge service.

The motor court drop-off is to be compared to a courtyard entry into a mansion.

The lobby is a pre-function room allowing visitors to wait in a comfortable situation.

The units are only four per floor and two per elevator bay. Thus giving a feel of privacy.

The units are designed as houses in the sky. Distributed from a gallery limiting the corridors to the minimum.

The bathrooms have windows, terraces are outdoor rooms.

A flexibility of choice was given as per the layout. Open plan or cluster plan, each one giving a set of possibilities adapted to different lifestyles.

The use of material has been chosen to give the building as quiet flair as possible. Great emphasis was given to light control (bay windows in master suite) and integration of exterior space as part of the apartment. In addition meeting rooms, spa, and pool are part of the project.

Every thing was designed with the intent of recreating the level of intimacy and privacy a house offers.

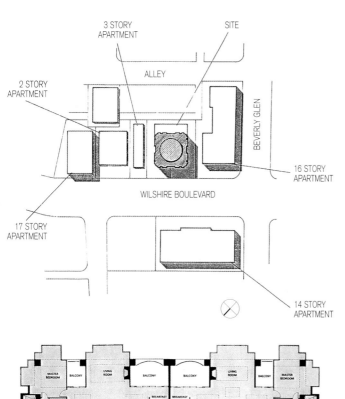

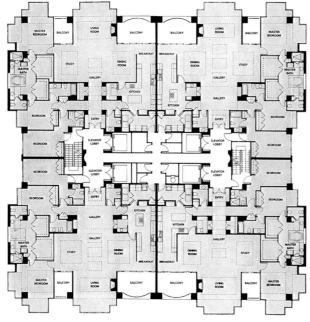

opposite top left   Site plan

opposite bottom left   Floor plan, floors 4–20

opposite right   Two apartment styles were offered, open or with a gallery, like in a house. One important point was to give windows to bathrooms, which happens so rarely in towers. The corners of the building are expressed by the huge bay window of the master suite.

left   The entrance on Wilshire Boulevard features pedestrian access to a double-height lobby/motor court area giving the building some sense of entry

above   All the elements of the plan are identified on the façade; bay window for master suite and outdoor rooms on the terraces

Pacific View

135 m/443 ft
39 stories
Residential
1991

Hong Kong SAR, People's Republic of China
P&T Architects and Engineers Ltd.

48

Located at the seafront, overlooking Tai Tam Bay and the Stanley Peninsula on Hong Kong's south side, the tower contains 376 apartments with sizes ranging from 120 square meters/1292 square feet to 200 square meters/2153 square feet. Car parking and a clubhouse are contained in a podium structure.

The five interconnected towers are arranged into a fan-shaped plan, maximizing the magnificent views of Tai Tam Bay.

Standard accommodation units have two or three bedrooms. Sea views are maximized through full-height windows in the living rooms and master bedrooms, which also provide a strong visual accent to the extensive tower façade. The podium is dominated by monumental columns, clad in granite, which weave round the perimeter of the sea-facing façade.

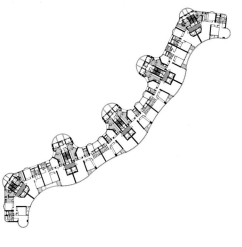

opposite   Club house
left   Front view
top right   Detail of stone work at entrance level
above   Typical floor plan
photography   P&T Photographic Department

Queen's Garden

167 m/548 ft
35 stories
Residential
1991

Hong Kong SAR, People's Republic of China
P&T Architects and Engineers Ltd.

50

Overlooking the Central district and Victoria Harbour layout, this luxury apartment tower is designed to maximize the views provided by its location at Old Peak Road.

Three towers, linked and arranged in a fan-shaped configuration, provide a total of 173 luxurious split-level apartments, with a unit size of 240 square meters/2583 square feet.

Double-height living rooms optimize the views. Car parking and clubhouse with a swimming pool for residents is provided in the base structure.

above   View from stair rotunda
right   Entrance
opposite left Front view
opposite right Typical floor plan
photography   P&T Photographic Department

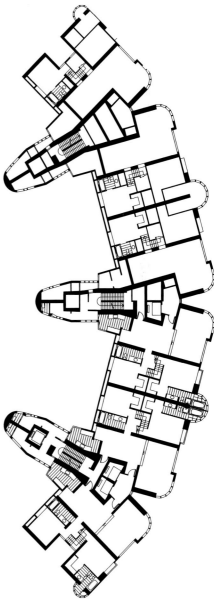

Le Mondrian (formerly Le Grand Palais)

125 m/410 ft
42 stories
Residential
1992

New York, New York, USA
Fox & Fowle Architects PC

This 179-unit apartment building was designed to fit in with the contemporary midtown surroundings of 54th Street and Second Avenue. The units are substantial and comfortable, ranging from studios to three-bedroom apartments. Common facilities include a complete health club and a swimming pool exclusively for the use of residents.

The building form is a juxtaposition of two separate masses, one solid in façade treatment, the other more transparent, and unified by red accent bands and common window mullion spacing. It maintains its identity as a residential building among the office building giants of a prominent commercial neighborhood by means of articulated balconies and punched windows along Second Avenue, and a stone-clad tenant entrance on 54th Street.

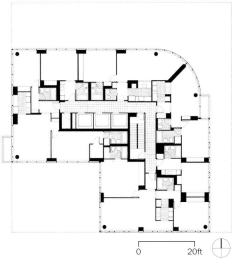

opposite left   Aerial view from northeast
rendering   Howard Associates
opposite right   Elevation
photography   Andrew Gordon
left   Exterior from southwest
photography   Andrew Gordon
above   Typical floor plan

0   20ft

Marine Prospect Housing

90 m/295 ft
23 stories
Residential
1992

Tanshui, Taipei County, Taiwan

C.Y. Lee & Partners

Environmental concern
These high-quality residential towers give the open space back to the residence, creating a good outdoor environmental space in this crowded city.

Flowing open space
Open space is not only located at the ground floor but also at B1 level and the third floor. This three-dimensional garden area completely covers the bottom four floors. The four towers sit on top of the base in order to give the residences more privacy.

The metaphor of "flower"
This is not just a building. It is a live object—like a flower that grows each day. Following the idea of utilizing the natural curve, the concept of four flowers has become the spirit of this project, instead of four towers. The interior space also works with this idea.

right Overall view
below Site plan
opposite top left City scale
opposite middle left Powerful roof top
opposite right Roof parapet

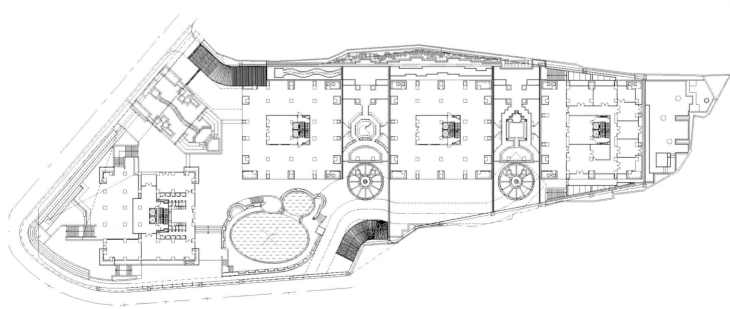

Permanent Mission of India to the United Nations

New York, New York, USA

Charles Correa Architects/Planners; Bond Ryder and Associates

The site, just down the road from the UN Headquarters in New York, consists of two Manhattan city blocks connecting adjacent streets, forming a narrow strip of land 60 meters/197 feet long, with a frontage of 12 meters/39 feet along 43rd Street, and a mere 6.3 meters/20 feet along 44th Street. Into this crevice, a complex program of offices had to be inlaid for the Permanent Mission of India and an exhibition gallery (with direct access from 44th Street) located in the four levels of the podium, surmounted by a tower with residential accommodation for five different categories of staff, ranging from the security personnel

(15.5 square meters/167 square feet) to the Dy. Consul General (200 square meters/2153 square feet in a triplex apartment with terrace gardens, at the top of the building). This wide range of apartment sizes was accommodated in the same envelope (a tower 14 meters/46 feet wide and 15.5 meters/51 feet deep), wrapped in a taut metal-paneled skin. The larger apartments at the top are interlocking duplexes—somewhat like the Kanchanjunga Apartments in Bombay (1969–83), but with the double-height areas glass-enclosed (so as to remain useable in the North American winters).

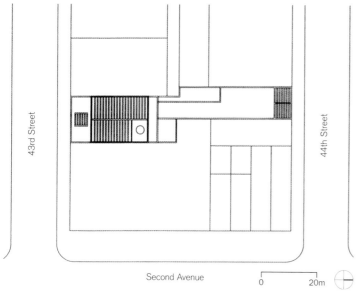

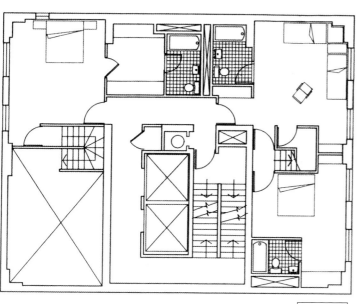

Sceneway Garden

100 m/328 ft

29–35 stories

Residential, commercial, public transport interchange

1992

Kowloon, Hong Kong SAR, People's Republic of China

Dennis Lau & Ng Chun Man Architects & Engineers (H.K.) Ltd
(formerly Ng Chun Man & Associates Architects & Engineers (H.K.) Ltd)

58

Sceneway Garden is built directly above the eight-lane Kwun Tong Road expressway that is one of the main arterial routes of Hong Kong. The project is also built above the Lam Tin MTR station and incorporates a major public transport interchange serving the many points in the New Territories and Hong Kong Island.

The creation of a very long span podium deck above the station and expressway created a tranquil and spacious landscaped environment for the private estate. All commercial and transport activities are contained in the podium. The effectiveness of the estate in remedying the problems of noise and other pollution was recognized by an Environmental Award organized by the Hong Kong Government's Environmental Protection Department

opposite left   Podium and residential superstructure. The podium absorbs the fall in the site.

opposite top right   The estate viewed from the podium deck

opposite bottom right   Rotunda

left   The formal landscape of the podium deck

below   Trellis

bottom right   Clubhouse

photography   Frankie Wong and Michael Tse Photography, Hong Kong

The Alexandria

79.3 m/260 ft
28 stories
Residential
1992

New York, New York, USA

Frank Williams & Partners, Architects; Skidmore, Owings & Merrill LLP

The architectural design of The Alexandria is trying to show respect for the existing built context of the upper west side of Manhattan and tries to respond to this important corner of the upper west side in scale and spirit. The granite-base building incorporated design elements that are contextual with the upper west side, such as the multicolored brickwork, limestone trim, and decorative ironwork.

This 28-story building anchors the corner of Broadway and 72nd Street. The floors are set back every floor above the 15th. This design provides a stepped profile that suggests the mansard roof of the existing landmark building, The Ansonia, located one block to the north on Broadway. The strongly articulated corner also echoes the Ansonia.

Three levels of retail space are also provided at this important intersection. At the top of the residential tower is a glazed, octagonal mechanical penthouse, forming The Alexandria's beacon on Broadway at West 72nd Street.

At each setback, new apartment layouts were created and the column system was repositioned accordingly and the loads were transferred. This stepping has created wonderful continuous terraces for the residences, above the 15th floor setback.

right   At the corner of Broadway and West 72nd Street the residential tower is shown in its contextual relationship with the Ansonia residential tower, which is a New York landmark

opposite left   Aerial view of residential tower within context of Upper West Side and its relationship with the Hudson River

opposite top right   Floor plan, upper level residences

opposite bottom right   Floor plan, lower level residences

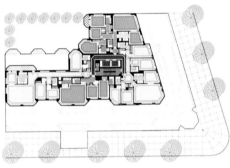

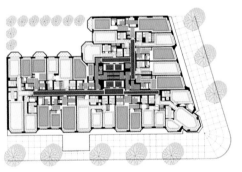

888 Beach Avenue

Northwest tower: 88 m/290 ft;
southeast tower: 54 m/176 ft
31/18 stories
Residential, retail
1993

62

Vancouver, British Columbia, Canada

James KM Cheng Architects Inc.

The project consists of two residential high-rise towers (31 and 18 stories) rising out of predominately low-rise street-oriented townhouse forms. The low-rise built form at the perimeter ranges from three to seven floors, with three-story townhouses on the east, west, and south sides and four-story apartments over townhouses on the north edge, facing the park. A small amount of retail space is included at street level.

This is one of Vancouver's earliest efforts at creating street-oriented urban row housing, which defines the street and creates pedestrian-level interest and surveillance (safety). The two north–south streets and southerly waterfront mews elevation are particularly successful, with the use of brick cladding adding to the quality of the streetscape. The transition from public sidewalk to private front door is finely calibrated, with the use of classic architectural devices such as grade changes, bay windows, screening, and recessed front stoops.

The interior courtyards are beautifully landscaped, although designed primarily to be appreciated by the residents as semi-private gardens. No public views into or through the site have been provided, although narrow gaps from the street give restricted visual access.

This project constitutes an exemplary response to the area's urban design master plan and was an important harbinger of higher density urban housing in downtown Vancouver. It provided many lessons for addressing the increasing conflicts, which come with maintaining livability and making a positive contribution to the public streetscape in the face of increased density.

above   Interior courtyard at east end
top right   Interior courtyard facing west
opposite left   False Creek view toward north
opposite top right   View of an interior suite
opposite bottom right   Northeast corner from street level
photography   James KM Cheng

MBf Tower

111 m/365 ft
31 stories
Residential, offices
1993

Penang, Malaysia

T. R. Hamzah & Yeang Sdn. Bhd.

64

This tower is a development of the architect's tropical high-rise ideas where the upper parts of the tower have a large two-story-high "skycourt" as the building's key feature, to provide better ventilation and deck space ("places-in-the-sky") for plants and terraces.

The lift lobbies are naturally ventilated with bridged walkways leading to the apartment units. Stepped landscaping planter-boxes are located on the main façade of the building.

The site consists of a rectangular-shaped lot along the Julan Sultan Ahmad Shah, Penang. The site is close to Persiaran Gurney and faces the north beach head of Penang. The land is about 3.2 kilometers/2 miles from the town center and is along the road that links the beach hotels further down in the Tanjung Bungah area to Georgetown.

The structural frame is constructed out of reinforced concrete with slip-form for the service cores and lift shafts. The typical floors are designed column-free. The lower block for the apartment is reinforced concrete frame construction with brick infill. The tower columns are located at the periphery of the apartment units and are transferred to the columns at the podium.

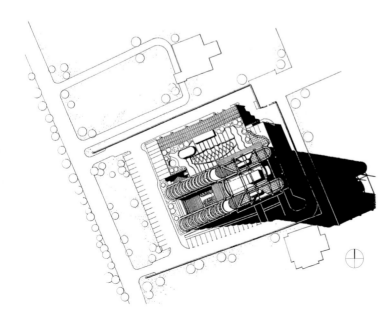

top left   Lobby view
left   Site plan
above   View of terraces
opposite left   North view
opposite top right   Ground level plan
opposite bottom right   Façade view
photography   Courtesy T. R. Hamzah & Yeang Sdn Bhd

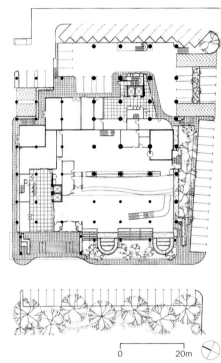

The Indigo

74 m/243 ft
27 stories
Residential, commercial
1993

Toronto, Ontario, Canada

Architects Alliance (formerly Wallman Clewes Bergman Architects)

A compact downtown development that combines enviably high density with a well-mannered street presence. Constructed on a small site in the central downtown section of Toronto, the project shares characteristics with the high-density financial core to the west, and the small scale turn-of-the-century warehouse buildings to the east.

The project incorporates a 27-story point-block residential tower and an eight-story, 3530 square-meter/38,000-square-foot office building. The small footprint of the tower provides significant views and natural light by presenting at least two exterior exposures to each suite.

The building includes an innovative mechanical system that uses steam from the Toronto District Heating System for winter heat, and an ice storage tank for summer cooling.

The Indigo won the *City of Toronto Urban Design Award* in 199

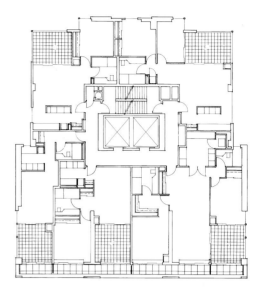

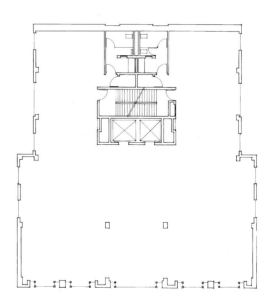

opposite top left	An aerial view of downtown Toronto shows The Indigo site, located on the boundary between the city's historic 19th-century downtown and the modern financial district
photography	Waginski Architectural Photography Services
opposite bottom left	The south façade, as seen from below Lombard Street
photography	Steven Evans
opposite right	View from the northeast on Church Street
photography	Waginski Architectural Photography Services
left	View from the southeast, across historic St. James Park
photography	Lenscape/Jones
above	Plan of residential floors 7–12
top right	Plan of third floor

Villa Athena

94.85 m/311 ft
27 stories
Residential
1994

Hong Kong SAR, People's Republic of China
Ronald Lu & Partners (HK) Ltd.

68

Villa Athena is a large-scale luxury residential development consisting of 10 blocks, each 27 stories and situated in the foothills of Ma On Shan overlooking Tolo Harbour and the YMCA Wu Kai Sha Youth Camp. The optimization of views was a primary consideration in the design of the towers. Each comprises four units per floor with all rooms facing Tolo Harbour.

Landscaping and extensive recreational facilities are provided at podium level which, due to the extreme length of the site, have been articulated as a series of different activity spaces, each with an individual design character.

An open space with a grand staircase and waterfall at the western end of the site acts as the main pedestrian connection with the neighboring retail/residential area of Ma On Shan New Town.

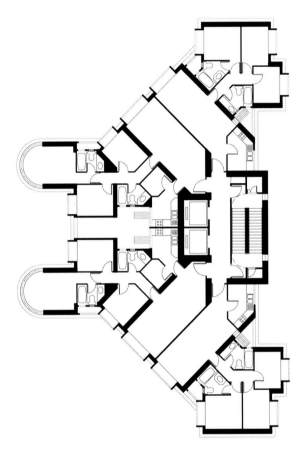

above   Typical floor plan
right   Elevation detail
opposite left   View of development from east side
opposite right   Site plan

SkyCity Tower

130 m/427 ft
34 stories
Offices, residential, retail
1995

Chung Ho, Taipei County, Taiwan
KRIS YAO / Artech Inc. Architects & Designers

This 34-story, mixed-use development features office/suites, residential units, and retail stores. Situated on a 100-meter/ 328-foot by 60-meter/197-foot site, the building is oriented east–west and recesses on north and south sides to create public plazas for its surroundings. The retail space, arranged at the base of the building from first to fourth floors, acts as a podium for the complex, while the office and residential quarters split into three towers from the fifth floor and above. To differentiate the functions and to provide privacy to the residents, the independent tower holding the office/suite space sits in front, and the paired towers accommodating residential/family units recess at the back.

One of the major design concepts of the project is to provide an economical use of living space in a city that isolates its residents

in their own vertical living units. Therefore, the paired residential towers are connected by horizontal terrace planes at the fifth, 14th, and 24th levels. These landscaped pool terraces or sky gardens not only provide the city residents with open outdoor spaces at interval of every 10 levels, but also stimulate more activities and neighborhood interactions.

The exterior façades are clad with aluminum panels to reduce the structural loading. Tinted reddish-brown and black interwoven on an imitated natural granite color surface, these panels form a modern, lively appearance. At daytime, natural light flows through the large view windows to brighten the interior, and at nighttime, residents sit in their living rooms and can view the quiet cityscape under the dark sky.

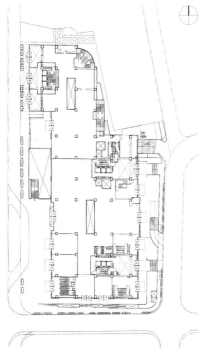

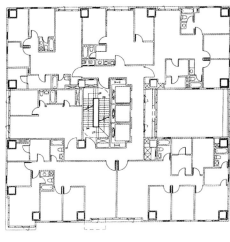

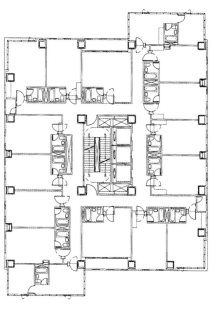

opposite top left   Site plan
opposite bottom left   Sky garden view
photography   Jeffrey Cheng
opposite right   South elevation
photography   Synpac Development Inc.
left   Connected sky gardens between
   residential towers
photography   Jeffrey Cheng
top right   Residential tower, typical floor plan
above   Office tower, typical floor plan

Golfhill Terraces (formerly Golf View Terraces)

64 m/210 ft
18 stories
Residential
1996

Jakarta, Indonesia
Development Design Group, Inc.

Golfhill Terraces makes imaginative use of a small site to create a 200-unit luxury condominium complex that gives each resident a view of the Pondok Indah golf course. A V-shaped design opening out toward the course, and the heavily serrated towers that create more corner views, are the keys to creating the necessary sight lines.

Another challenge was creating a complex of this size on a small site in a region with strict building-height regulations. Designers resolved this problem by breaking the complex into two identical towers in close proximity to each other. The towers share a common porte cochere and fountain courtyard as well as a garden, a pool, tennis courts, a jogging trail, and other amenities. A covered walkway connects the towers at the ground level. A grand stone stairway marks the transition from the arrival location to the pool and garden.

The complex's one-, two-, and three-bedroom luxury apartments all have trademark octagonal entry foyers. Paving patterns in granite and limestone and intricate tile designs are among other design features.

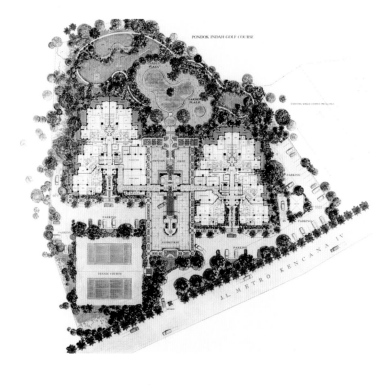

above   Site plan
right   View from garden walkway
opposite left   East building from pool terrace
opposite top right   Elevator lobby
opposite bottom right   View from Pondok Indah golf course
photography   Tim Griffith

Le Park Tower

160 m/525 ft

50 stories

Residential

1996

Buenos Aires, Argentina

Mario Roberto Alvarez y Asociados, Alvarez-Kopiloff-Alvarez-Rivanera-Bernabó

Le Park Tower is a residential building that is one of its kind in Argentina and South America. It is located in an area of Buenos Aires that, before its construction, was a completely depressed area of the city. The development is built on a full sector of 10,000 square meters/107,640 square feet—this made it possible to construct a unique and outstanding tower of 50 levels (160 meters/525 feet). Today, six years after its inauguration, the project is comparable to that of a building of urban scale.

Its base level, with modest use of the ground area, has been modified into a park, which changes the image of the four neighborhood boundaries. The inversion status plus the quality of the project have transformed the land cost of the area.

The district, which used to be a marginal zone with a low land prices, has been transformed into one of the most sought-after areas of the city, generating, in the near future, another four new projects.

Le Park Tower, either as a real estate development or as an architectural project with urban concepts, will definitely improve the city.

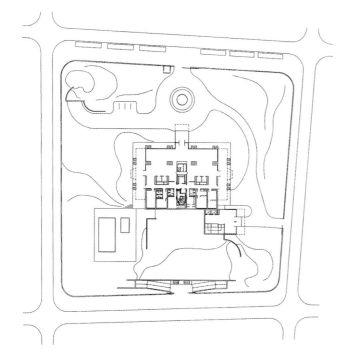

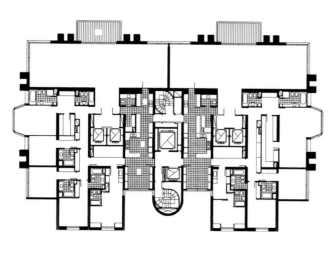

opposite top left   Site plan
opposite bottom left   Typical floor plan
opposite right   View from the park
left   Cerviño Street view
below   Tower lobby
photography   Daniela MacAdden

Libertador 4444

Buenos Aires, Argentina

Mario Roberto Alvarez y Asociados; Alvarez-Kopiloff-Alvarez-Rivanera-Bernabó

Two lateral buildings: 50 m/164 ft;
central tower: 130 m/427 ft
15/40 stories
Residential
1996

76

The typical block in Buenos Aires gains its structure through building with dividing walls that conform ring blocks to a common lung. Due to the cost of land in some districts, building schemes have to be varied in order to increase the volume and occupy less ground space. These towers in Buenos Aires, whose advantage is the creation of green spaces, had the disadvantage of having to leave bare the dividing walls of the old buildings—worsening this well-known urban landscape.

The studio, with experience in the development of projects in the city, corrected this situation by creating a new typology that was adopted by the Urban Planning Code. This typology nominated a "semi-free border", that consisted of upholstering the bare dividing walls with new buildings.

In the case of Libertador 4444, this allowed the construction of two lateral building covers, with a tower of 40 floors. The result is an absolute coexistence of typologies of units included in the same complex. The repetition of this concept for other sites in the city offers a substantial improvement and also a contribution to the urban space.

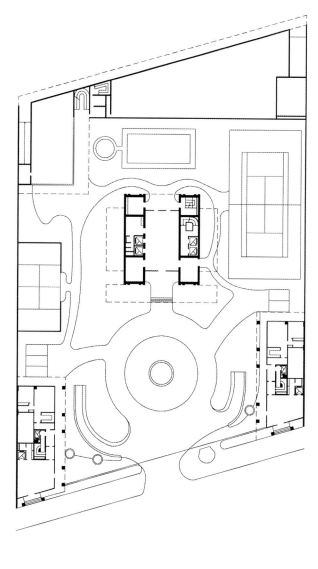

above   Site plan
right   Lateral building
opposite left Tower
opposite top right   Tower entrance
opposite bottom right Tower typical floor plan
photography   Jorge Leberato

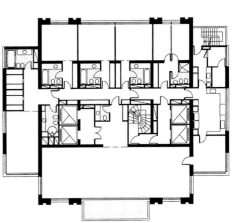

Nexus Momochi Residential Tower

87 m/285 ft
27 stories
Residential
1996

Fukuoka, Japan

Michael Graves & Associates; Maeda Construction Company, Ltd

Michael Graves, Architect was commissioned to design a 27-story luxury apartment tower on the bay in Fukuoka. The tower, the tallest building in the internationally acclaimed Nexus residential district, occupies one of the most prestigious sites in this development. The building's exterior consists of a slender ochre precast concrete frame applied over a glass curtain wall and horizontal balcony system. The transparent quality of the frame system gives the tower a luminous presence, as seen from the water, making it seem like an abstract version of a lighthouse.

The minimal cladding also provides the apartments with generous amounts of fenestration from which to appreciate the spectacular view. In addition to the building's exterior and public spaces, Michael Graves, Architect was also commissioned to develop, in their entirety, six penthouses for the 27th floor. The building received the *Tenth Fukuoka Urban Beautification Award* in 1997.

above   Night view
above right   View of pergola
right   Typical floor plan, 13th–19th floors
opposite left   View from the southwest
opposite right View of lobby
photography   Maeda Corp.

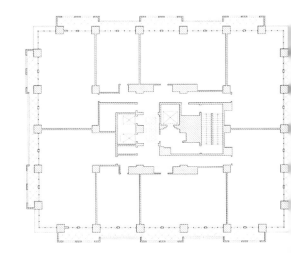

Palisades

Vancouver, British Columbia, Canada

James KM Cheng Architects Inc.

East tower: 91 m/300 ft;
west tower 67 m/219.8 ft

33/24 stories

Residential

1996

80

These two residential towers are the result of up zoning a 1957 apartment/office complex from a density of 3 FAR (Floor Area Ratio) to 6, effectively doubling the original amount of density. Furthermore, the area has since evolved into a high-end residential/hotel/retail district. Hence, the existing eight-story office building and one of the three original 23-story rental apartment towers were imploded to make way for the new high-end condominiums, and the remaining two rental apartment towers are converted into a boutique hotel with retail fronting onto Vancouver's premiere shopping street. The boutique hotel provides room and housekeeping services to the condominiums, and the amenities of the hotel, such as swimming pool, spas, and so on are also made available to the condominium owners.

The shape of the towers is derived directly from maximizing the views of another hotel tower behind, and are turned away from each other slightly to minimize overlooking. The oval shape also minimizes the blunt impact to the hotel behind.

Floor-to-ceiling glass is used throughout to maximize the view to the harbor and to let in as much daylight as possible. By refining a special window wall system, the windows are manufactured off site in panels for assembling on site. These panels are finished on both sides, hence, no further work is required once the assembly is complete. This method of construction allowed the construction to save several months from its schedule.

Incorporated into the base of the building are major public art (sculpture and fountain) that serves also as a physical barrier to separate the public from the residence without compromising the privacy of the residents. An oriental garden provides a sense of seclusion within the bustling city and a visual relief when viewed from above.

right   site plan
below   Rear view of towers
below right Front view of the entrance from
            Alberni Street
opposite left View of towers from corner of
            Alberni Street and Bute Street
opposite right View of the interior lobby
photography Peter Aaron/Esto

ALBERNI STREET

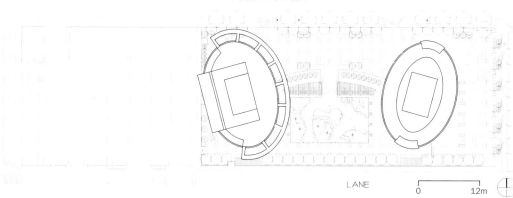

LANE

0   12m

Schielandtoren

102 m/335 ft

32 stories

Residential, retail

1996

Rotterdam, The Netherlands

de Architekten Cie.-Amsterdam; Pi de Bruijn

This tower block is part of "Beursplein," a multi-functional complex with facilities for shopping, leisure, dwelling, and parking. Situated at the junction of a major boulevard (Coolsingel) and an urban plaza (Beursplein) in the heart of Rotterdam, the complex consists of two parts: the sunken and partially underground shopping mall running below Coolsingel, and the building block between Beursplein, Coolsingel and two smaller streets, Bulgersteyn and Korte Hoogstraat.

Schielandtoren is the residential component of the building block, which otherwise contains the new premises of two big stores,

C&A and Kreymborg, a shopping arcade, and a parking garage. Occupying the back line of the complex, at a slightly further remove from Coolsingel, it accords in height and position with nearby office towers such as Helmut Jahn's Fortis Bank premises (1996) and Wim Quist's Robeco building (1991).

The residential tower block rises up 32 stories, conspicuous in its reddish-brown cladding embossed with metal bays. Tower, garage, and access courtyard of the surrounding shops are all entered from Bulgersteyn, the small street to the south.

photography   Daria Scagliola and Stijn Brakkee

Searea Odaiba Tower-4

105.1 m/344.8 ft
33 stories
Residential
1996

Tokyo, Japan

KAJIMA DESIGN; Urban Development Corporation

This residential tower, the first in the Tokyo Waterfront Odaiba District, was developed with the goal to achieve a new model for housing complexes in the 21st century. The building was designed as a skyscraper to serve as a landmark in the district.

Situated at a splendid location on the waterfront, facing the Odaiba Kaihin park with a view that extends to the Rainbow Bridge, this rental apartment building offers a variety of apartment layouts that range from 1DK to 3LDK.

The ceiling height was raised on the highest floor and the "skip-floor" configuration was employed to provide generous living places. A meeting room was located on every fifth floor to encourage interaction between residents. A high reinforced concrete structural system (reinforced concrete structural system for skyscrapers) was adopted, and a 24-hour ventilation system was installed in all units.

top left   Site plan
top right   Exterior view (west)
bottom left   Entrance lobby
bottom right   Residential unit
opposite left   Exterior view (southwest)
opposite right   Typical floor plans
photography   Hisashi Takenami

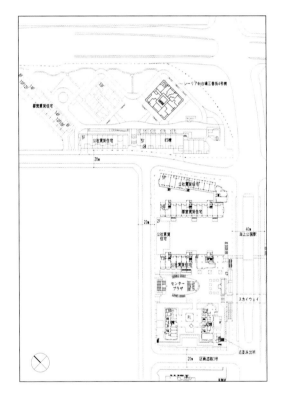

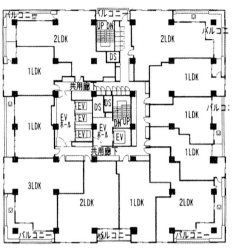

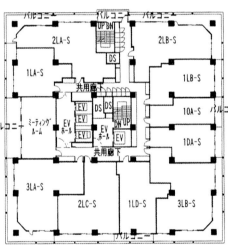

Horizon Apartments

139 m/456 ft
43 stories
Residential
1997

Sydney, New South Wales, Australia

Harry Seidler & Associates

The 43-story tower is shaped to gain the widest sweep of harbor outlook, centered on Sydney's Opera House and the Harbour Bridge. The rest of the site, excavated to house a five-story, 500-car garage, accommodates on its deck a 25-meter/82-foot swimming pool and tennis court, which is overlooked from the terraces of surrounding low-rise split-level apartments.

The tower contains two penthouses, 18 three-bedroom apartments (135 square meters/1453 square feet), 157 two-bedroom apartments (100 square meters/1076 square feet, 105 square meters/1130 square feet and 115 square meters/1238 square feet), and 54 one-bedroom apartments (55 square meters/592 square feet). The townhouses consist of 22 one-bedroom/studio apartments, eight two-bedroom apartments, and one three-bedroom apartment.

The apartment tower planning divides the floor space evenly between living and bedroom portions, making these interchangeable in plan, which makes possible combinations and side reversal of two-bedroom and three-bedroom apartments.

To maximize the magnificent sweep of views toward the harbor, Opera House, Harbour Bridge, and city skyline, the tower is shaped to reflect the view arc from north to west.

As the views become increasingly dramatic with increased height, taking in the Pacific Ocean as well as Sydney Harbour, the orientation of the balconies changes in the top quarter of the tower, which contains the larger apartments.

To take full advantage of the spectacular views, living and main bedrooms have full glass walls, with narrow horizontal windows to kitchens and second bedrooms. All windows are sun-protected either by the terrace overhangs or special exterior awnings to obviate the need for venetian blinds (which would block the view).

Approximately 20 percent of the site is covered by buildings, with the remainder extensively landscaped, and containing a swimming pool, barbecue area, and tennis court.

below	Site plan
below right	View of tower from gardens across swimming pool
opposite left	View looking up at tower from entry drive
opposite top right	Floor plan (levels 7, 9, 11, 13, 15, 17, 19, 21, 27, 29)
opposite middle right	Apartment interior view
opposite bottom right	View from apartment toward city and harbor
photography	Eric Sierins

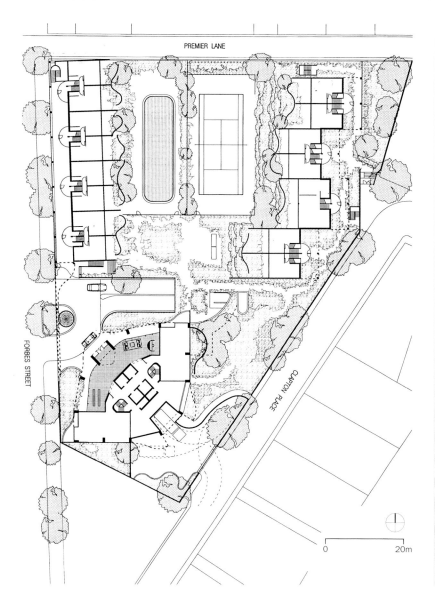

Portofino Tower

136.2 m/447 ft

45 stories

Residential

1997

Miami Beach, Florida, USA

The Sieger Suarez Architectural Partnership

88

Portofino Tower, a 45-story, 228-unit condominium tower built on the southernmost tip of Miami Beach with a future retail component, was completed in 1997. In addition to being designed by The Sieger Suarez Architectural Partnership, its landscape architect is EGS2 Corporation.

This new oceanfront community is a joint venture development of Marquesa Development and Related Companies.

Portofino Tower encompasses one-, two-, and three-bedroom condominium townhomes and penthouses on the 28th floor ranging up to 650 square meters/7000 square feet in area. Its landmark location, alongside Government Cut, affords residents magnificent "floor-through/see-through" views of Miami Beach to its north and Fisher Island, Key Biscayne, and Biscayne Bay to its south, the Miami skyline to its west and, to its east, the Atlantic Ocean.

Upscale retail boutiques and gourmet restaurants are located at ground level.

top left   Artist's rendering
rendering   Art Associates Inc.
top right   North view of tower from Washington Avenue
photography   John Adams
opposite left   Southwest view of heath spa, skydeck, and town
homes with crowning top element take
opposite right   South view of tower from across Biscayne Bay inlet

The Floridian

Quarry Bay, Hong Kong SAR, People's Republic of China
Dennis Lau & Ng Chun Man Architects & Engineers (H.K.) Ltd

The Floridian consists of two residential towers above a
two-story-high podium carpark.

Towers one and two are respectively 26 and 22 stories high.
A residents' clubhouse is situated on the first floor of tower two
and a swimming pool, changing room, and covered children's
playground are situated on the podium roof.

above	Square and garden
right	South elevation
opposite left	North elevation and west gable end
opposite top right	Swimming pool
opposite bottom right	Typical apartment interior
photography	Frankie Wong and Michael Tse Photography, Hong Kong

Watertower Entrepôt

60 m/197 ft
22 stories
Residential
1997

Amsterdam, The Netherlands

atelier PRO architekten

The Watertower is the finishing touch in the Entrepôt-West housing project carried out by Atelier PRO.

The introduction of a residential tower meant that the diversity in dwelling arrangements could be enhanced to the maximum. At the same time the tower has become a point that helps identify the new area and the bridge.

The tower has three apartments on each level and has been positioned over the existing embankment, which means that a large part of it is standing in water, hence the name "Watertower." The stepped finish at the top gives it a striking appearance. At this level there are two penthouses. From behind the arched façades, the residents have a magnificent view out over the city.

Just above water level, where the storage area is located, jetty sections have been constructed in keeping with the harbor atmosphere. The bays, which have been placed along the side façades, make it possible to look out along the long water line from outside the outer wall.

The entire tower has been rendered in a bright white plaster finish. The dark grey strips unite the corner windows, which creates a playful visual effect where the outside walls meet. Strips of tiles, which have been used as transition between the two colours, accentuate this effect. The windows have black powder-coated aluminum frames and are of the tilt/turn type.

The round grilles in the façade provide an intake for the outside air for the balanced ventilation system. Next to this grille is a small round window that lets the outside light into the bathroom like a porthole. A dark red steel structure against the east façade marks the fire escape stairs.

This also marks the spot where the building touches the water, well as being the highest point of the tower. The tower has bee positioned to form one line with the buildings on either side of th water. The entrance hall projects like a box of glass building blocks over two levels out from the building's edge, which make it easy to see and find.

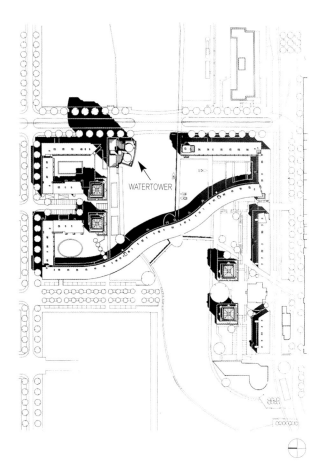

WATERTOWER

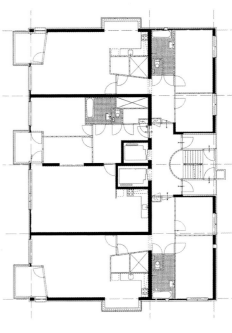

opposite left   Map of Entrepôt-West area
opposite top right   Southwest corner of tower
opposite bottom right   Eastside of tower
left   Westside of tower
above   Ground-plan of apartments
photography   Luuk Kramer

Baan Piya Sathorn

102 m/335 ft
34 stories
Residential
1998

Bangkok, Thailand

Palmer & Turner (Thailand) Ltd.; Concept International Design

94

Baan Piya Sathorn is a 34-story luxury residential development situated on 3344 square meters/35,995 square feet of land in the heart of Bangkok's central business district. The building responds to its context with the orientation of the six-story podium matching that of the main road and adjacent buildings. The tower plan, however, is rotated 45 degrees to this grid to maximize the views from each apartment.

The X-shape of the tower is derived from a highly efficient floor plate with a slot of space between each of the four wings. This provides privacy and security as well as natural ventilation suitable for the local climate.

An elegant image is achieved through the careful articulation of the façade elements and subtle use of a classical vocabulary.

Colored tile cladding combined with dark anodized aluminum and clear glass windows regulate the tower elevation, which sits comfortably on the more solid podium base.

Behind the podium façade are housed the main support faciliti 200 car spaces, and recreational areas including a swimming pool and jacuzzi in the garden on level seven.

Within the tower there are three passengers lifts and one servi lift, which efficiently transport residents to each of the four win At levels 8–14 each wing houses two apartments, which reduc from levels 15–30 to allow for increasingly spacious and more luxurious apartments.

At the higher levels, the building steps back in a series of terraces that contain the duplex penthouse suites. At this point the building culminates in a copper-clad pyramid roof crowned with a lantern feature and arrestor pole at over 100 meters/ 328 feet in height. The entire roof is illuminated, which makes the building glow and stand out among its surroundings at nigh

right   View at night
opposite left   Front view
opposite top right   Entrance lobby
opposite bottom right   Interior
photography   P&T Photographic
Department

Del Bosque

Mexico City, Mexico

Cesar Pelli & Associates Inc.; Diseño y Arquitectura Urbe; Kendall Heaton Associates

Del Bosque comprises the 13-story North Latin American headquarters for Coca-Cola, two 31-story residential towers, a 465-square-meter/5005-square-foot health club and a three-level below-grade parking facility. The four buildings are situated on a triangular piece of land in the Polanco District and have been designed with multi-curved plans that maximize the panoramic view of Chapultepec Park.

The headquarter's building has a curved triangular plan form that responds to the geometry of the site and marks the corner of the block. The building is clad in Brazilian green granite,

semi-reflective insulated glass, and has a polyfluorimer painted aluminum curtain wall. The granite spandrels have recessed moldings to bring forward the glass wall and intensify the desig intent of a taut skin.

The apartment buildings are twin towers designed as sculptural pylons with a multiple curved plan, setbacks, and balconies to maximize views and enhance their residential quality. The buildings are clad in alternating bands of butt-glazed and red precast terrazzo spandrels with accents of glazed Mexican tiles.

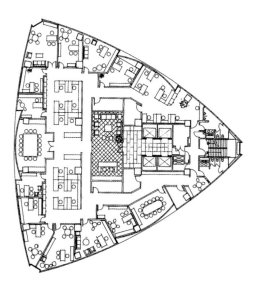

opposite top left   View from Chapultepec Park
opposite bottom left   Site plan
opposite right   View up towers
top left   View from Chapultepec Park
middle left   Drop-off area
bottom left   Residential tower lobby
above   Office building typical floor plan
photography   Aker/Zvonkovic Photography LLP

Elsa Tower 55

185.8 m/610 ft
55 stories
Residential
1998

Kawaguchi City, Saitama Prefecture, Japan
Takenaka Corporation

Elsa Tower 55 is conveniently located in Kawaguchi City, a place that has developed as a "bedroom community," only 30 minutes from Tokyo station. Standing at 185.8 meters/610 feet high, Elsa Tower 55 is presently the tallest residential apartment building in Japan.

As superhigh-rise apartment buildings have become more established, there has also been some criticism of the problems caused by "super density" and "super scale," which come from the important business aspects that are the basic characteristics of superhigh-rise apartments. Therefore, the aim was to make a large improvement to the characteristics of superhigh-rise apartments that comes from the idea of "a vertical dimensional community," in order to try and solve these problems.

Creation of a town space consisting of a territorial hierarchy
Formation of a territorial hierarchy based on towers, "neighborhoods" and "floors."

"Town plazas" where "neighborhoods" meet, as places where people can get together
The places where "neighborhoods" meet, which are the floors where people change elevators to go to different elevator banks, are the same as the "crossroads" in contemporary towns, and

Japanese and western-style rooms with accommodation facilities have been built to give these "neighborhoods" "town plazas," with the function of bringing people together.

"Community core"
"Community cores" that can also be used as meeting places have been built in the neighborhoods, which are perceived as daily life and management units. However, it is not an overstatement to say that the people who live in the apartments have some degree of negative reaction to the word "community." Therefore, active use of these spaces has been promoted by allowing people to do things that they could not usually do in their own homes, thereby enabling mutual exchange between neighborhoods.

"Sky pocket park"
Up to now, play lots have been built in towns. In this project "sky pocket parks" have been built about every 10 floors, for children and infants to play in. With the positions of these parks, in respect to the up-and-down direction, a lot of consideration has been given to the movement range as a walking zone for infants. Also, consideration has been given so that adults can see into these parks, by having them adjoin the common-use town plaza and community core spaces.

below left   Garden with a pond
below right   Void space
opposite left   Elsa Tower 55
opposite top right   Site plan
opposite bottom right   Typical floor plan
photography   Masayuki Miyagawa

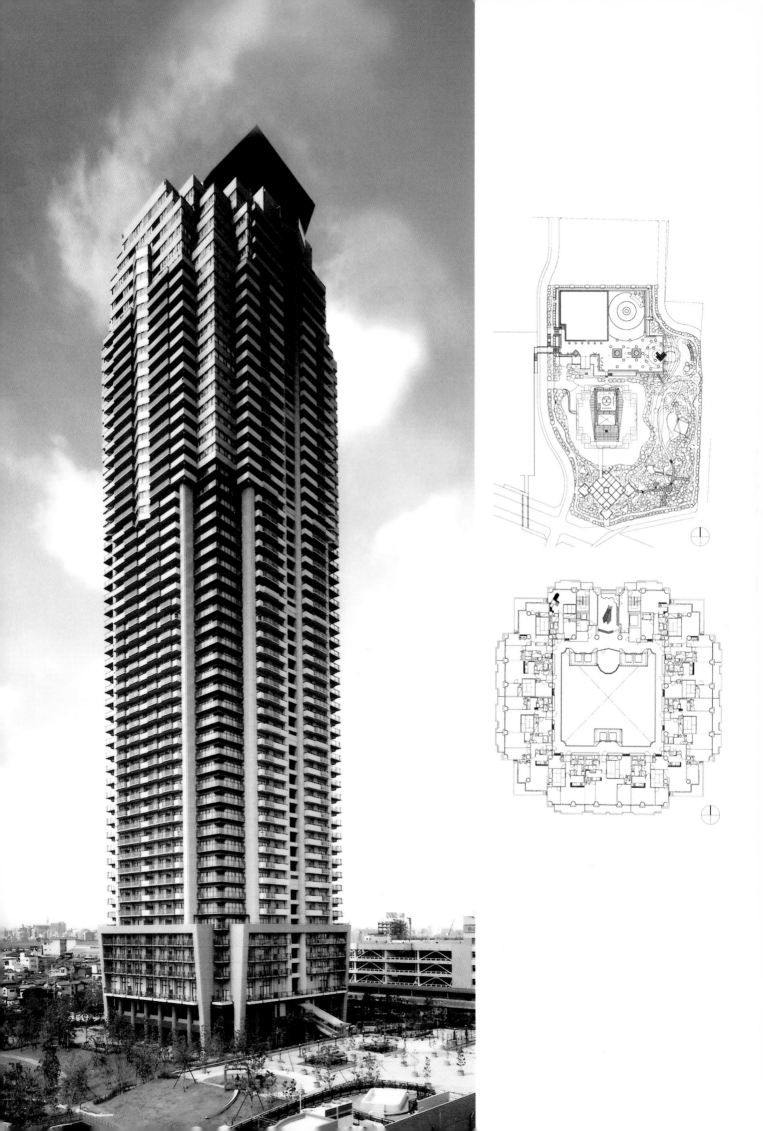

Lotus Village

95 m/312 ft
23–28 stories
Residential
1998

Hsichih, Taipei County, Taiwan
C.Y. Lee & Partners

Trend
From a digital technology and energy ecology viewpoint, a future city shall develop toward minimization and centralization.

Evolution
The minimization and centralization of a future city certainly promotes a compound residence architecture that evolves toward a "great gathering."

Great gathering
Oriental cultural thinking points out that "gathering" leads to prosperity, since a collective life can last longer. The gathering of a real entity can manifest the virtual entity, while something with capacity is great. The virtual entity refers to a spiritual, heart-orientated, artistic, and natural space. The future compound residence tends to develop toward a "great gathering" form, and will finally develop into clusters of different basic residential units directed by public value, in order for people to be in a great virtual space where "gathering of real entity can manifest the virtual entity," with a high level of contact with heart, art, and nature, facilitating the limited real environment experience to be upgrade to the development of an unlimited life.

Something with capacity is great
"Lotus Hill" is decorated with trees and flowers, surrounded by Golden Dragon Lake, and embraced by forest. Its natural atrium area of 80,00 square meters/861,120 square feet enables human beings to be in contact with nature, so as to further facilitate the inner human life to be filled with nourishing vigor, and internalized to be the everlasting vitality of human beings. This is the true denotation of a "great gathering."

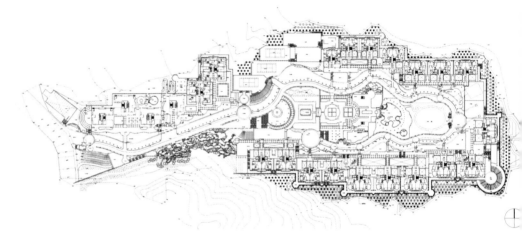

right — Site plan
bottom left — Central Park
bottom right — Arcade
opposite top & bottom left — Landscape
opposite right — Typical floor plan
photography — Jeffrey Cheng

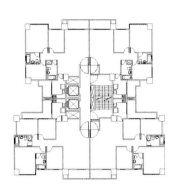

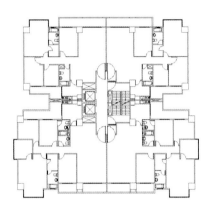

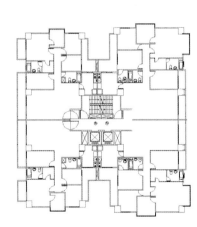

Quayside Marina Neighborhood

(Phase I: Aquarius; Phase II: Marinaside; Phase III: Quay West)

Vancouver, British Columbia, Canada

James KM Cheng Architects Inc.

Aquarius (4 towers): 95 m/312 ft, 89 m/292 ft, 43 m/141 ft, & 40 m/130 ft; Marinaside (3 towers): 88 m/289 ft, 67.3 m/221 ft, & 38.5 m/126 ft; Quay West (2 towers): 69 m/227.7 ft & 95 m/312.3 ft

Aquarius (4 towers): 33, 30, 14, & 12; Marinaside (3 towers): 32, 22, & 12; Quay West (2 towers): 24 & 34 stories

Residential, commercial, office, retail

Aquarius: 1998; Marinaside: 2001; Quay West: 2002

Quayside is a master-planned self-contained neighborhood of approximately 139,350 square meters/1.5 million square feet of market and non-market residential/commercial density along one of the many waterfronts in Vancouver. The urban design concept was to maximize the water view for as many units as possible while maintaining a sense of community. Three pedestrian mews were introduced to connect Pacific Boulevard to the waterfront. These mews afforded additional frontages to the townhouses lining them. Convenience commercial units such as major supermarkets, Starbucks Coffee, banks, restaurants, and offices line the major street to complement the community center across the way. This area has become the heart of the neighborhood.

The public realm is designed as the major environmental asset and is part of the total setting of public waterfront walkways and bikeways; marina; mews; and a neighborhood park. Other public amenities include a neighborhood daycare center and playground (skateboard and basketball).

Public art is interspersed along the crescent that bounds the marina. Small ferries connect the marina to Granville Island, a celebrated market place nearby.

Living rooms of the units at the rear are projected out in round forms to give owners a view of the waterfront. In this manner, almost all units manage a prized water view.

The towers and townhouses provide a friendly pedestrian scale to the street; at the same time they provide privacy to a secluded internal podium garden, where residents are safe and secure. Amenities such as a clubhouse, indoor swimming pool, and business center are located in this podium.

Base construction is reinforced concrete. Again, window wall systems are used for efficiency. Other major exterior materials selected are Alucabond metal panels and brick for their low-maintenance characteristics.

above   False Creek view of neighborhood
right   Street view
opposite left   Waterfront luxury mid-rise building
opposite top right   Commercial/retail corner
opposite bottom right   Interior view of suite
photography   James KM Cheng

Residences on Georgia

Vancouver, British Columbia, Canada

James KM Cheng Architects Inc.

West tower: 100 m/330 ft;
east tower: 98 m/322 ft

36 stories

Residential

1998

104

The "Residences" on Georgia Street is a noteworthy high-density residential development in downtown Vancouver. It is comprised of two 36-story towers, three-story townhouses, and the restoration and conversion of a heritage house on the site into five condominium apartments. The site is strategically located on Vancouver's premier downtown ceremonial route: Georgia Street.

The urban design responses are exemplary. The two handsome towers are oriented where they contribute to the street's character as a tower-lined grand boulevard. A raised private green court separates the towers. The green court, with its cascading water wall along the sidewalk edge and lush landscaping, also creates an elegant foil to the busy street, and screens the town housing that extends between the towers.

The towers have been carefully located about 61 meters/ 200 feet apart to minimize view impacts from adjacent upland towers. The east tower has been designed with a broad,

generously landscaped sidewalk, steps, landscaping, and a public art installation. The west tower in turn is set well back so that the restored heritage house is not overwhelmed.

The townhouses front onto the street and add significantly to the street's emerging residential character. The units are repetitively articulated and scaled to respond to the narrower, lower-scaled street. Each 4.5-meter/15-foot-wide unit has direct front door access from the sidewalk. The ground floor is raised up a few feet from the street in the traditional "porch" or "stoop" arrangement, and screened by a low retaining wall, railing, and small landscaped front yard, thus creating a handsome transition between the public sidewalk zone and the private front door.

The Residences on Georgia demonstrates not only an exemplary response to the city's premier downtown ceremonial route's urban design guidelines, but also a keen understanding of good urban design in a high-density urban context.

JERVIS STREET

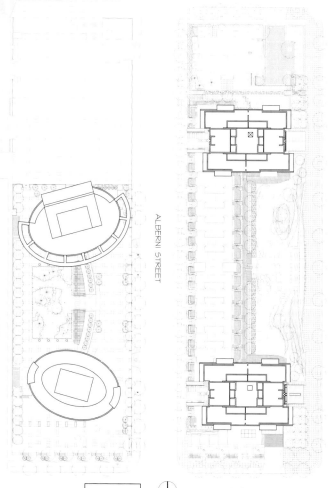

ALBERNI STREET

LANE

0   12m

BUTE STREET

GEORGIA STREET

opposite left	Site plan
opposite right	View from Georgia Street and Bute Street
top left	Georgia Street "Green Court"
middle left	Street view of courtyard townhouses
bottom left	Interior view of townhouses
below	View from Alberni Street
photography	Peter Aaron/Esto

SEG Apartment Tower

60 m / 197 ft
25 stories
Residential, offices
1998

Vienna, Austria
COOP HIMMELB(L)AU

Located between Wagramerstraße and Kratochwilestraße and adjacent to the "Alte Donau" metro station, the 60-meter/ 197-foot-high SEG Tower from COOP HIMMELB(L)AU forms, in conjunction with two other projected high-rise buildings, the new district "Donau City." The tower includes 70 apartments, nine eating facilities, offices, and practices on 25 floors.

The complete arrangement is captivating as a result of its immediate proximity to the city core and the shopping center "Donauzentrum," as well as by its location in one of the favorite leisure districts of Vienna. Also captivating are its striking height and quality of space, which are determined by different typological concepts.

Two major considerations were important for the design of the outer form of the COOP HIMMELB(L)AU building: on one hand, the concept of the tower is based on the idea of placing two houses, one on top of the other, to create a common space at the intersection. This common space—called a sky-lobby— is then used for the accommodation of a venue, a playground, a "teleworking café," and a sundeck. On the other hand, the concept of the so-called climate façade was developed, which is the linking and surrounding element between the two components.

This is an "intelligent" glass façade that regulates, together with the "air box" on top of the roof and the circulation core (planned as heat accumulator), the cooling of the apartments in summer and the heating in winter. This well-calculated system offers a higher level of comfort during hot weather and a minimizing of costs during the heating period. Besides its function as sound protection, the climate façade provides space for glazed loggias placed in front of the apartments, comprising two or three floors. These loggias allow green spaces, not normally seen in high-rise buildings, and a view to the city and of nature, also uncommon in urban living.

The concept of the glass skin surrounding the building enables an orientation of all buildings toward the south.

All apartments (ranging from 55 square meters/592 square feet to 130 square meters/1399 square feet) are based on a loft concept with an open plan and without load-bearing walls. This concept enables a flexible layout of all the apartments. A concierge located in the two-floor entrance lobby will provide optimal service for all the residents.

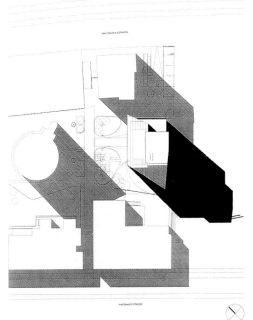

opposite left   View from southwest
photography   Gerald Zugmann
opposite right   Air space between apartment and façade
photography   AnnA BlaU
left   View from southeast
photography   AnnA BlaU
top right   Site plan
above   Orangery in front of skylobby
photography   AnnA BlaU

Terminal City Club Tower

91 m/300 ft

30 stories

Residential, hotel, offices, retail

1998

Vancouver, British Columbia, Canada

James KM Cheng Architects Inc.; Musson Cattell Mackay Architects

Terminal City Club, one of the oldest private clubs in the city, decided to tear down their old facility for a new mixed-use tower in order to raise funds for their new premise. This tower contains a 6967-square-meter/75,000-square-foot clubhouse with associated banquet and sports facilities. The remaining density consists of: revenue-producing retail at grade, strata offices, a 60-room hotel to be operated by the club, and 75 high-end strata residential units for sale. The proceeds from the sale of the residential and strata office portions provided the funds for the new construction, while the income from the 60-room hotel, the retail at grade, and the underground parking garage provided ongoing operating revenues.

The tower contains the retail at grade with the five floors of strata offices on top. The 60-room hotel sits on top of the offices, and residential condominiums fill in the remainder of the tower. A bustle to the rear (toward the water/mountain view) contains the new club. The club provides housekeeping and room service to the condominium owners. Separate elevators service the office, residential/hotel, and the garage. Separate and secured parking are provided for the residents.

The shape of the building is derived principally from orienting the units to maximize the water view. The canopy at the top of the building provides wind protection for the penthouse roof terrace and is lit at night to provide interest to the skyline.

opposite left   View from Waterfront Hotel
opposite right   Building view as seen from the
    termination of Hastings Street
left   Building as seen from Burrard Street
below   The building façade is divided into smaller
    sections to reflect the rhythm of the
    heritage façades across the street
photography   Roger Brooks

Three Sails Tower

70 m/230 ft
24 stories
Retail, residential
1998

Abu Dhabi, United Arab Emirates

WZMH Architects (Webb Zerafa Menkès Housden Partnership Architects);
A.E.C. (Architectural & Engineering Consultants)

110

The Three Sails Tower residential development on the Corniche in Abu Dhabi is designed to be a landmark on the waterfront. As a building of distinction it will stand out from its neighboring surrounds and become a prominent symbol on the western stretch of the city.

The design concept recognizes the full development potential of the site with attractive massing, modern architectural character, and an eye-catching skyline image.

The massing concept responds well to this spectacular site, inspired to capture the breathtaking views of the Gulf shoreline and the city. The building portrays its location on the Corniche by emphasizing its two façades: one facing the water and the other facing the city. The magnificent color of the Gulf is a sparkling blue-green. The building responds to this by a north façade of aqua-sparkle blue reflective glass. The shimmering quality of the reflective glass is meant to convey a monochromatic color palette that will distinguish the aesthetic image and quality of this development from any vantage point. The south façade faces the city, and as such, is clad with a slightly more solid material with metal and glass.

The Gulf and its history also provided inspiration for the building most distinctive feature, recalling the great days of the sailing Dhows trading with India and East Africa. Integrated in the building design is a dramatic top of silver metallic "sails." The poetic shape of the three triangular sails is a geometry which is inspired by the national heritage of the Emirates. Three vertical masts support the sails and emphasize the verticality of the glass tower.

The lobby is finished with rich marble with geometric patterns. A cascading wall of water maintains the imagery of the Gulf, bringing it into the building. The units range in size from 195 square meters/2099 square feet to 225 square meters/2422 square feet and are oriented such that 80 percent of the suites have Gulf views.

A health club, restaurant, and terrace are located on the roof top below the sails, which provide shade for the terrace.

opposite top   Three Sails Tower as seen from across
                  the bay
opposite bottom   Typical floor plan
left   North elevation
above   Detail of sails
photography   Charles Crowel

TriBeCa Pointe

122 m/400 ft

42 stories

Residential

1998

New York, New York, USA

Gruzen Samton Architects Planners & Interior Designers LLP

The residential building is composed of three significant architectural elements: a 42-story tower placed in alignment with Manhattan's street grid, a seven-story base oriented orthogonally to the powerful axis established by the West Side Highway and the Hudson River, and crystalline elements set within the tower which bring resolution to the two different grids by rotating from one into the other.

The tower soars over 122 meters/400 feet and becomes a beacon on the northernmost reach of New York's Battery Park City. Its brick façade with punched windows is reminiscent of New York's finest apartment buildings, while the introduction of curtain wall elements becomes a reminder of Battery Park City's office function, both of which must be acknowledged by the tower. These glassy elements have been carefully positioned to proportion the tower and to establish relationships with neighboring structures in accordance with the Battery Park City Design Guidelines.

The base of the building is conceived as a continuation of the masonry pavilions of the adjacent Stuyvesant High School, and it establishes a sensitive human scale along the beautiful waterfront esplanade. Light brick harmonizes with the school, and double-height windows create a scale commensurate with it. A granite and limestone base, recessed brick detailing, and a glass marquee bring richness to the lower levels and recall the architectural character of the nearby Tribeca neighborhood.

The design of the 340 apartments (80 percent market rate, 20 percent subsidized) maximizes the opportunities offered by the magnificent site. Curtain wall windows have been projected beyond the surface of the brick tower, enabling nearly all units to have corner views. Apartment windows have been extended to the floor, which allow tower apartments to have views down to the river activity below.

The two-story lobby was placed at the river's edge and provides splendid views shared by all tenants. Both the health club and laundry have been located with water views, and the rooftop terrace and solarium provide one of Manhattan's finest views for all residents.

above   Apartment interior
right   View from the north
opposite left   North façade relating to adjacent school
opposite top right   Canopy detail
opposite bottom right   Lobby looking toward river
photography   Paul Warchol Photography, Inc.; Stan Ries Photography

Canal Town West Housing–7

118.5 m/389 ft
37 stories
Residential
1999

Kobe, Hyogo Prefecture, Japan
KAJIMA DESIGN KANSAI; Urban Development Corporation

114

This building completes the urban development in front of Kobe Hyogo Station, called "Canal Town West," which uses the Hyogo Canal as a motif.

As the only skyscraper in the district, this building, which is located at the end of the canal, takes on the role as the landmark of the district, commemorating the rapid recovery from the devastating Hanshin-Awaji earthquake.

One of the unique features of the residential tower is the irregular octagonal layout with a central atrium that relates to the streetscape with various expressions. The color pattern of the façade, which accentuates its verticality, is further emphasi[?] at night with the key colors of each floor seen through the larg[e] balcony openings. The slanted grid handrailing and the deep balconies provide a sense of dimension and elegance to the overall architecture with the subtle sensitivity required for residential design.

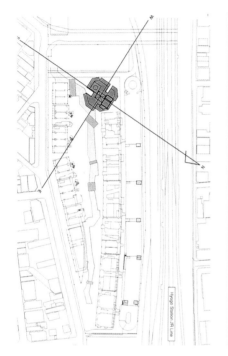

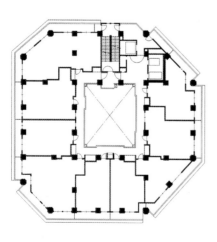

opposite top left   Site plan
opposite bottom left   Typical floor plan
opposite right   Exterior view (streetscape)
left   View from canal
below   Exterior view (balcony)
bottom right   Central atrium
photography   SS-Osaka Inc.

Eurotheum

110 m/361 ft
32 stories
Retail, offices, residential
1999

Frankfurt, Germany
Novotny Mähner Assoziierte

116

The architectural office of Novotny Mähner Associates (NMA) was awarded the commission to design this building in 1996.

The Eurotheum is not the first high-rise tower designed by NMA; it is one of a total of 10 high-rise towers that have been realised or are currently being realised over the 50 years of the company's existence.

At 110 meters/361 feet high, the Eurotheum is a dwarf tower and the architects have paid the greatest attention to maintaining the highest quality and finesse for the building.

The three outstanding features of Eurotheum are:

1 The combination of flats and offices in a high-rise building. The Eurotheum is the first example of this form in Germany.

2 The glazed lift shaft housing six panorama lift cars.

3 Effectiveness and flexibility in combination with a high standard of fittings.

The 74 apartments in the seven uppermost stories (23rd to 29th floors) are operated on the American model of a doorman concept. The apartments are furnished in various styles. The doorman sits in the so-called Euro-lounge on the 22nd floor. Additionally there is a bar, a lounge, and a small conference suite.

At the start of designing, the brief was to provide as many tenancy units as possible.

Today, the European Central Bank is the principal tenant of all the office space. Separate access to the apartments and offices is achieved by providing each user group with its own lift lobby. Bank employees enter at the first floor and residential tenants at ground floor.

Although both user groups use the same group of lifts, control of the lifts was altered so that intermixing is not permitted.

Acceptance of the building by its users, as the first few months have shown, is high, which is connected in no small part to the successful circulation.

above   Avantgarde
right   Central hall
opposite left   Eurotheum at night
opposite top right   Romance
opposite middle right   Residential floor plan
opposite bottom right   Ground floor plan
photography   H. G. Esch

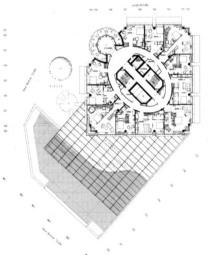

Highland Park

Hong Kong SAR, People's Republic of China

Ronald Lu & Partners (HK) Ltd.

Blocks 1 and 2: 96 m/315 ft;
blocks 3–6: 101 m/331 ft

28–30 stories

Residential

1999

118

This "Sandwich Class" government subsidized housing development was designed in 1995 for 1456 families whose financial position did not allow them to purchase their own private housing units during the property boom.

The site is situated on a hilltop overlooking the Kwai Chung Area, Kowloon Peninsula, and Victoria Harbour. A linear master layout for six 28–30-story residential towers was used to capture the panoramic peninsula and harbor view for most of the residential units. The tower and podium portion were arranged to minimize the site formation works on the existing platforms and facilitate a large, flat, and coherent podium garden on top of the car-parking areas.

Environmentally, a sun path analysis was carried out which substantiated the construction of a solar screen projection to the large glazed façades of the living room areas facing west. Large ventilating wells were also created at Blocks 3 to 6 to facilitate the air flow of the ventilated corridor on the typical floors. The podium landscaping area was placed to receive the southeast monsoon wind during summer. All public areas, car-parking floors, and the residential units were designed for cross-ventilation to minimize the use of mechanical extraction or air-conditioning.

A spatial hierarchy was intentionally created from the development entrance/shuttle lift lobby to the common and lift lobby of the towers. The oval-shaped plaza and the swimming pool echo the curvilinear form of the building mass.

A modular, flat layout was adopted to control the construction cost during the property boom. Variation to the building form was achieved by means of modifying the master bedroom modules and the addition of balconies on upper floors, which reduced the use of new timber form works for the construction.

opposite top left   Site plan
opposite bottom left   View of swimming pool
opposite right   View of north east
left   View of south west
below   Typical floor plan

Hollywood Terrace

128 m/420 ft

35 stories

Residential

1999

Hong Kong SAR, People's Republic of China

Rocco Design Ltd

120

The development consists of two 35-story towers on a five-level podium, which in turn sits on a steep slope. There is a total of 532 residential flats, amounting to about 40,780 square meters/438,956 square feet of domestic gross floor area.

Situated within the colorful, dense, and highly textured urban fabric of the old Central/Western Districts, and sandwiched between Hollywood Road and Queen's Road Central against a slope with a level difference of 23 meters/75 feet, the site calls for a careful response in terms of its environment, connection to context, and an appropriate interaction between the private and the public realms. On one hand, it poses a challenge for the development of typically dense residential accommodation (with a plot ratio of 9) under highly constrictive environmental and geological constraints. On the other, it offers an opportunity for urban regeneration and integration to complement and complete the existing open space, traffic, and circulation systems in the neighborhood.

Under the lease conditions, a certain amount of public space needs to be provided with part of the lot zoned as a public amenity. These are developed as a landscaped garden and a series of landscaped terraces that, together with the stairs and lifts, form part of an elaborate public route connecting Queen's Road Central with Hollywood Road that allows 24-hour pedestrian access through the site. This is carefully interwoven

with the private access route for residents, from both Queen's Road and Hollywood Road, to the residential tower lobbies and their own private amenity areas. The two routes intertwine but remain segregated.

The residential portion is developed into two towers of 35 storie These are, by marketing necessity, typically compact units with eight flats clustered around each core. But the units are carefu configured so that they all face predominantly north or south. Overlooking between units is essentially avoided and most living areas, despite the small unit size, are capable of being cross-ventilated.

The towers are set back as much as possible from noisy Queen Road, which helps to maximize the openness of the podium terraces in front to alleviate the harshness of the encroaching adjacent buildings. Nevertheless, the visual continuity of the street frontage is maintained, and the rhythmical arrangement of vertical piers both along Queen's Road and Hollywood Road makes a subtle reference to the traditional tenement buildings which once proliferated in the neighborhood. In particular, the ro of shop units along Hollywood Road, defined by the piers, are intended to reconnect the line of popular antique shops on eithe side of the site and to re-affirm Hollywood Road's status as "Th Antique Street" of Hong Kong.

below	Site plan
below right	Physical separation and visual connection of private and public spaces—view from private footbridge toward public walkway
opposite left	Public scenic lifts and private residential entrance on Queen's Road Central
opposite top right	Private footbridge looking toward public lifts at Hollywood Road level
opposite bottom right	View of development from Queen's Road Central

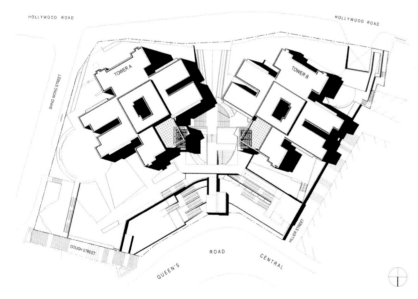

Republic Tower

110 m/361 ft
36 stories
Residential
1999

Melbourne, Victoria, Australia

Nation Fender Katsalidis Pty Ltd

Republic Tower is a 36-story residential building that rises from a five-story, mixed-use podium on the corner of Queen and Latrobe streets, Melbourne, and contains 87 single-story and two-story apartments. The apartments range from 150 square meters/ 1615 square feet to 600 square meters/6458 square feet, and the complex includes a restaurant, gymnasium, and a 25-meter/82-foot lap pool.

Typical floor layouts consist of four apartments with uninterrupted corner views of the Melbourne skyline. All of the penthouses comprise complete floor plates with 360-degree views. The external building fabric consists of stainless steel, dark glass, and precast concrete. A three-story-high curved wall has been dedicated to the community for displaying public art works.

This development is characterized by an unprecedented degree functional clarity and aesthetic sophistication that has set new standards for high-rise apartment design in Australia.

opposite left   Republic Tower detail
opposite right   Art installation at Republic Tower
               (by Howard Arkley)
left   South elevation façade
below   View from corner of Queen and
               Lonsdale streets
photography   John Gollings Photography

A: 102 m/336 ft; B: 180 m/591 ft;
C: 165 m/540 ft; D: 132 m/432 ft;
E: 109 m/359 ft

A: 31; B: 48; C: 46; D: 40; E: 33 stories

Residential

A: 2003; B: 2002; C: 1999;
D: 1999; E: 2001

Riverside Boulevard at Trump Place

New York, New York, USA

Costas Kondylis & Associates PC; Philip Johnson/Alan Ritchie Architects for 200 Riverside Blvd (C),
180 Riverside Blvd (D), 160 Riverside Blvd (E); Costas Kondylis & Partners LLP for 240 Riverside Blvd (A),
220 Riverside Blvd (B)

Eventually reaching from 59th Street to 72nd Street along the
Hudson River, Trump Place blends the serenity of its waterfront
location with the excitement of Manhattan's sophisticated upper
west side. Residents enjoy a friendly neighborhood ambience,
incredible open spaces, and unobstructed panoramic views.
Trump Place beautifully blends the energy of the city with the
rich tapestry of the river and sky, creating a place that is unique
to New York, and on par with the finest residential neighborhoods
in all the world.

top right Western skyline view
right Model of western skyline
photography Architecturalphotography.com

240 RIVERSIDE BOULEVARD (Building A)
opposite top left Site plan
bottom left Perspective view from
 the park
opposite bottom right Western elevation
photography Architecturalphotography.com

220 RIVERSIDE BOULEVARD (Building B)
opposite top middle Site plan
opposite top right Western elevation
photography Architecturalphotography.com

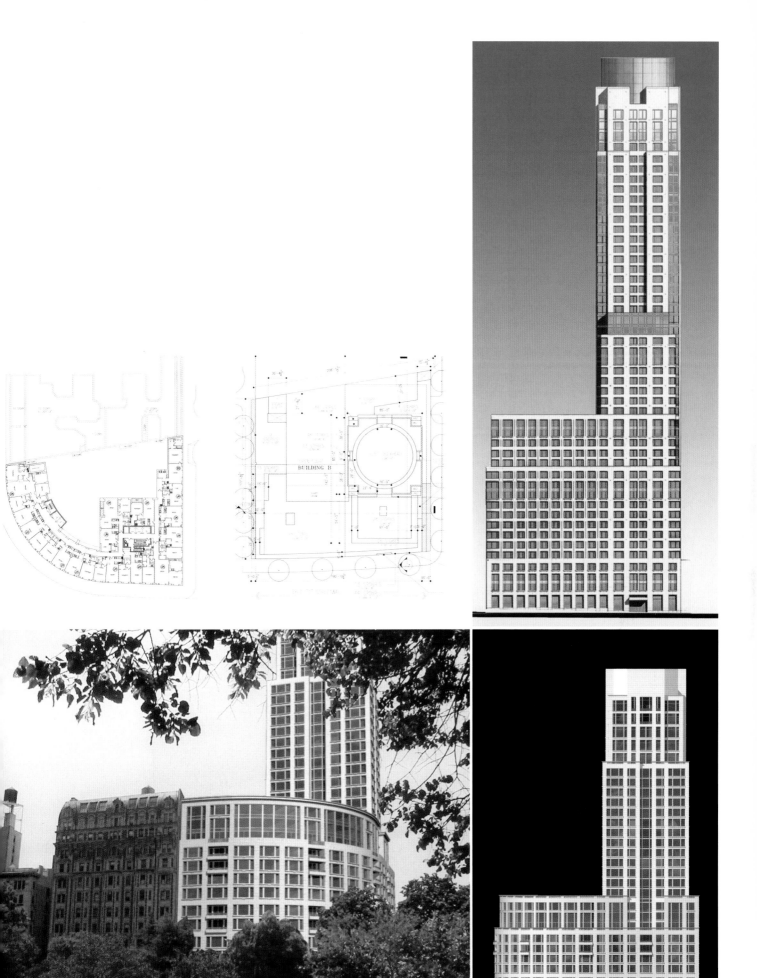

BUILDING B

126

200 RIVERSIDE BOULEVARD (Building C)
right   View from street
          (180 and 200 Riverside
          Boulevard)
below right   Site plan
photography   Architecturalphotography.com

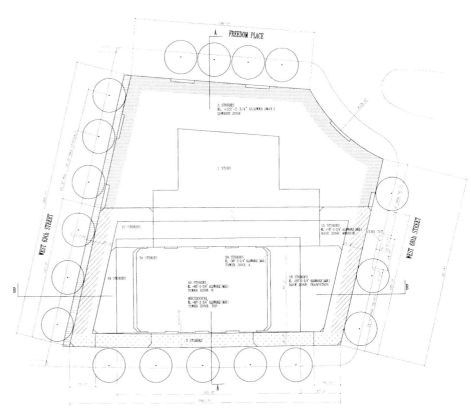

RIVERSIDE BOULEVARD (Building D)
below   Entrance
bottom left   Site plan
photography   Architecturalphotography.com

160 RIVERSIDE BOULEVARD (Building E)
below   Rendering of façade
bottom right   Site plan
rendering   Telsa

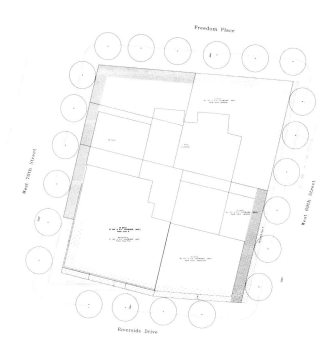

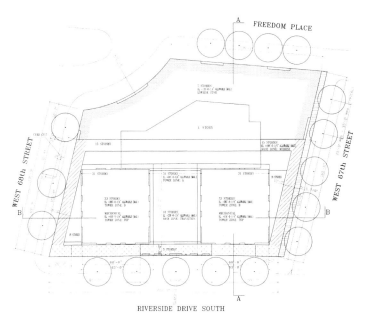

Royal Pavilion

129 m/423 ft
39 stories
Residential
1999

Shanghai, People's Republic of China
Dennis Lau & Ng Chun Man Architects & Engineers (H.K.) Ltd

The Royal Pavilion Development comprises two 39-story apartment towers located in a residential neighbourhood of Shanghai. At the time of completion the twin towers were the tallest residential buildings in Shanghai.

The towers are united at ground floor by a spacious central lobby.

The developer's management policy permitted the adoption of a centralized air-conditioning plant that is housed in the distinctive stories.

The development includes two levels of basement parking, a clu house, outdoor swimming pool, tennis courts, and basketball co

above — View of the forecourt entrance to the grand lobby shared by the twin towers
opposite left — View of the twin towers
opposite top right — Site plan
opposite bottom right — Typical floor plan
photography — Frankie Wong and Michael Tse Photography, Hong Kong

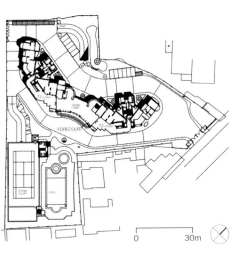

0   30m

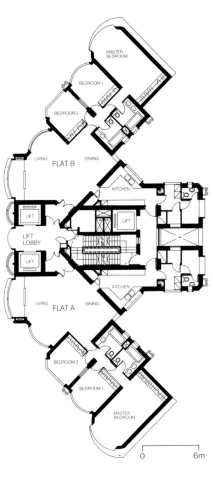

0   6m

The Bristol

149 m/488 ft
42 stories
Residential, retail
1999

Chicago, Illinois, USA

Solomon Cordwell Buenz & Associates Inc. (SCB)

Slender and elegant, this high-end, 190-unit condominium building rises 42 stories above Chicago's renowned Gold Coast, just off the Magnificent Mile. Charged with creating the most elegant atmosphere possible, Solomon Cordwell Buenz & Associates designed a unique structure shaped like a double diamond to give each of the six units per floor a corner view. Floor-to-ceiling windows flood the units with natural light, while providing spectacular cityscape views.

In keeping with the bustling, upscale urban neighborhood, the pedestrian-scaled first two floors feature retail space clad in granite while the building's articulated upper floors create classic lines that situate the building in the larger urban context. The s[...] level parking facility matches the residential tower in fenestrati[...] to create a unified expression.

above   Typical floor plan
right   View from Rush Street
opposite left   View toward Lake Michigan
opposite right   Corner detail
photography   Mark Ballogg of Steinkamp/Ballogg
             Photography, Chicago

The Golden Bay Garden

100 m/328 ft

25–31 stories

Residential

Phase I: 1999; Phase II: 2001

Futian, Shenzhen, People's Republic of China

Wong & Tung International Limited

132

The Golden Bay Garden project is located at the southern edge of Fu Tian district in the city of Shenzhen. The site enjoys the privilege of being situated at the northwest junction of the Fu Yong Road and Sa Zui Road stretch along the Shenzhen Bay, which enjoys the open landscape and overlooks the magnificent seaviews to the south. The site is well connected with easy access to all major traffic thoroughfares: southeast along Fu Yong Road into the urban district of Shen Zhen or northwest to the airport and expressway to Guang Zhou.

The design of Golden Bay Garden was intended to capture the advantage of the view of Shenzhen Bay. In order to enhance the spaciousness and allow for high visibility of each unit, the 10 tower blocks are divided into three different zones from east to west with harmonious array and disposition. The residential blocks are erected on top of the podium deck, facing south and enjoying the visual access to the coastline and the uninterrupted seaviews.

The ground and basement level of the podium are arranged to accommodate all the service facilities and car parking spaces.

By separating the circulation of residents and vehicles, the development provides a comfortable and tranquil space for a very favorable living environment.

With the site area of 42,500 square meters/457,470 square feet, the Golden Bay Garden provides about 1020 residential units with a total gross floor area of 123,500 square meters/1,329,354 square feet. This development consists of 1 residential blocks with varying heights of 25 to 31 stories. The residential units come in variety of configurations, from the smallest, which consists of 86 square meters/926 square feet, 138-square-meter/1485-square-foot standard units, to the larg 160–200-square-meter/1722–2153-square-foot duplex units, and the 180-square-meter/1937-square-foot to 240-square-meter/2583-square-foot penthouse units occupying the four to stories. Facilities include a kindergarten, swimming pool, and tennis courts, as well as an extensive landscaped podium garde and children's playground. A separate clubhouse is also implemented for residents' use.

below left   Master plan layout
below right   Landscape podium
opposite left   Poolside, clubhouse
opposite top right   Typical floor plan
opposite bottom right   Phenomenal view of Shenzhen Bay
photography   Wong Tung & Partners Ltd.

Wohnpark Neue Donau Tower

100 m/328 ft
33 stories
Residential
1999

Vienna, Austria

Harry Seidler & Associates

In 1993, Harry Seidler & Associates were commissed to design the complex consisting of seven six-story apartment blocks, a 100-meter/328-feet-high apartment and office tower, a multipurpose center (with 14 movie halls), and a variety of other facilities including a kindergarten, community centers, and a three-story carpark for 1500 vehicles.

The brief had suggested placing the apartment building across the expressway parallel to the spanning girders. Seidler, however, suggested angling the buildings across the expressway to distribute the load. This enabled the height of the buildings to be increased to nine stories.

The scheme created expansive and far more interesting spaces between the apartment buildings. More importantly, it ensured that nearly all of the 900 apartments in the complex enjoyed the views of Danube. It also created view corridors for three existing residential towers inland from the new complex.

The apartment blocks are profiled to step down toward the river giving the rooftop terraces views across the river to the old city the distance. This could be read as a subtle reference to the post-war tradition of Viennese public housing, recalling as it doe the Wohnpark Alt-Erlaa (1974) and Am Schöpfwerk (1974–81) both of which made a feature of terracing—private green space to complement public green spaces and wide range of commun amenities.

The complex tensions of the structural linearity of the buildings with the curvilinear features of the balconies, courtyard walls, rooftop lift enclosures, and walled public walkways create visual interest (assisted by the Lin Utzon murals on the end walls of th apartment buildings) and spatial variety. Landscaping and tree planting aim to create a sense of transparency without compromising privacy.

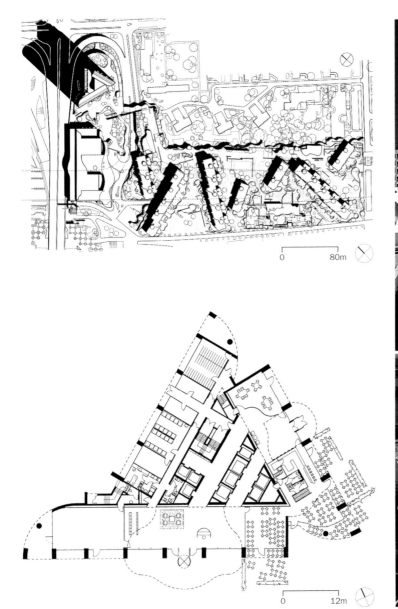

0   80m

0   12m

opposite top left   The total development
opposite bottom left   Tower ground level plan
opposite top right   Low housing and 35-story tower
opposite bottom right   View from tower over Danube
left   The tower with communication mast
bottom left   The view of the recreation area
below   The tower facing the plaza
photography   Eric Sierins

300 Park Avenue

152 m/500 ft
44 stories
Residential
2000

Atlanta, Georgia, USA

Burt Hill Kosar Rittelmann Associates

Located in the Atlanta suburb of Buckhead, this 44-story luxury condominium complex was designed as the first of several signature properties targeted to high-end residents. Its success was immediate, with all but five units sold before the occupancy permit was issued.

The project posed a number of design challenges to the architects. Municipal zoning required 12-meter/40-foot setbacks and a maximum of 37,160 square meters/400,000 square feet in apartment units. It also faced an FAA height restriction based on proximity to the local airport. The challenge was to fit the required number of units on a constricted site without sacrificing amenities.

The structure is comprised of a pre-stressed concrete frame with an 80-percent glass curtain wall of an energy-efficient type that minimizes heat gain. Streamlined curves and arched architectural forms create a dramatic silhouette.

The expansive lobby features art glass mirrors and doors, marble flooring, bronze wainscot, and decorative metal railings with hardwood trim. Other shared amenities include a wine cellar, a fitness center, a pool, and a clubroom. Reached by private elevators, individual units feature broad balconies and panoramic vistas, as well as standard features such as hardwood moldings and trim, oversized showers and whirlpool tubs, marble and hardwood flooring, granite kitchen counters, and high quality residential appliances.

The project has won an *Outstanding Achievement Award* from the American Concrete Institute, Georgia Chapter.

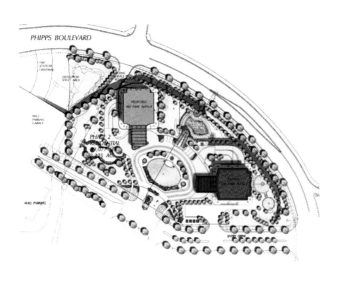

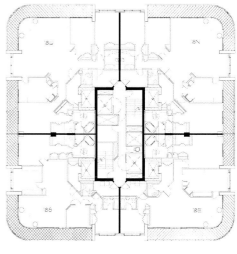

opposite top left	Entrance detail
opposite bottom left	Site plan
opposite right	Exterior from south
left	Exterior from below from west
top right	Floor plan
above	Lobby with seating
photography	Brian Gassel

515 Park Avenue

157.3 m/516 ft

43 stories

Residential

2000

New York, New York, USA

Frank Williams & Partners, Architects

At the time Frank Williams designed 515 Park Avenue, it was the first new residential tower on Park Avenue in nearly 20 years. The 43-story tower acts as a transition between the Park Avenue landmark residential district north of East 60th Street and the Park Avenue midtown office district south of East 60th Street.

The architectural design of 515 Park is closely tailored to the classic Park Avenue residential buildings which line the avenue from East 60th Street to 96th Street. Park Avenue has always been one of the most dignified streets in New York. The context of strong masonry buildings with punched windows and the classically strong corners are the predominant architectural features that characterize Park Avenue and whose design principles have been incorporated into the architectural design of this building. The architectural design of 515 Park Avenue would

make little sense in Los Angeles, Houston, or for that matter, a city other then New York. The architectural design starts with a strong 14-story street wall base of the tower, and there are two graceful setbacks. All of the setbacks are capped with a two-story series of pilasters and decorative balconies—this crowning occurs at each of the three setbacks in the residential tower.

The important site demanded the use of the finest materials. The architects proposed the use of French Magny limestone as the basic exterior material, accented by beige brick. The windows were carefully proportioned to complement the vertical proportions of most of the windows along Park Avenue. The "punched windows" provide a very strong tie to the existing Park Avenue architectural character.

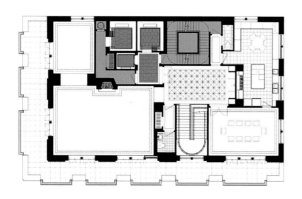

Edgewater Apartments

59 m/194.6 ft

15 stories

Residential

2000

West Vancouver, British Columbia, Canada

Robert A.M. Stern Architects; Lawrence Doyle Architect, Inc. (LDA)

The massing of this tower, containing 15 luxury units—three townhouse apartments at the base, 11 full-floor tower apartments, and a two-story penthouse apartment—responds to street setback and height zoning requirements, while the disposition of rooms within each apartment is influenced by the views of English Bay to the south and west and West Vancouver's uplands to the north.

The pedimented vault at the roof creates dramatic interior space in the penthouse apartment while masking mechanical function that would otherwise be intrusive to neighbors on the nearby hillside. It also helps distinguish the building from its largely unconsidered high-rise neighbors.

right   Pool
below right   Site plan
opposite top left   Top of building
opposite bottom left   View from English Bay
opposite top right   Lobby
opposite bottom right   Plan, floors 2–11
photography   Peter Aaron/Esto

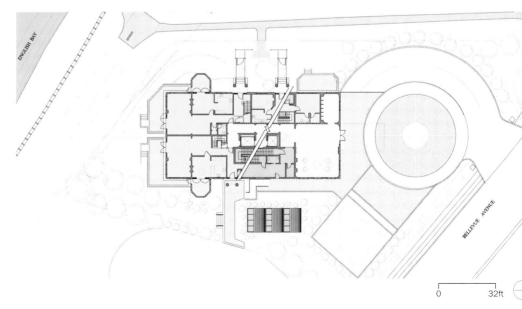

0   32ft

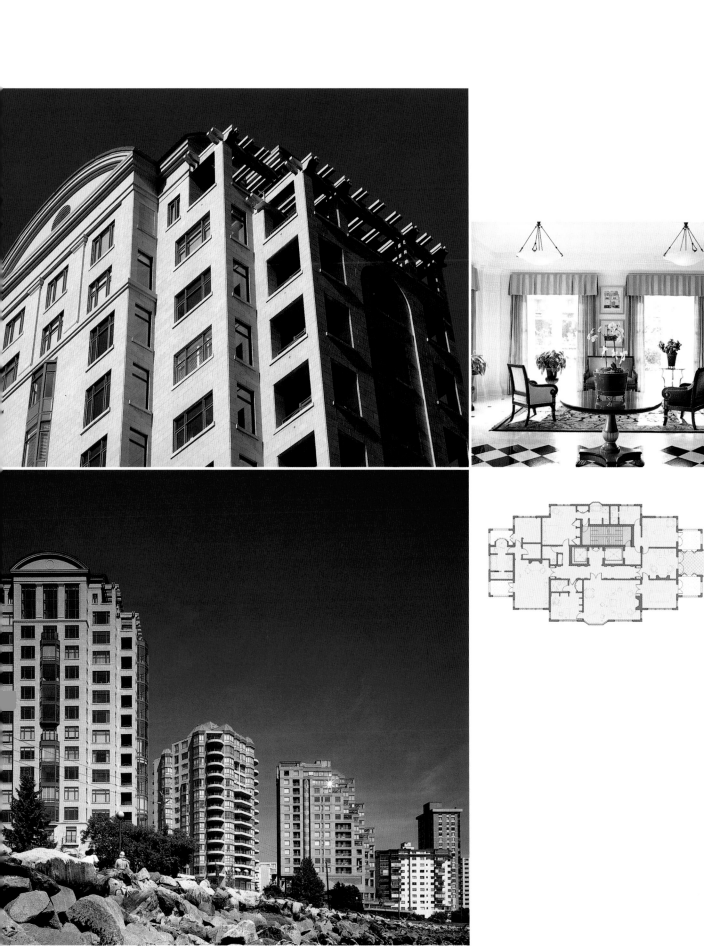

Florencia

75 m/246 ft

23 stories

Retail, residential

2000

St. Petersburg, Florida, USA

Sydness Architects, P.C.; Gillett Associates, Inc.

142

Sydness Architects has designed a two-phase, mixed-use project that will form the centerpiece of a revitalization for downtown St. Petersburg, Florida. The project, known as Florencia, includes a 23-story luxury condominium tower with retail at ground level and parking in a podium. On half of the adjacent block, a three-story retail and office building is planned with a courtyard entrance.

The project is on the site of the former Soreno Hotel across Beach Drive from the St. Petersburg Yacht Club and Fine Arts

Center, both of which are local landmarks designed in the Mediterranean style. The new buildings include elements that relate to these historical buildings and are built with stucco and clay-tile roofs. Arched windows and arcades at ground level wo to unify the downtown area architecturally.

Phase 1, the residential tower, opened in 2000. Phase 2, the retail and office building, opened in late 2001.

opposite top left   Club room
opposite bottom left   Penthouse master suite
opposite right   Aerial view looking west
top left   Front elevation from bay
left   Third level terrace
below   Typical tower floor plan
bottom right   Site plan
photography   George Cott/Chroma, Inc.

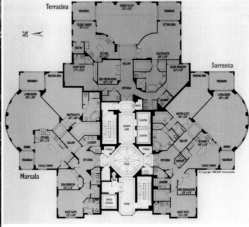

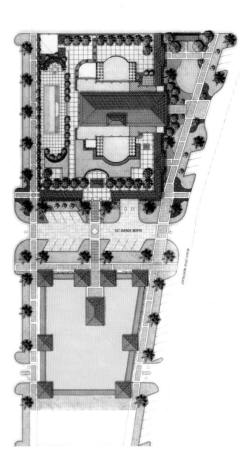

Glorietta 4/The Oakwood

116 m/380 ft
26 stories
Residential, retail, hotel
2000

Makati City, Philippines

Architecture International Ltd. (John P. Sheehy, FAIA, RIBA; William J. Higgins, AIA; Sherry Caplan, IIDA); GF & Partners

144

The Glorietta 4 hotel apartments are the newest addition to the 25-year evolution of an old city center, comprised of one- and two-story shops, into the contemporary Ayala Center, a mixed-use development. A master plan established separate "quads," each with its own mix of hotels, apartments, retail space, and feature parks. An unused outdoor space was covered to create a central "Glorietta," tying each of the quads together.

It was Ayala Land's desire that the Glorietta 4, a 26-story hotel-apartment complex, provide a new signature identity for the center. The overall retail space of the center was expanded by adding five levels of restaurants, cinemas, high-end shops, and

a food court, which service the long-term-stay hotel apartments above. It was necessary to create an effective entrance/drop-off for the Glorietta 4 retail and hotel and also integrate the hotel apartments with their park setting.

The landmark design for the Glorietta 4 provided a unique skyscape, its lantern effect lighting the skyline at night, and providing a distinguishing identity during the day. Front door identities were provided for the hotel and retail shops to distinguish their entrances. By integrating the park with the drop-off area, carrying its geometry and landscaping into the entrance, a special arrival experience was achieved.

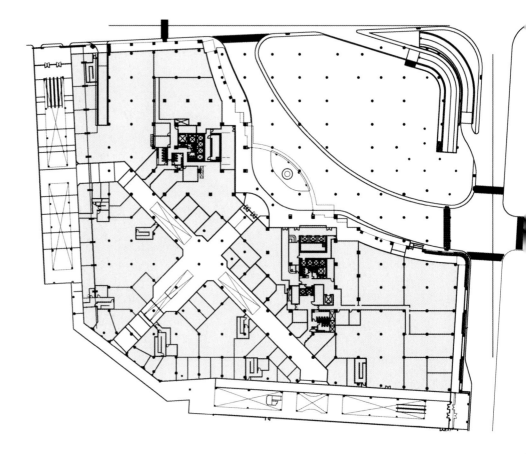

top right   Ground level plan
right   Rendering
rendering   Phil Ishimaru & Lawrence Leong
opposite left   View of The Oakwood at Glorietta 4
photography   Danny Feliciano
opposite right   Typical floor plan, 13th–18th floors

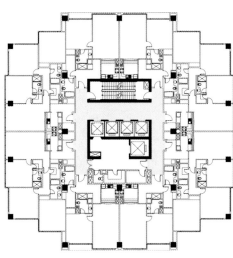

Miranova

86.9 m/285 ft

27 stories

Residential

2000

Columbus, Ohio, USA

Arquitectonica; HKS Inc.

Miranova is a mixed-use "community within a city" built on a 2.5-hectare/6-acre site on the Sciotto Riverfront south of downtown Columbus. It is just far enough from the downtown core to command a panoramic view of the entire skyline.

The residential tower is composed of two thin, curved volumes, one glassy and transparent, the other solid and opaque, bypassing each other racing downstream together with the Ohio River rapids. The curve exposes the main rooms of all the 120 luxury residential units to the views of downtown Columbus. The glass volume, facing downtown, curves in plan to emphasize the panorama notion. A more solid stone masonry volume acts as backdrop for the glass volume and emphasizes the frontality to

downtown. The two volumes appear to slide past each other. This articulation makes the building appear as two very thin sla The solid volume is taller and projects beyond the glass volume making itself evident from downtown (and, by the way, hiding elevator overruns and mechanical areas). The building profile curves upward toward the river like two sails making a dynamic composition, implying movement and conveying the sense of a lighter building. The tower rises from a three-story parking and amenities podium whose arcade aligns with a new street that is part of this new neighborhood at the edge of downtown.
The balance of the project, also designed by Arquitectonica, includes two office towers, retail, and a riverfront walk, all part of the re-urbanization of Columbus.

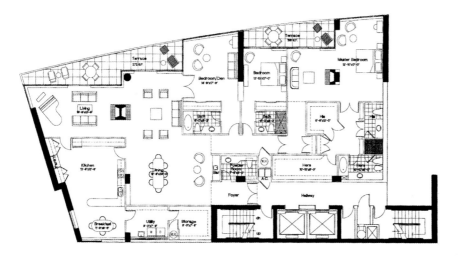

opposite top   Miranova is sited on the Sciotto River, south of downtown Columbus, Ohio, just far enough from the downtown to command a panoramic view of the entire skyline

opposite bottom left   Typical floor plan

opposite bottom right   Site/Landscaping plan

left   The residential tower is composed of two thin, curved volumes, one glassy and transparent, the other solid and opaque. The more solid stone masonry volume acts as backdrop for the glass volume making the two volumes appear to slide past each other.

above   The residential tower, to the left, rises from a three-story parking and amenities podium, whose arcade aligns with a new street that is part of this new neighborhood. The office building to the right, also designed by Arquitectonica, is the first of two office towers and a retail component that will connect to a new riverfront walk.

photography   Brad Feinknopf

Monte Vista

116.9 m/384 ft
30 stories
Residential
2000

Hong Kong SAR, People's Republic of China
Ronald Lu & Partners (HK) Ltd.

Monte Vista is a private residential development comprising 12 residential towers with a two-story podium, a three-story clubhouse, and a three-story basement carpark. Being triangular in shape, the 30-story residential towers are sited in a V-shape in order to maximize the exposure of the residential flats toward both the sea view in front and the mountain view at the rear.

The clubhouse forms a prominent element of the whole development where residents can enjoy the grandeur of the triple-height entrance foyer with a water feature at the front. Footbridges with skylights and planters were adopted to create natural surroundings, enriching the user's journey to and from the residential towers.

Many green elements are introduced such as a lotus pond, lawn, naturalistic stream, water feature, and a reinforced concrete grid plantation along the slope, in order to achieve the concept of "architecture in nature."

above — Indoor swimming pool
above right — View of development from north side
right — Site plan
opposite left — View of development from outdoor pool
opposite top right — Club house lobby
opposite bottom right — Typical floor plan

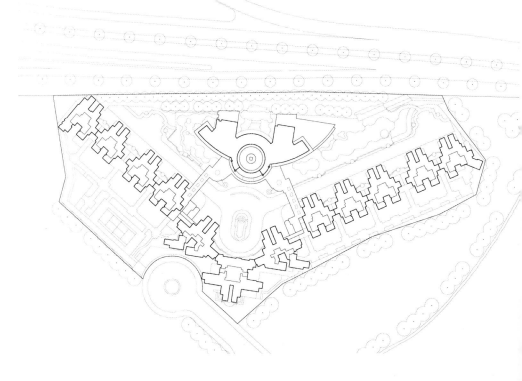

Olympic City

120 m/394 ft
35–39 stories
Residential
2000

Hong Kong SAR, People's Republic of China
P&T Architects and Engineers Ltd.

150

One of the major projects along the new Lantau Airport Railway, straddling both sides of the West Kowloon Expressway and the new MTRC station, are two sites linked by pedestrian bridges. Along the edges of the site are nine upmarket residential towers, 35–39 stories tall, that capture the prime sea view. The buildings are oriented to create a large central landscaped deck above the clubhouse and carpark.

As an important landmark and emerging new focus for the city, the development is seen as an opportunity to create a city with a city, distinguished by its clean, contemporary design.

above   Overall site view
opposite left   View of major façade
opposite right Typical floor plan
photography   P&T Photographic Department

Park Tower

251 m/825 ft
67 stories
Residential, hotel, retail
2000

Chicago, Illinois, USA

Lucien Lagrange Architects (formerly Lucien Lagrange and Associates); HKS Inc.

Lucien Lagrange has focused on creating architectural design that meets the street in a gentle way, enhancing the pedestrian's experience with the building and contributing to the experience of the neighborhood. Park Tower is a significant achievement in this approach.

"I thank Mr. Lagrange for what I consider to be a true triumph of contextual design. The respect that his building shows to its immediate adjacent properties, the detail with which that has been carried out, its contextual sensitivity to Chicago's historic Water Tower, and indeed to the Michigan Avenue streetscape is a true triumph", said Reuben Hedlund, Chairman of the Chicago Planning Commission.

The first two stories are clad in buff-colored limestone with architectural precast concrete above. The building is topped with a pitched, copper roof with four spires. The richness of detail and attention to materials increases at the building's base, a significant enhancement that adds value to the building and interest to pedestrians. Lucien strove to design a tall building that

rises from the ground while engaging people at street level. The result is that people love this building.

Elegantly designed to assume a prominent place on Chicago's Magnificent Mile, this structure intelligently combines a 20-story luxury hotel and 47 stories of high-end condominium space with eight full-floor penthouses. Optimal views of the lake and city are provided in all the residences. The building is the tallest precast concrete-faced residential building in the world. It sits on a 2601-square-meter/28,000-square-foot site and includes a 200-car parking structure on four floors at the back of the site, cleverly hidden behind a well-articulated façade.

The verticality of the building is softened with classic design features including setbacks and curved balconies to create a sculptural effect. The building's scale and design relates to specific buildings in the surrounding area. The landmark building to the north was incorporated into the hotel design and its façade was renovated and preserved.

below left   Residential entry
below right   Residential entry detail
opposite left   Overall view
opposite top right   Penthouse floor plan
opposite bottom right   Elevation
photography   Barbara Karant
floor plan   Lucien Lagrange
Architects

Tavistock II, Aigburth, and Valverde

Tavistock II: 166 m/545 ft;
Aigburth: 183 m/600 ft; Valverde:
119 m/390 ft

Tavistock II: 46; Aigburth: 47;
Valverde: 36 stories

Residential

1999/2000

154

Hong Kong SAR, People's Republic of China

Wong Tung & Partners Limited

Located near the peak of Hong Kong Island, TAV Redevelopment (Tavistock II, Aigburth Hall & Valverde Redevelopment) is a two-phase luxury residential development.

The first phase of the project, Valverde Tower, consists of a 36-story tower, housing 82 units ranging in size from 71 square meters/764 square feet to 271 square meters/2917 square feet. All units are disposed to face Hong Kong Harbour. The massing of the rooftop spires, influenced by the art deco age, provides the duplex and triplex penthouses with generous rooftop terraces. At the base of the tower, a double-height lobby, a carpark, and a residents' club have been accommodated within the compact and steeply sloping site. The club features a tennis court, pool, fitness centre, function room, and a children's play area.

The second phase of this development consists of two new residential blocks, Tavistock II and Aigburth Towers (36 and 36 stories respectively), and a renovated existing residential block of 13 stories. The towers sit atop an 11-story podium, which houses a residents' club unparalleled in Hong Kong. Among the facilities provided are two outdoor pools, an outdoor tennis court, an indoor badminton and basketball court, squash court, gymnasium, aerobics room, billiard room, function rooms, mahjong rooms, and children's play area. Extensive landscaping at the podium deck provides a natural garden for the residents and includes a dramatic three-story waterfall linking the upper and lower pools. Units range in size from 140 square meters/1507 square feet to the 600 square meters/6458 square feet of living space found in the Aigburth duplex penthouse.

below   Site plan
bottom right   Edgeless pool
bottom left   Valverde typical floor plan
opposite left Aigburth Towers
opposite top right   Valverde main elevation
opposite bottom right Tavistock II, Aigburth, and
               Valverde from the peak
photography   Wong Tung & Partners
               Limited

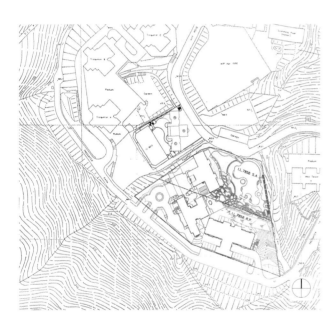

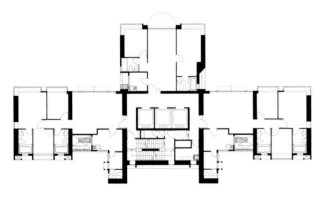

The Chatham

122 m/399.5 ft

32 stories

Retail, residential

2000

New York, New York, USA

Robert A.M. Stern Architects; Ismael Leyva Architects, P.C.

156

This 21,460 square-meter/231,000-square-foot tower consists of 2044 square meters/22,000 square feet of retail and 94 apartments.

The base of the building rises to 26 meters/85 feet and follows the property line. Above the base, the building sets back as per New York City zoning laws. On the 65th Street side is the entrance for the condominium tower. The entrances to the retail spaces are along Third Avenue.

The brick and limestone façades and the building's massing recall those of the highly respected luxury apartment buildings along Park Avenue. The two-story base is limestone and above the façades are brick with limestone accents. The façades are articulated with French balconies, bay windows, and subtle changes in plane in the shaft of the building. The top of the building consists of a series of setbacks culminating in a lantern.

above   View of retail along Third Avenue façade
right   View from north down Third Avenue
opposite left   View from south up Third Avenue
opposite top right   Lobby
opposite middle right   Plan, floor 32
opposite bottom right   Plan, floors 16–21
photography   Peter Aaron/Esto

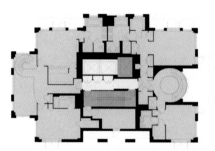
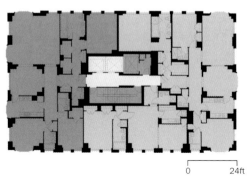

0   24ft

Trinity Place

79 m/260 ft
18 stories
Residential. retail
2000

Boston, Massachusetts, USA

CBT/Childs Bertman Tseckares, Inc.

158

Trinity Place is located at Copley Square in Boston's Back Bay. The 22,296-square-meter/240,000-square-foot, 18-story building provides 836 square meters/9000 square feet of street-level retail and restaurant space on Huntington Avenue, 104 high-end and luxury housing units, and three levels of below-grade parking. Amenities for residents include private balconies and a health club.

Distinguished neighbors of the new building include the Boston Public Library, designed by McKim Mead & White in 1888; H.H. Richardson's Trinity Church, designed in 1872; and the Copley Plaza Hotel by Henry Hardenbergh, erected in 1912. Immediately to the south are the high-rise towers of the Marriott and Westin Hotels at Copley Place.

The prominence of the site, together with the significance of neighboring buildings, necessitated the resolution of a number of urban design challenges. To maximize views and the impact of

the library for those traversing Dartmouth Street and Huntington Avenue, the new building was set back from the full extension of its unique triangular site. By further setting back the higher stories, shadows on the square as well as the library could be minimized.

A collision of sorts takes place on the site between the Back Bay and Huntington Avenue grids. To acknowledge this urban design reality, the building was designed to reflect the geometry of both entities. The lower stories of the building preserve the street wall of Huntington Avenue, while the high-rise portion is oriented with the grid of the Back Bay.

The building's design is intended to distinguish it from the more box-like towers located nearby. Materials are stone or precast concrete with stone detailing, and an architectural metal roof caps the building. Bay windows provide an additional reference to the architecture of the Back Bay.

top left   Ground floor retail; Salamander, one of the city's most popular restaurants

photography   Edward Jacoby, Jacoby Photography

top right   Exterior front façade

photography   Edward Jacoby, Jacoby Photography

opposite top left   Exterior front façade as seen from Copley Squ

photography   Edward Jacoby, Jacoby Photography

opposite bottom left   Window detail with Boston Public Library in th background

photography   Edward Jacoby, Jacoby Photography

opposite right   Lobby interior of Trinity Place

photography   Courtesy Gauthier Stacy

COSCO Brilliant City

48–100 m/157–328 ft

15–34 stories

Residential, commercial, school, kindergarten

2001–2004

Shanghai, People's Republic of China

East China Architectural Design & Research Institute Co., Ltd. (ECADI)

160

below   View of first-stage slab-type plan
bottom left   View of first-stage spot-type residences
bottom right View of first-stage slab-type residences
opposite left First-stage view from the river
opposite top right First-stage spot-type residences' plan
opposite bottom right Fountain plaza
photography   Ni Yian

COSCO Brilliant City will be comprised, when fully completed, of 11,000 apartment units spread among 33 buildings over a total of 1.6 million square meters/17,222,400 square feet of which 770,000 square meters/8,288,280 square feet are already completed.

Concerning the reform of an old urban district in Shanghai, its high investment, high habitation density and high FAR are of an unavoidable reality. How to transfer this realistic crux into a superiority of the planning design itself is the target that this project strives to attain.

The planning attempts to appropriately integrate the functions of residences, parking lots and commercial facilities by adopting a highly integrated method. At the same time, it attempts to meet the demand of social communication and the different high standards of modern life; it also makes every effort to efficiently lower the architectural density to enable the green environment become the true theme of the residential space.

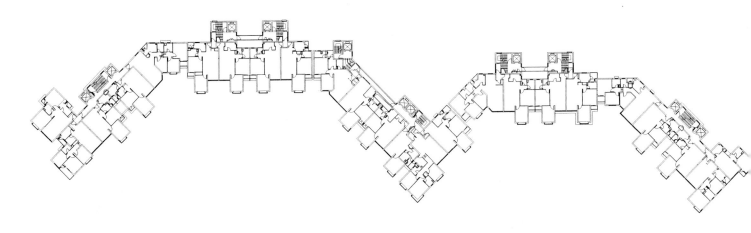

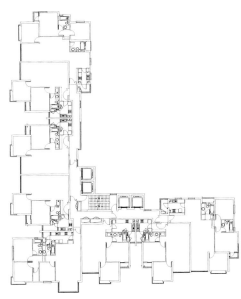

Elit Residence

150 m/492 ft
39 stories
Residential, retail, fitness center
2001

Sisli, Istanbul, Turkey
BSB Architects, London

Elit Residence is located in Sisli, central Istanbul, in a densely populated residential and commercial part of the city, which was mainly developed after the 1950s. However, there was a large area of undeveloped land, which includes the site of Elit Residence, with a large shopping center under construction on one of the adjoining sites and further high-rise residential and commercial developments on the other side.

The tower block of Elit Residence contains 61 apartments of various sizes, ranging from 125-square-meter/1345-square-foot two-bedroom units to 250-square-meter/2691-square-foot three- and four-bedroom apartments, with some larger two-story penthouses at the spiraling top. All apartments have panoramic views over the city toward the Bosphorous and the Marmara Sea in the distance. Five stories of podium levels below the tower contain a health club with a swimming pool, gymnasium, squash courts, and saunas; a restaurant; shops; garden terrace with tennis courts; and service areas and underground car parking.

The reinforced concrete structure of the building is designed to resist earthquake forces. The main structural elements of the tower are the cross-walls dividing the elliptical plan into four quarters with additional columns on the external perimeter. The wet areas of the flats are located in the central part of the ellipse, allowing continuous windows for the habitable rooms to enjoy the views.

BSB Architects were appointed in June 1996 following a concept design presentation. Construction started on site in April 1998 and was completed in June 2001. The building was nominated by an international jury for 2001 MIPIM Awards as one of three projects in the residential category.

above   Living room of larger apartments
right   Living room of smaller apartments
opposite left   View from northwest
opposite top right   Typical floor plan with three apartments
opposite bottom right   Site plan
photography   Courtesy Yapi Kredi Koray

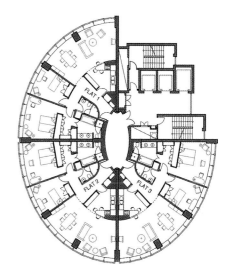

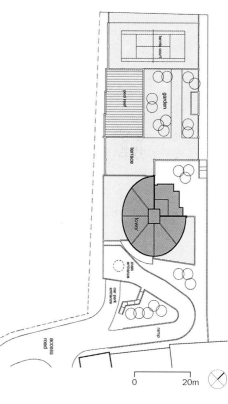

0   20m

Hoge Erasmus (formerly Erasmus Tower)

90 m/295 ft
29 stories
Offices, residential
2001

Rotterdam, The Netherlands
Klunder Architecten/Ir. B.J. Sybesma

164

Hoge Erasmus is situated near the foot of the new city bridge, which connects the north and south banks of Rotterdam. In the concept, seen from a town-planning viewpoint, the point of the intersection of the city axis and the right riverbank of the river Meuse is marked by three high-rise accents.

For more than four centuries this area was a maritime destination, where shipyards, ropeyards, and dockyards were situated. Today, a great number of shipping companies still have their offices in the area.

The massive black substructure with its heavy, steel V-shaped column base gives the building a maritime character. The curved façade, facing the riverside, refers to the specific location on the bank of the river Meuse where the inside bend turns into the outside bend.

The ground floor has a public character. The substructure contains offices and the floors above contain apartments of various sizes. As a result of the low apron walls in all the apartments, magnificent views of the city and the river, with its lively shipping activities, are offered in all the apartments.

above — East façade, night view
right — South façade, view from street level
opposite left — North façade, view from street level
opposite top right — Floor plan, 28th level
opposite bottom right — East and south façade
photography — Marcel van Kerckhoven

Leninsky Prospekt

Moscow, Russia

George Mailov & Archizdrav's Partners

116-1: 114.6 m/376 ft;
128-1: 106.7 m/350 ft

30 stories

Residential

1998/2001

This project, the reconstruction of a large Moscow residential quarter, has been the most important and significant project for "Archizdrav." This work was approved by the Moscow government and began in 1993. The site plays an important role in Moscow city's urban unit because it is enclosed between Leninsky Avenue and Vernadsky Avenue, and Lobachevsky Street and Kravchenko Street, and covers 118 hectares/292 acres.

More than 850,000 square meters/9,149,400 square feet of housing are currently under construction and a significant amount has been completed.

The multifunction development consists of 30-floor residential buildings, with two–three levels of underground parking; 25-story municipal residential buildings; 9-, 12-, and 15-story blocks of flats; schools; supermarkets; and business centers. The reconstruction is based on building the new housing on empty sites and then the demolition of existing dilapidated, five-story houses.

The most interesting and important part of this project is that it represents a holistic architectural ensemble: one style, one image, and one structure. These five residential buildings (two of them have been built and the others are under construction) are situated on Leninsky Avenue. They are successfully integrated into the existing urban environment.

The construction of these buildings is based on using reinforced monolithic concrete, finished with brick, instead of the standard panel construction that is so widespread in Russia. This allows the creation of spacious and glazed interiors, with 9-meter/30-foot spans for securing maximum living comfort. It also provided the opportunity to create many glazed surfaces, which make the façades expressive and unique for dwelling. While the overall appearance is welcoming and inviting, the internal layout is functional and practical, allowing for smooth circulation and maximum usable space.

opposite	Residential building 116–1, lobby interior
photography	JSC Kvartal 32–33
left	Panoramic view, quarter 32–33
photography	Architectural-Planning-Artistic Firm Archizdrav Ltd
bottom left	Residential Buildings 128–1 and 116–1, Leninsky Avenue, quarter 32–33
photography	Architectural-Planning-Artistic Firm Archizdrav Ltd & JSC Kvartal 32–33
bottom right	Quarter 32–33, site model
photography	Architectural-Planning-Artistic Firm Archizdrav Ltd
below	Residential building 128–1, lobby interior
photography	Architectural-Planning-Artistic Firm Archizdrav Ltd

Millennium Place

Boston, Massachusetts, USA

Gary Edward Handel + Associates; CBT/Childs Bertman Tseckares, Inc.

North building: 114 m/375 ft;
south building 122 m/400 ft
33/37 stories
Residential, hotel, retail, theaters
2001

168

Millennium Place is an important part of the revitalization of one of Boston's toughest neighborhoods, formerly known as the "Combat Zone." It achieves this by bringing the "critical mass" of mixed-use residential, retail, and entertainment venues to the area. The program includes a total of 400 luxury residences, 200 Ritz-Carlton five-star hotel rooms, 3900 cinema seats, and a 9290-square-meter/99,998-square-foot state-of-the-art fitness and recreation club housed in two high-rise buildings, which are a stunning addition to the Boston skyline, integrating subtly into the neighborhood and marking the energy and dynamism of the 21st century. The program also includes the renovation and re-use of the 1934 Paramount Theater, previously in disrepair.

The challenge was to create a vital environment in a formerly dangerous and depressed area. Millennium Place achieves this by housing the entertainment, retail, and fitness club in a full block base, which reinforces the street line and the mid-rise texture of the surrounding 19th- and 20th-century commercial buildings.

Each corner of the base relates to the surrounding urban fabric of Boston and invites people in by being given a special function. The natural bend in Washington Street at the Avery intersection is marked prominently using a bold figural "basket" element. This acts as a visual marker for entry into the building, drawing people down Washington Street from the Downtown Crossing retail area. All entries to the building are from the street, with no internal pedestrian mall, encouraging pedestrian activity in the neighborhood. The theater entry is located at the busy intersection of Tremont and Avery streets, overlooking the Boston Common Park with easy access to the Park Street subway station. The condominium towers rise above the base, but are extended down and visually connected to street. The hotel guest rooms form a "bar" along Avery Street mediating between the building's tower and base. At the skyline, the residential towers mark the southeastern corner of the park, framing the intersection of Avery and Washington streets.

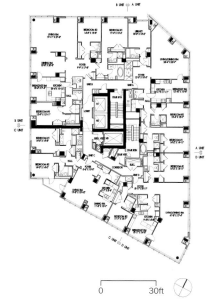

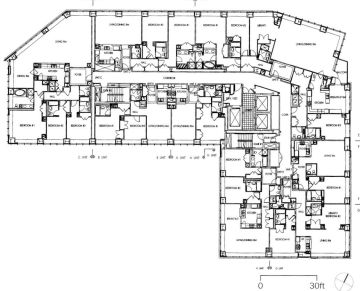

opposite top left   View from Boston common
photography   David Desroches
opposite top right   Lobby
photography   David Desroches
opposite bottom left   North residential tower floor plan
opposite bottom right   South residential tower floor plan
left   Millennium Place
photography   Steve Dunwell
above   View along Tremont Street
photography   David Desroches

Neguri Gane

150 m/492 ft

41 stories

Residential

2001

Benidorm, Alicante, Spain

Peréz-Guerras Arquitectos & Ingenieros; Urbano Igaralde Telletxea

As the project site is located in the high part of the city and at an approximate distance of 1 kilometer/0.6 mile from the sea, Pérez-Guerras and his team stylized the design of the building (the base plan is 27 meters/88 feet by 22 meters/72 feet) to have a direct view of the sea. A community pool is also located on the 26th floor, which provides the opportunity to swim while enjoying the magnificent view of the Mediterranean Sea and its shores. This floor, designed with more height than the rest, allows the sun to enter the swimming pool area and the two terraces. This sun and light intake is also increased as the shape of the building is narrower from this floor to the top of the building.

The sea and its waves are prevalent in the design of the tower, inspiring the curve of its façades and balconies, which are cut by the straight lines of the concrete structural walls. The hanging vegetation will also add to this sense of movement. In this way, the 40th-floor plan changes its form as the building rises.

The building, with its 145-meter/476-foot height, is much higher than its neighbors (Cibeles Building and Neptuno Building) and at present, the highest apartment building in Spain.

The structure of the building, made of high-resistance concrete, is designed with vertical walls that follow a radial scheme around a huge column that resists the different structural strains of the building.

For emergency evacuation, two staircases were designed in concrete and joined to the general volume of the building.

The top of the building is finished with a hat-shaped dome.

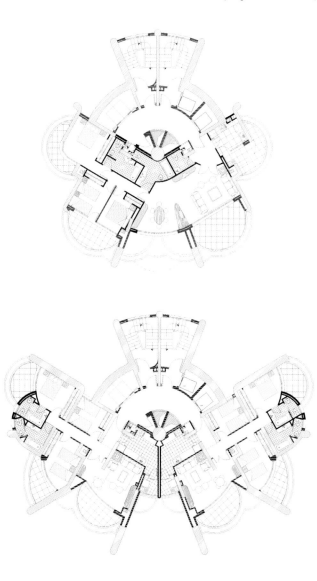

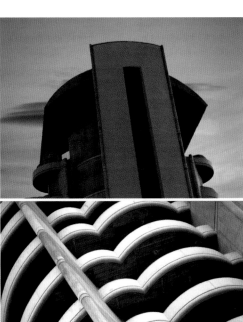

opposite top left   35th floor plan
opposite bottom left   11th–13th floor plan
opposite right   Front view
left   Lateral view
top right   Top of building
above   Terraces
photography   Fernando Marcia Domene

Ocean Pointe

172 m/564 ft
52 stories
Residential
2001

Hong Kong SAR, People's Republic of China

Dennis Lau & Ng Chun Man Architects & Engineers (H.K.) Ltd

Ocean Pointe comprises three 52-story towers above a podium carpark, clubhouse, and landscaped deck. Each of the blocks employs a "half-moon" plan that orientates all apartments outwards in order that they enjoy the dramatic views of the sea and the Tsing Ma Bridge.

In view of the coastal setting and unobstructed views of the si a resort atmosphere, reflected in both the building details and palette of materials used, was adopted.

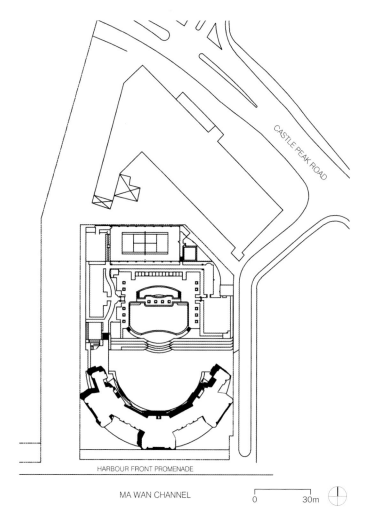

CASTLE PEAK ROAD

HARBOUR FRONT PROMENADE

MA WAN CHANNEL

0   30m

above   Site plan
right   Conceptual rendering of the project
opposite left   Ocean Pointe
opposite right Typical floor plan
photography   Frankie Wong and Michael Tse Photography,
             Hong Kong

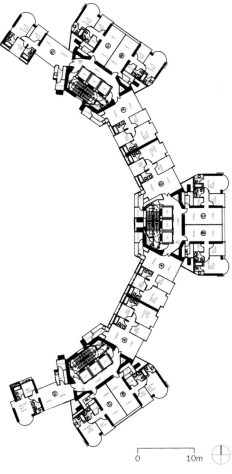

0   10m

One Wall Centre

137 m / 450 ft

46 stories

Residential, hotel

2001

Vancouver, British Columbia, Canada

Busby + Associates Architects

This is the second phase of the Wall Centre Hotel complex, the city's first "green" tower, and the tallest building in Vancouver.

At the highest point of land in the downtown core and at a height of 137 meters/450 feet, the unique elliptical tower shape is a distinctive and elegant landmark on the city's skyline. Appropriate for Vancouver's first tower of the new millennium, the building incorporates many technological innovations.

The 48-story tower is a combination of hotel space (25 floors) and private residential (17 floors) with a total building area of 42,955 square meters/462,000 square feet. Hotel amenities include a ballroom, restaurant, meeting rooms, boardrooms, and a business center. Universal access suites have special provisions for wheelchair and hearing-impaired guests. Three upper floors of the hotel are a time-share resort, with high-end finishes distinguishing these rooms from typical hotel suites.

The private residential units residing in the upper floors are large and luxurious, filled with natural light and expansive views. With only four units per floor and glass window walls, each suite is characterized by unparalleled views of mountains, ocean, and city. Residents are also able to take advantage of an impressive range of hotel amenities.

One Wall Centre leads Vancouver's environmental building standards, and is, according to the architect, the "greenest" high-rise building in the city. The four-sided structural silicone curtain wall-clad tower not only creates dynamic reflections of the surrounding cityscape, it also surpasses ASHRAE 90.1 energy requirements through a number of environmentally friendly design features:

- high-performance "three element" glazing system
- shading devices along the Volunteer Square façade
- operable windows in each unit, for natural ventilation
- energy-efficient light sources
- silver-coated clear glass maximizing interior daylighting
- electrical controls to regulate waste and recover energy
- low-water-consumption plumbing fixtures
- building orientation optimizes heat pump energy transfer between north and south façades
- interior finish materials with low-embodied energy.

The small building footprint, and careful positioning allowed room on the site for an important new civic space to be created—Volunteer Square will be at the corner of Burrard and Nelson streets, and is a public space specifically designed to honor the work and legacy of Vancouver's volunteer community.

above	Interior of restaurant
	photography Colin Jewall
right	Tower at sunrise
	photography Nic Lehoux
opposite left	Tower at sunset
	photography Nic Lehoux
opposite top right	Site plan
opposite middle right	Floor plan of typical residential floor
opposite bottom right	Floor plan of typical hotel floor

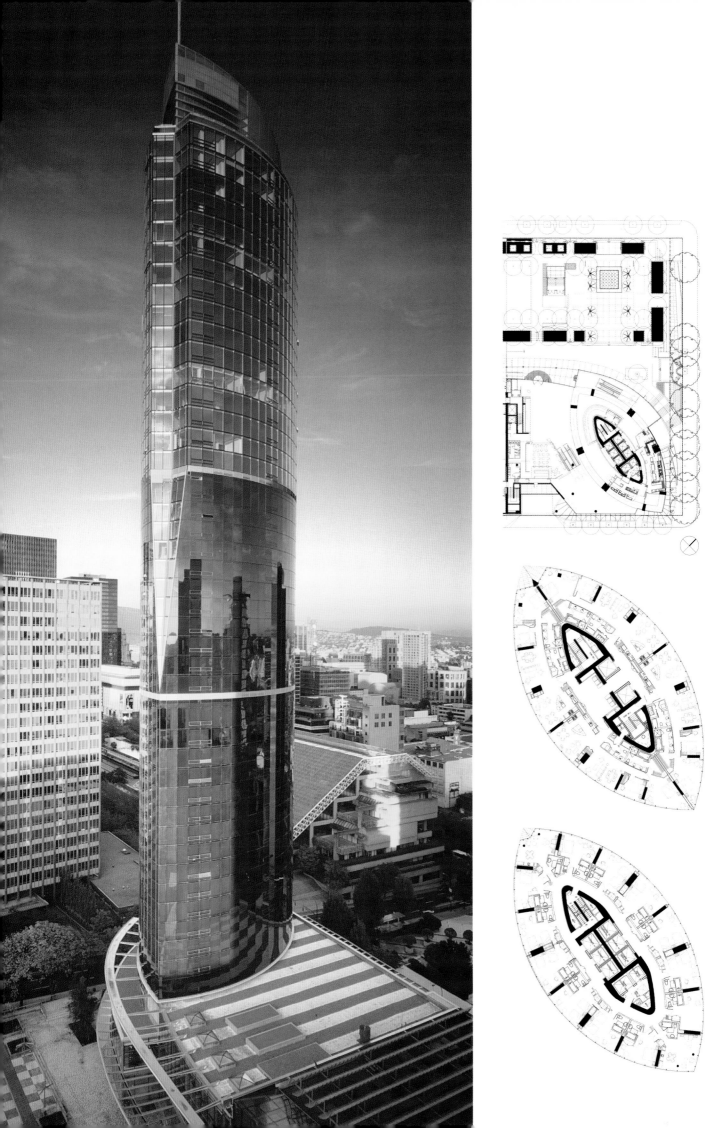

Orchard Scotts

Singapore

Arquitectonica; Ong & Ong Architects Pte. Ltd.

20-story towers: 64 m/ 210 ft;
18-story tower: 58 m/190 ft
20/18 stories
Residential
2001

This project in Singapore consists of 640 luxury serviced apartments, varying between one to four bedrooms, in three high-rise towers with a clubhouse, swimming pool, putting green, and other amenities.

The first tower is a perfect square with a central square cutout. It alternates gray glass and simulated blue stone striping with a horizontal orientation on its broad sides and a vertical orientation on its narrow sides. The second, more slender tower incorporates a curved roof for visual interest and is clad in reddish tones. The third and longest tower was designed as a green horizontal slab sheared at an angle with a vertical void subtracted asymmetrically. Each volume originates as a functional rectangular plan, and is then "carved" in section to create form and profile. This is

accomplished by removing a portion of buildings at its center o its edges. Each building earns its identity through its profile against the sky and the surrounding buildings. Their personality further defined by their individual colors. The colored glass stri vary in shades to create a moiré pattern, adding depth and a painterly quality to the skin.

The buildings rotate at angles about a central water landscape the focal point of the composition and of communal activities within the secure compound. The result is a setting in which the buildings act as monumental statements of form within a sculpture garden. From a distance, their graphic presence positions them as giant abstract canvases standing tall in the skyline.

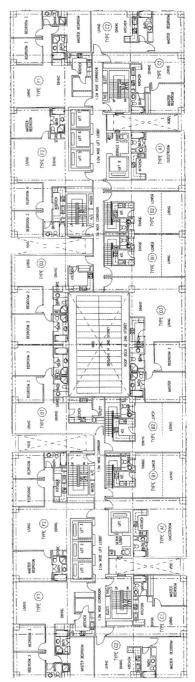

opposite A vertical void is subtracted asymmetrically from the center of this building, which angles toward the sky. Each building earns its identity through its profile against the sky and is reflected in the other two buildings, enlivening the façades.

left This building with green-colored glass is a horizontal slab sheared at an angle. The colored glass stripes vary in shades to create a moiré pattern, adding depth and a painterly quality to the skin.

above Typical floor plan, tower 1

photography Tim Nolan

Pacific Plaza Towers

170.8 m/560.4 ft
52 stories
Residential
2001

Makati City, Philippines

Arquitectonica; Recio + Casas

178

This project consists of two 52-story exclusive residential towers containing 400 luxury apartments. Each apartment has a "thru-view" living and dining area that provides a city view on one side and golf course view on the other. Each tower has its own helipad on its roof for use by its residents as well as for emergency evacuation purposes. The north tower has an undulating curve as its façade; the south tower is shaped like a crescent.

Each tower incorporates a sheer wall on its narrow end that wraps up over the rooftop; this not only adds optical drama, but also conceals mechanical equipment housed on the roof. Contrasting eyebrow configurations on each building create a dynamic juxtaposition of visual elements. The lighting scheme highlights the rooftops and helipads making an interesting profile in the nighttime sky. The complex includes an atrium space with skylight; a meditation room for residents' use overlooks the lush landscaped garden and waterfall that front the property.

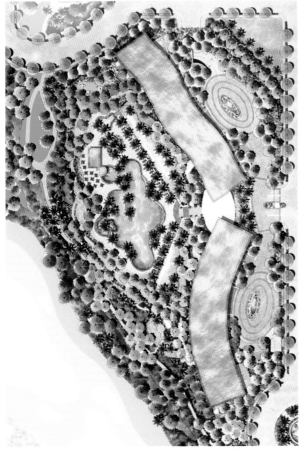

above   Site plan
right   The north tower's façade (left) is an undulating curve while the south tower façade (right) is shaped like a crescent. Each incorporates a sheer wall on its narrow end that wraps up over the rooftop, which not only adds optical drama, but also conceals mechanical equipment housed on the roof.
opposite top left   The lobby affords views of the beautifully landscaped gardens, which cover over 12,000 square meters/129,168 square feet of the site and which are the largest gardens of any residential project in Manila
opposite bottom left   The lighting scheme highlights the rooftops and helipads making an interesting profile in the nighttime sky
opposite top right   South tower typical floor plan
opposite bottom right   North tower typical floor plan
photography   Metro Pacific Corporation

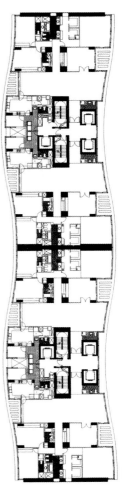

Régence Royale

133 m/437 ft
38/39 stories
Residential
2001

Mid-levels, Hong Kong SAR, People's Republic of China

Dennis Lau & Ng Chun Man Architects & Engineers (H.K.) Ltd

180

Régence Royale is located on the exclusive Bowen Road in a secluded part of the mid-levels area in close proximity to Hong Kong Park. All apartments are orientated to face the best views toward Victoria Harbour.

The roof of the podium is used for recreational facilities and residents' open space, whilst the roofs of the superstructures a designed with swimming pools and hard and soft landscaping fo the private gardens of the penthouse units of the blocks, each o which occupies a whole floor.

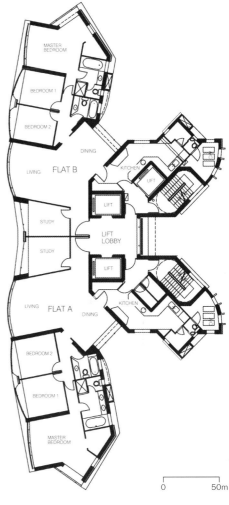

FLAT B

MASTER BEDROOM

BEDROOM 1

BEDROOM 2

DINING

LIVING

STUDY

STUDY

LIVING

FLAT A

DINING

KITCHEN

LIFT

LIFT

LIFT LOBBY

LIFT

KITCHEN

BEDROOM 2

BEDROOM 1

MASTER BEDROOM

0   50m

opposite   View from Magazine Gap Road
left   View from Bowen Road
above   Typical floor plan
photography   Frankie Wong & Michael Tse Photography,
Hong Kong

Roxas Triangle Towers

175 m/574 ft
50 stories
Residential
2001

Makati City, Philippines

Skidmore, Owings & Merrill LLP; Pimentel Rodriguez Simbulan and Partners

SOM's master plan brings housing to the central business district with two 50-story towers containing 372 luxury apartments (of which only One Roxas Triangle has been completed). Designed to complement the nearby Ayala Triangle business center development, the Roxas Triangle residential condominiums create a strong sense of place for the resident. These towers are set within lushly landscaped gardens atop a podium containing amenities and parking for over 3000 cars.

The towers' exterior form grew out of SOM's interior residential planning concepts. Each floor contains four units of approximately 300 square meters/3229 square feet and is designed to maximize views to the surrounding mountain range and cityscape. All bedrooms on the first 40 floors have bay windows, which form

a counterpoint to the solidity of the buildings' white metal panel. The final 10 floors step back as the lower floors give way to duplex units, which have floor-to-ceiling glazing. The top of each tower is defined with a boldly projecting trellis, which cantilevers out to support window-washing equipment and to shade the duplexes.

SOM designed each unit to provide a sense of privacy and ownership usually found only in low-rise residential prototypes. All units have their own front and back doors. Front doors are accessed via dedicated elevator lobbies, while service entries are separately accessed via the central elevator core. In designing the towers, SOM combined the best of local and international design standards by ensuring that every room has an operable window.

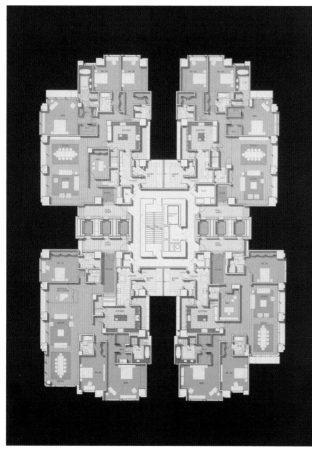

opposite left   Typical floor plan. The design for both towers reflects SOM's interior planning concepts.

opposite right   Rendering of Roxas Triangle Towers. The design of the 50-story twin towers complements the nearby Ayala Triangle business center, and creates a strong presence on the Manila skyline.

left   One Roxas Triangle. The complex, when fully completed, will contain 372 luxury apartments, bringing upscale housing to Manila's central business district.

photography   Brian Lee

The Melburnian

65.8 m/216 ft

29 stories

Residential, restaurants, offices, retail

2001

Melbourne, Victoria, Australia

Bates Smart Pty Ltd; HPA Architects Pty Ltd

The Melburnian occupies an outstanding site opposite Melbourne's Royal Botanic Gardens. Completed in October 2001, the complex is regarded as the leading large residential development in Melbourne.

The Melburnian combines luxurious larger apartments, more affordable one- and two-bedroom apartments, four-level townhouses, and home office facilities. Other components include two restaurants, a variety of retail spaces, a pool, and a gym. The location of these publicly accessible activities along the boulevard enhances the public realm of St Kilda Road as well as adding to the experiences of residents.

The scheme has three major components: a long lower building to St Kilda Road, a row of contemporary townhouses to the north, and two north-facing towers overlooking a sun-filled central garden. The design and placement of the residential tower take full advantage of the remarkable views over the Botanic Gardens and toward the city.

opposite top Tower plans
opposite top right Detail of east building
opposite bottom Townhouses as podium
top left View from north
left View from southeast
above Detail of south wall
photography Gollings & Pidgeon

The Ritz-Carlton New York, Battery Park (Millennium Point)

131 m/430 ft
42 stories
Residential, hotel, museum
2001

New York, New York, USA

Gary Edward Handel + Associates; The Polshek Partnership Architects

Located on Site I, the southernmost parcel in Battery Park City, this project at the tip of lower Manhattan overlooking New York Harbor creates a new gateway to Battery Park City. The project is comprised of the Ritz-Carlton Hotel on the lower floors with condominium residences above. The site is also the new home of the Skyscraper Museum, an exhibition space dedicated to the art of large-scale buildings and their impact on the urban fabric.

A landscaped park with restaurant and cafe defines the front approach. The 13th floor, located between the hotel and the condominium residences, features a restaurant with an outdoor terrace overlooking the harbor. This floor also allows access to additional amenities including a fitness center and spa, meeting rooms, and banquet halls. Constructed with a brick and curtain wall, the exterior is a composition of large and small elements relating to the scale and texture of both the existing buildings of Battery Park City and their harbor-front location.

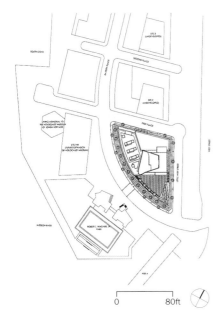

0   80ft

above | Site plan
right | View from Robert F. Wagner, Jr. Park
opposite bottom right | View from Robert F. Wagner, Jr. Park
opposite top right | Residential tower floor plan
opposite left | View along Battery Place
photography | David Desroches

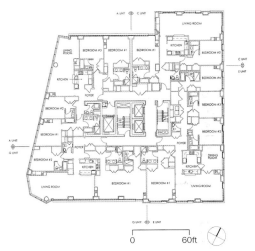

The Sterling

142 m/466 ft

48 stories

Residential, retail

2001

Chicago, Illinois, USA

Solomon Cordwell Buenz & Associates Inc. (SCB)

188

In designing the Sterling, Solomon Cordwell Buenz & Associates was challenged to create a building that would satisfy the top priority of high-rise apartment dwellers: the view. In response, SCB created the building with curved northwest and southwest corners, yielding a floor plan that provides the residents with broad, panoramic views over Chicago's Loop and Downtown.

In addition to 389 apartments, the 48-story building includes parking for 615 cars, 3530 square meters/37,990 square feet ground-floor retail space, tennis courts, an outdoor pool, fitness room, and a hospitality room. The building is designed as a modern structure with a "crisp" aesthetic and it provides a notable gateway to Chicago's Loop.

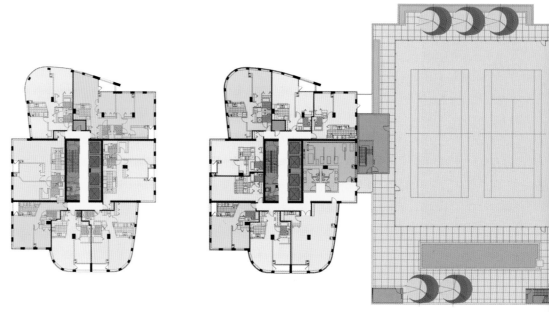

opposite top	Building entrance
opposite bottom left	Typical tower plan
opposite bottom right	14th floor
left	View from LaSalle Street
above	Lobby
photography	James Steinkamp of Steinkamp/ Ballogg Photography, Chicago

The Waverly

108.2 m/355 ft
35 stories
Residential
2001

Miami Beach, Florida, USA

Arquitectonica

190

The 35-story Waverly, within easy walking distance to South Beach's art deco historic district, is the area's first "up-scale" rental building. The issue of density is particularly sensitive in a city with such an important historic district, so the challenge was designing a tower with 399 units which did not seem out of scale or too dense for its surrounding context. The design solution was to split the massing into what appears to be two separate volumes, creating a much more dynamic form, with the added benefit of providing water views for almost every unit.

The design includes distinctive wave-forms along the roofline while bold patterns of colored grids and stripes give the project a bold graphic presence. Both small-scale and large-scale elements were used in the façade and are combined into three-story and five-story monumental squares. These design features make the

building an icon that can be seen from many different vantage points. One-story square elements add texture to the façade design from closer distances and squares in a grid pattern defir the three-level parking garage on the street giving it a more pedestrian scale. The façade seen from the city center (Lincoln Road) incorporates a clock on its façade for city residents. The façade's predominant color is white with yellow and blue accent that emphasize the design concept.

Lighting was carefully designed to enhance the bold design motifs and colors of the building at night with the curving parape visible from as far away as Miami. There are a total of 112 one-bedroom/one-bath units, 244 two-bedroom/two-bath units, 25 two-bedroom/two-and-a-half bath units, and a total of 18 penthouses in four configurations.

above   Lighting was carefully designed to enhance the bold design motifs and colors of the building at night with the curving parapet visible from as far away as Miami
right   Detail of windows and balconies that create bold patterns of grids and stripes giving the project a bold graphic presence
photography   Courtesy ZOM
opposite left   The 399-unit tower was designed to split the massing into what appears to be two separate volumes, creating a much more dynamic form, with the added benefit of providing water views for almost every unit
photography   Scott B. Smith
opposite top right   Fourth floor and lobby level plan
opposite bottom right   Ground floor podium plan

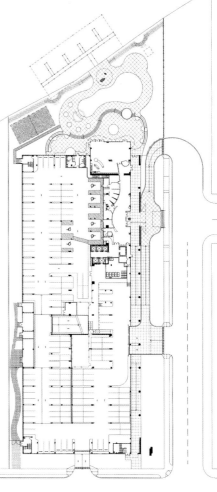

Trump World Tower

262 m/860 ft
72 stories
Residential
2001

New York, New York, USA

Costas Kondylis & Partners LLP

Overlooking the East River, United Nations Park, and First Avenue in New York City, Trump World Tower is surrounded by significant towers such as the Chrysler Building and the UN Secretariat. In this context, a rectangular, glass-sheathed prism rises 262 meters/860 feet in the air. At its bases, a landscaped plaza opens onto a light-filled lobby and two double-height dining spaces. Above are located 370 apartments with panoramic floor-to-ceiling views of Manhattan.

It is interesting to note that the building's elegant slenderness, a pleasing ratio of 11:1, is achieved by using a pioneering high-strength concrete in the shear walls and columns, as well as in a perimeter wall. The wall is engineered as a strengthening "belt" and is located one-third of the way up the tower. The integration

of formal qualities of an aesthetically simple mass with a highly innovative approach to engineering the structure of the building has won awards from The New York Association of Consulting Engineers, the Concrete Industry Board, and others.

The highly polished surfaces of the building, which capture the subtlest nuances of changes in light and shadow, are divided in an abstract grid by an open joint system. This state-of-the-art "windscreen" principle curtain wall, constructed entirely of glass and aluminum, is the first of its kind in the United States. Because water from the building's skin is forced by wind pressu directly into drainage channels, the building will never be discolored by leaking pigmentation from caulking or sealant compounds.

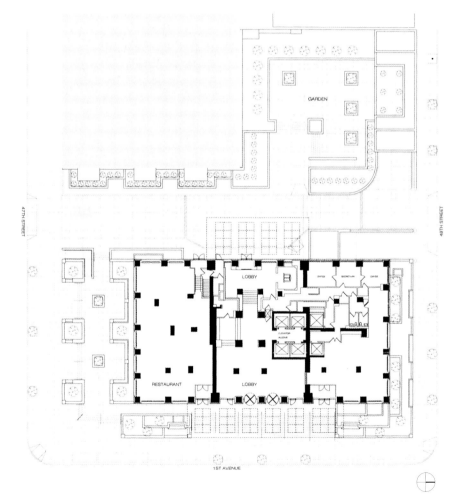

above   Site plan
above right   View from UN Plaza
opposite left   Eastern building façade
opposite top right   70th floor plan
opposite middle right   View from 70th floor
opposite bottom right   Eastern skyline view
photography   Architecturalphotography.com

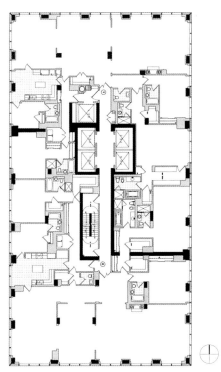

Harbourfront Landmark

230 m/755 ft
68 stories
Commercial, residential
2002

Kowloon, Hong Kong SAR, People's Republic of China

Dennis Lau & Ng Chun Man Architects & Engineers (H.K.) Ltd

194

The Harbour Front Landmark is a high-rise residential and commercial development comprising three towers of 61, 59, and 57 stories respectively, all built over a seven-story-high commercial podium. The towers are equipped with a damper tank to mitigate building movement on high floors.

Residents' facilities include a clubhouse at the seventh floor with an indoor swimming pool and an outdoor swimming pool on the podium roof. Ample outdoor landscaping is provided on the ground floor and on the podium roof.

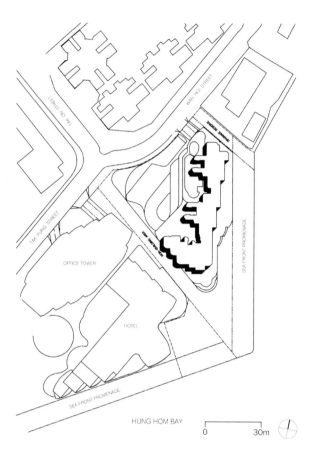

HUNG HOM BAY

0   30m

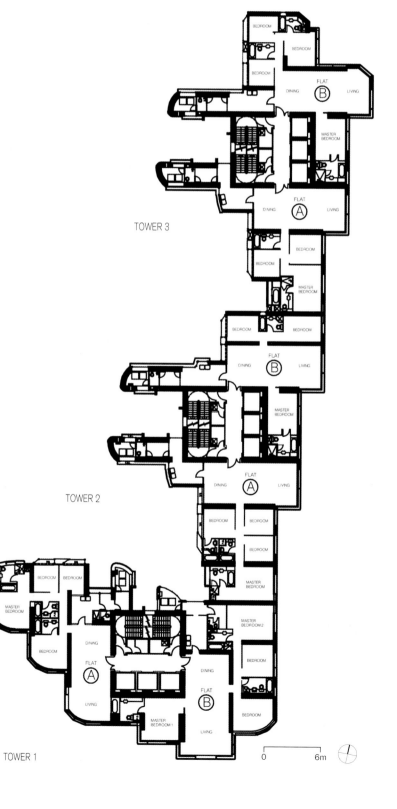

TOWER 3

TOWER 2

TOWER 1

0   6m

above   Site plan
left   Typical floor plan
opposite   View from Hung Hom Bay
photography Frankie Wong & Michael Tse
            Photography, Hong Kong

Les Saisons

Shau Kei Wan, Hong Kong SAR, People's Republic of China

Wong Tung & Partners Limited

139 m/456 ft–160 m/525 ft

44–50 stories

Residential

2002

196

The development provides 864 apartments of sizes ranging from approximately 60 square meters/646 square feet to 150 square meters/1615 square feet with four 160 m²/1722 ft² duplex penthouses in four towers sitting on top of a resident carpark and a podium clubhouse. It is on a site of about 7000 square meters/75,348 square feet within newly reclaimed land facing the Aldrich Bay of Sai Wan Ho.

A challenge of the project was to maximize the numbers of seaward apartments. The solution was to dispose the towers diagonally across the site in a curvilinear fashion, which not only increases the building frontage but also gives a distinctive building form and identity.

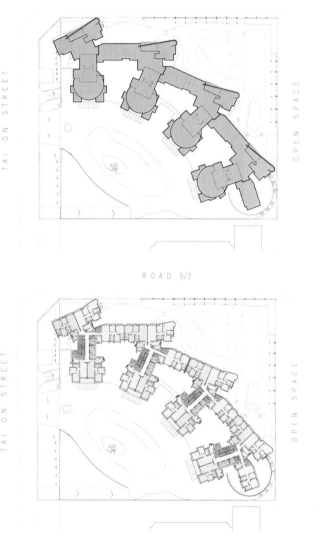

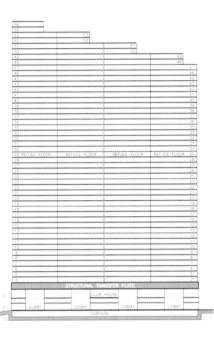

opposite top left   Block plan
opposite bottom right   Typical floor plan
above   Diagramatic section
photography   Wong Tung & Partners Limited

Residences at RiverBend

137 m/450 ft
37 stories
Residential
2002

Chicago, Illinois, USA

DeStefano and Partners, Ltd.

DeStefano and Partners is designing a phased mixed-use development currently under a 1990 Planned Urban Development plan with the City of Chicago. The 37-story Residences at RiverBend, overlooking Wolf Point, is the first tower to be built within this complex.

The high-rise residential tower has 150 condominium and townhouse units, all with eastern views. Two penthouses are also available. The condominiums range from one to three bedrooms, one-and-a-half to two-and-a-half bathrooms, and 102 square meters/1100 square feet to 353 square meters/ 3800 square feet of living space. Four riverfront townhomes are on a promenade level, three stories above a planned riverwalk overlooking the Chicago River.

Responding to the natural edge of the river, the Union Station commuter train tracks, and the city's guidelines for the Chicago River riverwalk development, the design for the Residences at RiverBend is oriented to face east–west. In keeping with the industrial nature of its west loop location, the building's units are designed with loft-like features, including 3.6-meter/11-foot-8-inch floor-to-floor heights, exposed concrete frame and ceilings, partial height room partitions, and natural light from both the east and west.

A single-loaded public corridor for each residential floor runs along the west edge of the building, providing all units with an east-facing orientation with views of the city skyline, the river, and Lake Michigan. Seven stories of valet parking are accessed via elevators. The entire fourth floor of the building is devoted to an executive business center with conference room, meeting facilities, and a private European spa and luxury health club.

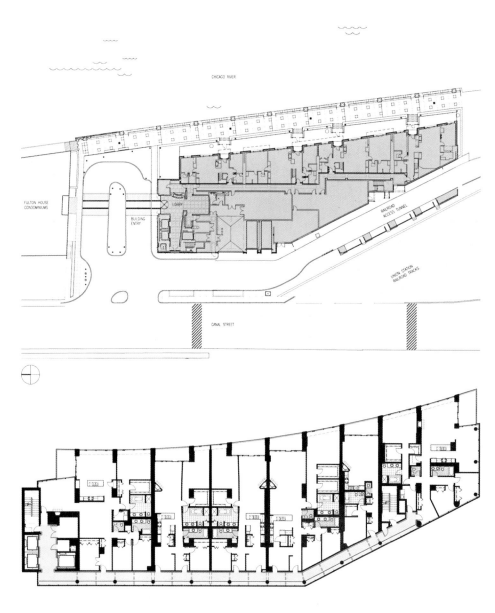

opposite top left   Site plan
opposite bottom right   Floor plan
opposite right   Residences at RiverBend
rendering   Gilbert Gorski
left   View from the southwest, showing corridor unit interface
below   View from the northwest of single-loaded corridor
bottom right   East view from the river
photography   De Stefano and Partners, Ltd.

River East Center Residential Tower

189 m/620 ft
58 stories
Residential, retail, hotel
2002

Chicago, Illinois, USA

DeStefano and Partners, Ltd.

Located on a full city block bound by Grand Avenue, Illinois Street, McClurg Court, and Columbus Drive, River East Center is a mixed-use development incorporating residential, retail, hotel, and entertainment components. The 1.2-hectare/3-acre, 185,800 square-meter/2-million-square-foot project is one of the first phases designed by DeStefano and Partners for MCL Companies' newly created River East neighborhood. On a site parallel to the north bank of the Chicago River with views to the lakefront, River East Center contributes to the development's importance as a retail link between Michigan Avenue and Navy Pier. The complex houses 13,935 square meters/150,000 square feet of space for shops and restaurants and a 21-screen multiplex theater.

Expanding on the existing residential stock of the River East community, MCL opted to include a high-rise of 620 one-, two-,

and three- bedroom condominiums as part of the new multi-use development. Situated on the east end of the property, the 58-story residential tower has been rotated 45 degrees to afford lake and city views from every unit.

The architectural style and exterior materials of River East Center are meant to recall grand buildings of the 1930s with gestures to the deco or modern style. Rendered with the most contemporary building techniques, the building simultaneously projects a high-tech edge and is compatible with its high-rise neighbors, the NBC Tower and Northwestern Memorial Hospital.

It is envisioned that the towers will have numerous light spires at the top that will serve as a beacon for the River East neighborhood.

above   Neighborhood view
above right   View from Lake Michigan
photography   Hedrich-Blessing
opposite top left   River East Center
opposite middle left   Aerial view
opposite bottom left   Base of tower
renderings   RM Design Studio, Ltd.
opposite top right   Typical floor plan
opposite bottom right   Site plan

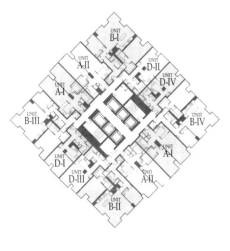

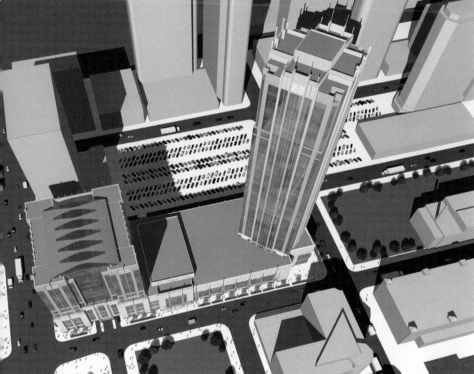

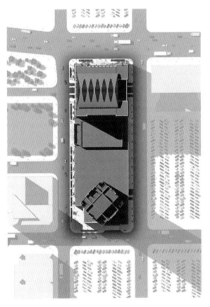

The Essex on Lake Merritt

69.2 m/227 ft
20 stories
Residential
2002

Oakland, California, USA

Architecture International Ltd. (John P. Sheehy, FAIA, RIBA; William J. Higgins, AIA; Sherry Caplan, IIDA); Philip Banta and Associates

202

This new apartment complex, located on a desirable site adjacent to the shores of Lake Merritt, at Lakeside Drive and 17th Street, is intended to meet the growing demands for housing in Oakland and contributes to the Mayor's goal of creating 10,000 housing units in Oakland. The project consists of a nine-story building that maintains the intimate residential scale of 17th Street, as well as a 20-story tower that is destined to become an instant landmark, with its unique profile on the Oakland city skyline.

The 270-unit development includes studio, one-and two-bedroom units with penthouse units located on the upper floors of 17th Street and the tower. A motor court provides direct access to parking and a sophisticated lobby. Fitness and business centers located on the ground level feature lakeside views. The close proximity to Lake Merritt and downtown Oakland, combined with private pool and clubhouse facilities on an elevated garden terrace, provides residents with panoramic views and opportunities for an active urban lifestyle.

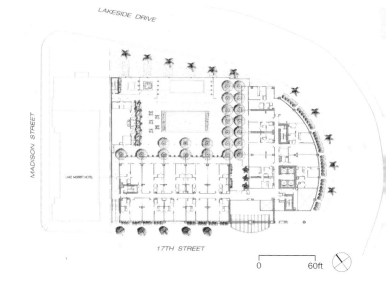

top left   View from Lake Merritt
top right   Approach to motor court entry
right   Site plan
opposite left   Signature spire
opposite top right   Residents lobby
opposite bottom right   Typical level plan
photography   Alan Blaustein

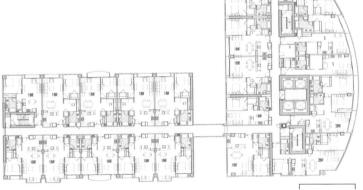

0   40ft

The Summit

207 m/679 ft
69 stories
Residential
2002

Mount Nicholson, Hong Kong SAR, People's Republic of China
Dennis Lau & Ng Chun Man Architects & Engineers (H.K.) Ltd

The Summit is a high-rise residential building located on a steeply sloping site on Mount Nicholson.

The project brief called for residences aimed at the top end of the Hong Kong market. The generosity of the space standards specified for the project permitted the adoption of a maisonette configuration for all units, which is normally not economically realistic in Hong Kong.

The typical units each have a double-height living room connected to two floors comprising the remainder of the maisonette. Upper floors are connected to the living room via internal staircases and feature "minstrel's" galleries overlooking the main voided space.

The elevation of the superstructure on a podium carpark that absorbs the fall in the site ensures that even the units on the lowest floors enjoy fine panoramic views.

Landscaping for the project to the podium deck and to the carpark elevations is elaborate and features both intensive planting and water features, including a waterfall, intended both to create a resort atmosphere and to merge the base of the building with the hillside.

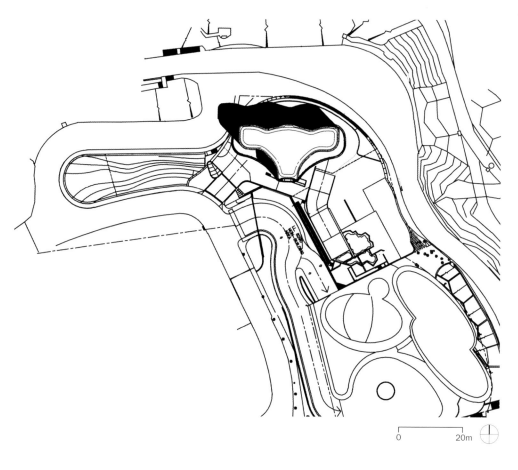

0   20m

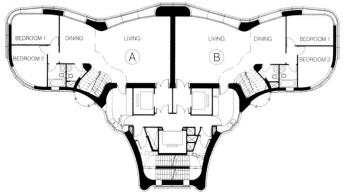

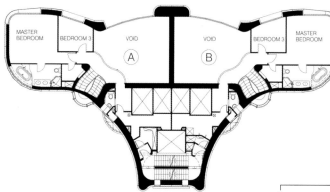

opposite top   Site plan
opposite bottom left   Typical floor plan –
    lower level of maisonette
opposite bottom right   Typical floor plan –
    upper level of maisonette
left   The Summit
photography   Frankie Wong & Michael Tse
    Photography, Hong Kong

BUILDINGS IN PROGRESS

510 West Erie

86 m/280.7 ft

24 stories

Residential

2002

Chicago, Illinois, USA

Lucien Lagrange Architects

The building is unusual in design and form. Its glassy condominium tower contrasts with the existing historically industrial environment of red brick buildings. The shape is a sleek parallelogram determined by its site that is bisected by an alley. The alley separates the building from its primary parking structure, which is connected by a bridge.

Residential space rises above the six-story base, which houses some parking, so that no residential views are blocked. The units are unconventional in design, evoking a creative, flexible, and high-tech lifestyle. Many rooms are unusually shaped and spaces are loosely blended together as in a loft.

"People are living differently today and these units provide an opportunity for people to enjoy a flexible space," says Lucien Lagrange, the building's designer.

rendering   Lucien Lagrange Architects

1322 Roxas Boulevard

190 m/623 ft

57 stories

Residential, retail

2002

Manila, Philippines

Architecture International Ltd. (John P. Sheehy, FAIA, RIBA; William J. Higgins, AIA; Sherry Caplan, IIDA); GF & Partners

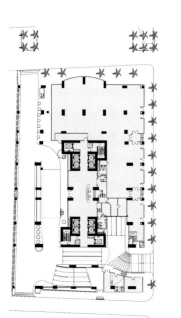

This 57-story luxury condominium will be located in one of Manila's best and most historical residential sites: on a corner property of Roxas Boulevard overlooking Rizal park in the historic Ermita District on Manila Bay and the South China Sea.

The soaring tower will meet the sea like the rounded prow of a ship, slicing through the trade winds. The green, blue, and white glass façades will blend with the colors of the tropical seascape and landscape. The rounded forms of the structure and the profile of the top of the tower will recall the sails on a ship at sea. This nautical imagery will be further expressed in horizontal metal sunshades, which will protect the tower from glare and heat, while allowing outstanding views.

The bio-climatic nature of the tower is uniquely designed to take advantage of this specific site. The building orientation, with the narrowest profiles of the tower facing east and west and long façades to the north and south, supports efficient energy conservation. The building will provide operable windows to capture sea breezes and large window openings to maximize views, light and air, with sunshades provided to minimize glare and heat.

At night, the tower lighting is designed to be a quiet beacon to identify what will be an important new landmark on Manila Bay.

rendering   Lawrence Leong & Phil Ishimaru

Embassy House

100 m/328 ft
32 stories
Residential
2002

Beijing, People's Republic of China

Hellmuth, Obata + Kassabaum (HOK);
China Architecture Design & Research Group

Embassy House is located in the Second Embassy District of Beijing just north of Dongzhimenwai Avenue. The project meets the requirements of a quality-conscious, primarily expatriate residential market, and provides the most prestigious address in this important international district of Beijing.

Photography   Georges Binder/courtesy Buildings
& Data s.a.

The 32-story tower is designed to respect its immediate neighbors. The floor plan will provide each resident with a south, east, or west light. A typical floor will have six apartments: three two-bedroom and three three-bedroom units—this design also allows flexibility for future market needs. The top three floors contain four four-bedroom penthouses, giving the building an additional level of prestige as well as special architectural expression at its summit. The exterior of the building is designed to complete a composition with the adjacent office building. The gently curved residential tower and circular office tower have similar and complementary, yet individual geometries.

Exclusively northern exposures for any apartments are eliminated and the impact of shadows on the office and residential buildings to the north is minimized. The entry provides a luxurious and formal arrival court, which will benefit from eastern and southern light. The site plan also provides a clear and safe traffic flow. The remainder of the site will have surface parking for 15 cars, the emphasis being given to landscaped areas creating a garden atmosphere at the tower's base. There are three basement levels which accommodate parking amenities, health club, swimming pool, and service areas.

Highcliff

252.3 m/828 ft
73 stories
Residential
2002

Hong Kong SAR, People's Republic of China

Dennis Lau & Ng Chun Man Architects & Engineers (H.K.) Ltd

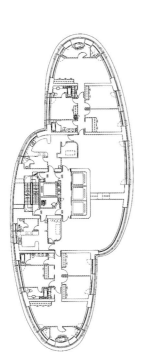

Highcliff, a 73-story apartment tower, is one of tallest residential buildings in the world.

The project is positioned in a prominent location with excellent views both of Hong Kong Island, Kowloon, and Victoria Harbour to the north and, from the higher floors, the South China Sea and outlying islands to the south. The project brief called for extremely generous planning, with only two apartments on each of the typical floors.

The superstructure has a streamlined form derived from the floor plan of overlapping ovals that announce the separate apartments.

The external envelope is clad in a light blue reflective curtain wall that provides floor-to-ceiling glazing for the living rooms and bedrooms. The development includes parking, swimming pool, clubhouse, and common areas of a standard that is in keeping with the luxurious specification of the apartments.

Multifunctional Business Center with Residential Apartments

118.5 m/389 ft
32 stories
Offices, commercial, residential
2002

Moscow, Russia

George Mailov & Archizdrav's Partners

210

This 32-story building is situated at the crossroads of Vernadsky Avenue and a local street. Taking into account the existing business center, the architects worked out an expressive composition of the building with a tall part situated further from the existing buildings. Thus, the building's overall shape represents a kind of cascade along the main road, Vernadsky Avenue.

The offices are situated in the tallest part of the complex. In addition, there are apartments on upper floors of the tower. All public and commercial facilities are placed in the main scope of the building and provided with a glazed upper lantern, which extends through most of the building. There are trading and exhibiting halls, a healthcare complex with swimming pool, fitness center, and beauty parlor, a nightclub, restaurants, and video hall.

This complex contains underground parking for 180 cars and there is also guest parking for 60 cars outside.

The rectangular floor plan reflects the desire to integrate the building into the existing context, while keeping in mind a dominating meaning of the situation and the desire to create contemporary architecture. Applying Russian and Western design philosophy and methodologies, the architects have striven to create a highly expressive form of architecture, perfection, and freshness in the design, and harmony with the existing environment.

Regent Tower

158.5 m/520 ft
45 stories
Retail, residential
2002

New York, New York, USA

Frank Williams & Partners, Architects

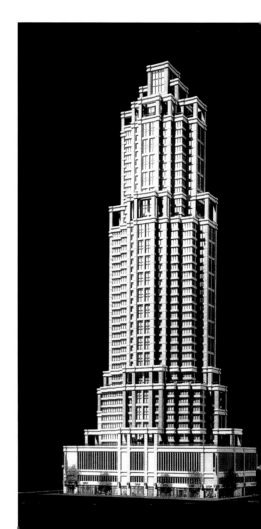

This 45-story residential tower sits in a very dense urban context. Fronting on Eighth Avenue between West 53rd and West 54th streets, it is an excellent location for families who would like to be close to work, shops, restaurants, and the theater district.

Using air rights from Studio 54 theater, the tower is organized by having a 41-story residential tower above a four-story public parking garage. There is retail continuity along Eighth Avenue, which is approximately 21 meters/70 feet deep. The residential lobby fronts on West 54th Street and has a service entry along West 53rd Street.

The new four-story public parking facility required a special permit from the City Planning Commission since there is presently a moratorium on parking below 59th Street. There was a public parking facility on the site, which parked 450 cars; however, structurally it was not designed for the new earthquake code nor was it designed to have a 41-story tower built above it. The special permit was required to replace the 450-car parking facility. Entrance and exits are provided from each of the crosstown streets.

The 41-story residential tower above has 345 rental residences. This is being built under 90 percent market rate and 20 percent subsidized unit program. The architectural design has developed a series of setbacks to give each of the living rooms two exposures. Also provided are dining rooms on the perimeter glass area to provide views. Trellised porches two stories in height are used at the major setback floors to add a residential scale to the tower.

photography   Jeff Goldberg/Esto

Skybridge

128 m/420 ft
39 stories
Retail, residential
2002

Chicago, Illinois, USA

Perkins & Will

This project is a 39-story condominium tower, which includes a four-story base of retail space and parking. The site of this extraordinary building is located in one of Chicago's revitalized neighborhoods, the West Loop District. To the east of the site is an eight-lane expressway, which demarcates the current boundary of the high-rises west of the loop. To the west is a section of Halsted Street known as "Greektown," which consists of low to mid-rise commercial and entertainment buildings.

The design is a base-and-lower scheme that reinforces these two urban conditions. A 39-story linear housing slab parallels the expressway on the eastern portion of the site, maximizing views of the Chicago skyline from the residential units. The mass of the tower is an urban marker defining the canyon created by the depressed expressway and marking the western edge of Chicago's downtown. The four-story base is a transitional element, consistent with the scale of buildings along Halsted Street.

Planning of the typical floor provides options, variety, and flexibility to prospective buyers. Each floor has six different layouts for one-, two-, and three-bedroom units, to create possible unit combinations as well. The design is based on the concept of a vertical urban village. The composition of the building, with its relationship between mass and void together with the contrast of opacity and transparency, work to produce this village-like quality.

St. Regis Museum Tower

146 m/479 ft
40 stories
Hotel, residential, cultural center
2002

San Francisco, California, USA

Skidmore, Owings & Merrill LLP;
Powell & Partners Architects

SOM has designed a new cultural center, condominium, and luxury hotel tower adjacent to the Museum of Modern Art at the corner of Third and Mission streets in San Francisco. The project will include a tower of approximately 40 stories with condominiums atop a 400-room hotel, and a 1858-square-meter/20,000-square-foot African-American cultural center.

The highly visible site is the last remaining Yerba Buena Center property to be offered for development by the San Francisco Redevelopment Agency. The proposed scheme is designed to sensitively address the unique character and urban design conditions of the area. The project also incorporates proposed solutions for site constraints including the historic Williams Building and vehicular access that will help to provide a unique, interesting, and stimulating pedestrian level condition.

The tower is positioned so that it is set back from both Mission and Third streets. This allows the podium elements to respond to the lower heights and scale of adjacent buildings along Mission Street and in Yerba Buena Center, including the San Francisco Museum of Modern Art, and opens up views between tall buildings back to the city from the Yerba Buena Esplanade. A proposed garden terrace above the ballroom is sited at the southwest corner. This public outdoor space is oriented to benefit from natural daylight and views of the Center for the Arts Water Garden, the Yerba Buena Esplanade, and the proposed Jessie Square.

Students Accommodation in Laakhaven

The Hague, The Netherlands

atelier PRO architekten

62 m/203 ft
21 stories
Residential
2002

The urban development plan for Laakhaven, which included the design of the Haagse Hogeschool (The Hague College of Higher Education), also provided for an extension of the strip with a tower for office space.

This area is now being filled with 309 student apartments in a way that retains the possibility of education premises in the extended strip in the future. It will be possible to combine different types of premises in the tower if desired.

The complex will offer a diverse range of single and two-bedroom units (ranging from 24 square meters/258 square feet to 45 square meters/484 square feet), long-stay apartments, communal areas, a laundry facility, and a bicycle-parking area.

The continuation of the strip will lead to a façade that will match the look of the existing façade. The façade will partly be rendered and on the side facing the water will have a recessed wooden curtain wall. Prefabricated concrete columns placed in front of the façade will provide a continuation of the existing row.

On the other side the new façade will join the existing rendered façade. A high gateway over the lowest floors makes deliveries to the front of the Hogeschool possible. The ground floor façade, which will also have the communal bicycle-parking facility located behind it, will fit in with the delivery façade of the Hogeschool. At the front, maisonettes will screen off the bicycle-parking area, which is readily accessible at ground level.

The tower (with a diameter of 25 meters/82 feet and a height of 60 meters/197 feet) will have red masonry with red mortar, which will form a strong colour accent in combination with the Hogeschool. The façade will have a high base and will match the height of the prefabricated columns on the side facing the water. In addition to the entrance hall, the ground floor will have an area for renting. Each standard floor in the tower will have 11 units (eight of 24 square meters/258 square feet and three of 30 square meters/323 square feet) and a communal area of 48 square meters/517 square feet. A laundry and a manager's area will be located on the first floor.

The top two levels will contain maisonettes. The roof terrace on the top level will be shielded by a full-length façade.

The interior walkways in the strip (with a total of 102 units) will have glass brick floors, which allow light to penetrate. Fire-escape stairs will be located at the narrow end joining the Hogeschool.

The Park Imperial at Random House

New York, New York, USA

Skidmore, Owings & Merrill LLP

207.5 m/681 ft
50 stories
Residential, offices
2002

When completed, the Random House project will bring to New York City for the first time a truly integrated mixed-use tower. To express the dynamic nature of the building's Broadway address, a granite base will serve as the podium from which the glass tower rises to form three sliding crystals in Manhattan's skyline. Wrapped by sculptural granite on the north and south faces to define the headquarters of Random House, the design both unifies and delineates the very different uses of the single building.

Taking advantage of views to Central Park and the Hudson River, the top 23 floors of the building will house the residential component of the project in the form of luxury condominiums. The residential component sits above 25 floors of class A office space that will become home to the headquarters of Random House, while the project's ground floor will provide prime retail spaces together with separate grand entrances for both Random House and residential lobbies.

digital image   Roy Wright

Two Towers

60 m/197 ft
22 stories
Residential
2002

Almere, The Netherlands

de Architekten Cie.-Amsterdam; Frits van Dongen

cons of present-day urbanity and domestic culture.

Like two dramatic urban beacons, these residential owers physically express the ongoing revitalization f Almere's city core. Situated on the border etween land (the city centre) and water Weerwater lake) they strike a key note in the rban landscape and announce a new, decidedly n-Dutch domestic culture.

With a respectful nod to Mies van der Rohe's Lake Shore Drive apartments in Chicago, the two dentical towers stand in an L-shaped composition, vith the repetition projecting an element of armony and quiet and the rotation a subtle sense f energy. This composition moreover has ontextual significance: the future route extending rom the station by way of OMA's new city center s deflected at the towers and led back into the xisting shopping center. Thus the L-shaped onfiguration spatially articulates the new main oute curving through the city center, stitching old nd new together as it proceeds.

The towers orchestrate Almere from the other side of Weerwater too by giving it a metropolitan skyline. To bolster their landmark character and to satisfy the many views to be had of the towers from the city, the façades have a deliberately abstract rendering in industrial glass, so that from a distance it seems more as if two crystals have settled there on the shores of the lake, with the mosaic of door and window frames revealing from closer up the great wealth of housing types the two contain.

The towers are, at the same time, icons of a new Dutch domestic culture.

Aside from the scintillating context (a hub of urban activity within the vast reaches of the dormant polder) and the wide variety of dwellings (20 types all with the spatial composition up front), the plinth on which the towers stand boasts a broad spectrum of communal facilities, from marina and winter garden to sauna and gym.

West One

108.5 m/356 ft
41 stories
Residential
2002

Vancouver, British Columbia, Canada

Hancock Brückner Eng + Wright Architects

This elegant and well-scaled proposed tower is designated a "landmark" tower to provide a visual focus at the southwest end of Pacific Boulevard, between Cambie and Richards streets. The form of the tower, with its curved façade, relates to its counterpart landmark tower at 1009 Expo Boulevard. The tower height and floorplate are also designed to enhance this relationship. The tower fits generally within the overall site as conceived in the approved beach area neighborhood plan. The tower steps back above the 34th floor and the mews is framed by four three-story townhouses.

The proposed tower is designed to be slender in the east–west direction, and more substantial in the north–south width to achieve its desired prominence with minimal impact on adjacent upland residents.

60 West Erie

74 m/242 ft
26 stories
Residential
2003

Chicago, Illinois, USA

Lucien Lagrange Architects

214

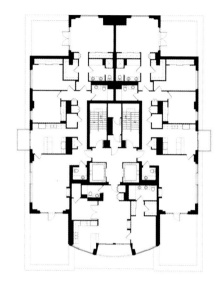

The building includes 30 spacious condominium units from one to three per floor. Several of the units are duplexes. Most units have balconies and several have terraces created by setbacks.

The building is clad in precast concrete rising above a base of buff-colored stone. An articulated screen wall conceals the parking and enhances the classic, art nouveau-inspired design of the façade. The first three floors are devoted to parking—they are wrapped around the central service spine.

Every unit faces south with unobstructed views. The site is tight with only 24 meters/80 feet of street frontage and confined on the other three sides by public alleyways.

235 West 51st Street

178.2 m/584.6 ft
52 stories
Residential, offices
2003

New York, New York, USA

Fox & Fowle Architects PC

Fox & Fowle Architects has designed a new luxury rental apartment tower on 51st Street in Manhattan's midtown theater district for The Clarett Group. This 52-story building is located on a narrow site adjoining the former Mark Hellinger Theater, between Broadway and Eighth Avenue.

On the lower floors, the building houses office space for the Times Square Church, the current owners of the Hellinger Theater, as well as mechanical spaces. The eighth through 46th floors contain 316 first-class studios, and one- and two-bedroom apartments. The top five floors contain 15 luxury two-bedroom apartments.

On 51st Street, a 18-meter/60-foot-high brick masonry base will rise from the street with a scale and detailing complementing the early 20th-century modernist style of the adjoining Hellinger Theater. The base will form a stone portal to an expansive glazed sky-lit plaza leading to the residential entrance. The masonry base extends over the west

annex of the Hellinger Theater to match the width of the tower and return the theater to its original composition. The setback façades feature corner windows that progressively increase in size at the upper floors reducing the mass of the building while opening up views for the occupants. The carefully articulated masonry walls will have projecting bay windows bordered by brick masonry frames. The masonry continues to the top of the tower where the articulated top echoes the early modernist features of the Hellinger Theater.

The residential lobby will provide quiet repose from the street for the building occupants with carefully detailed stone, wood, and glass finishes. The residential apartments feature 9-foot/2.7-meter ceilings with large bay windows at the eighth through 46th floors. At the 47th through 51st floors the penthouse apartments have 3-meter/10-foot ceilings with wrap-around windows at the living areas and bedrooms providing an abundance of natural light and many unobstructed views of midtown to the south and east, glimpses of the Hudson River to the west, and Central Park to the north.

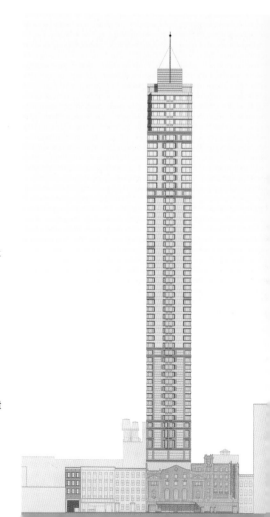

250 East Pearson
(The Pearson)

120 m/395 ft
36 stories
Residential
2003

Chicago, Illinois, USA

DeStefano and Partners, Ltd.

DeStefano and Partners is designing two luxury condominium towers as part of a master plan in the Streeterville neighborhood of Chicago. Using neotraditional planning strategies, the buildings will create a streetwall on Pearson Street that will help to define Lake Shore Park and enhance its importance as the center of the neighborhood. The 36th floor features a hospitality room with sweeping views of Chicago's skyline and Lake Michigan. 250 East Pearson consists of 180 units and parking.

To reduce foundation costs, the building was designed to reuse the foundation system and basement walls of the building originally on the site. The parking garage was designed so that it blends in with the building's façade, which creates an almost seamless transition from its use to the residential units above.

photography   ImageFiction

425 Fifth Avenue

188 m/617.1 ft
67 stories
Residential, retail, offices, recreation
2003

New York, New York, USA

Michael Graves & Associates;
H. Thomas O'Hara, Architect, PLLC

his 67-story mixed-use tower on Fifth Avenue contains ffices and 176 residential units on the northeast corner f Fifth Avenue and 38th Street. The building is 27,870 quare meters/300,000 square feet including the asement, and 26,012 square meters/280,000 square et above ground. Michael Graves & Associates began ork on it after another architect had completed design evelopment, and subsequently redesigned the building açade, as well as the interiors.

he base of 425 Fifth Avenue is articulated to reflect nd maintain the scales of the nearby New York Public ibrary and the Gotham Building by McKim Mead & Vhite. The base contains two floors of retail, with four f offices above. Above the ninth floor the building has rotected views of uptown and downtown Manhattan, ncluding an excellent view of the Empire State Building.

he 38th Street residential entrance to 425 Fifth venue, a building designed by Michael Graves & ssociates to embody the casual elegance of life in Manhattan, adjoins a vestpocket park designed by oted landscape architect Tom Balsley. Entering the

building through an elliptical vestibule with four decorative niches, one proceeds into the hippodrome-shaped residential lobby.

Other portions of the first floor include the office lobby, and the first of two stories of above-grade retail space. The third through sixth floors contain office space. The seventh floor, ringed on the exterior by a loggia, is a floor of recreational facilities, including men's and women's locker rooms; a treatment room; a steam room; and showers, sauna, and an "endless" lap pool.

A sky lobby on the eighth floor leads to the reception area (with lounge and bar) of "The Fifth Avenue Club & Spa," the residential hotel component of the building, which provides service apartments for long-term executive stays. A business center includes a conference room, a cinema room, children's playroom, and a fitness center, linked by an open stair to the locker rooms and pool below. The Fifth Avenue Club units occupy floors 10 through 26 (with the ninth floor as a mechanical floor), and 27 through 54 contain residential condominium units. Apartments have 2.7-meter/ 9-foot-high ceilings throughout. For The Fifth Avenue Club Michael Graves & Associates selected or designed furniture, fabrics, and carpet, in addition to designing the kitchens and bathrooms.

rendering   Michael Graves & Associates

840 North Lake Shore Drive

99 m/325 ft
26 stories
Residential
2003

Chicago, Illinois, USA

Lucien Lagrange Architects

216

A grand structure was needed for this site on the corner of Pearson and Lake Shore Drive, one of Chicago's premiere addresses and communities. The tower is the cornerstone, and the corner, of a three-building complex. Each building has a unique identity and all fit into the grand ambience required for the site. Together they create an elegant new street wall.

This Parisian-inspired building has 73 luxury residential condominiums. The building is designed as an extended private mansion and is topped with a two-story crested Mansard roof clad in zinc. A rounded, glass-enclosed corner tower will offer spectacular views of the lake and city.

photography   Lucien Lagrange Architects

Al Hitmi Residential/ Office Complex

101 m/331 ft
26 stories
Residential, offices
2003

Doha, Qatar

NORR Group Consultants International Limited

Located on a prominent site on the Doha corniche, this project allows spectacular views out to the ocean. The design of this 26-story, mixed-use residential and office development, is the result of the owner's requirement to maximize ocean views for the building occupants.

In response to this brief, the building is configured in an S-shaped curvilinear form, resulting in a unique new landmark project in Doha.

The site is accessed from the public road to the west. A landscaped driveway leads to a fountain and drop-off area immediately in front of the building entrance. Vehicular ramps provide access to basement parking with a capacity of 220 cars, while additional on-grade parking is provided adjacent to the drive.

The bold massing of the residential building is composed of four glass elements rising from a three-story stone podium.

The podium, containing lobbies, retail, and office functions, is clad in polished beige-colored limestone. The level immediately above the podium houses the building's health club and other shared recreational facilities. The podium roof terrace provides open-to-sky health club facilities including a swimming pool and jacuzzi.

The four glass elements, containing a total of 328 apartment units, are clad in blue-tinted glass set in a silver aluminum curtain wall system. The first 20 floors of these glass elements contain one-, two-, and three-bedroom units while the top two floors contain four-bedroom duplex units. Panoramic elevators provide vertical transportation to all levels, rising through a 26-story-high glazed atrium with dramatic views to the ocean and the city.

Interior finishes for the lobbies and atrium are a combination of granite, wood, glass, and stainless steel in various finishes. Finishes in the apartments will be of the highest standards reflective of the exclusive tenant mix targeted by this development.

Al Jaber Complex

199 m/653 ft
44 stories
Residential, hotel, offices
2003

Dubai, United Arab Emirates

NORR Group Consultants International Limited

Situated on a prestigious site on Sheikh Zayed Road, this 44-story twin-tower complex is a landmark development in Dubai.

In marked contrast to the glass box towers prevalent in Dubai, the architectural expression of this project is reminiscent of the early 20th-century New York skyscraper. The exterior of the two granite-clad towers is designed with a strong emphasis on the vertical, reflective of the tubular structural design of the buildings. The first 30 floors of the towers rise uninterrupted, with setbacks at the transfer floor and at the top. The cladding of the towers consists of beige-colored Brazilian granite, blue-tinted glazing between piers, and silver aluminum fins and mullions.

The project combines a variety of uses, including the five-star Shangri-La Hotel and related functions, rental apartments, and speculative office

floors. The lower floors of the towers contain a dramatic four-story-high entrance lobby, restaurants, health club, and business center. Levels five through eight consist of open-plan office floors. Levels 5 through 8 consist of apartments, comprising eight levels each of long-term apartments and serviced apartments operated by the hotel. The upper floors of the tower, from levels 29 through 41, consist of the 300-room hotel. The very top of the towers contains a presidential suite, executive health club, and restaurant/bar with dramatic views to the ocean and downtown Dubai.

The design of the vertical transportation system for the various user groups has been organized into three centrally located cores, with a total of 11 high-speed elevators and five dedicated service elevators.

A stand-alone parking structure, with a capacity of 450 cars, is connected to the towers by a pedestrian sky-bridge. The basement of the parking structure contains loading docks and service areas, while the roof deck features a 25-meter/82-foot swimming pool.

Cove

160 m/525 ft
45 stories
Residential
2003

Sydney, New South Wales, Australia

Harry Seidler & Associates

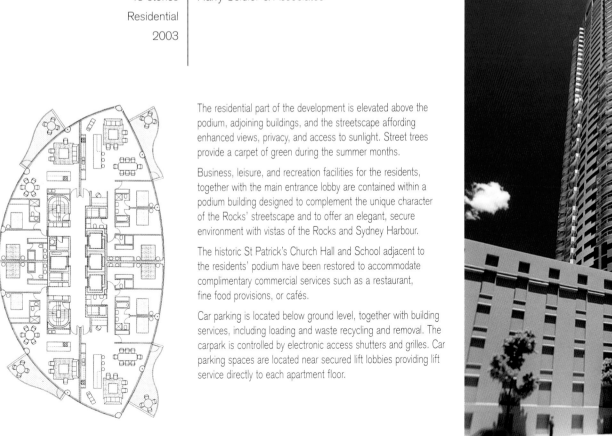

The residential part of the development is elevated above the podium, adjoining buildings, and the streetscape affording enhanced views, privacy, and access to sunlight. Street trees provide a carpet of green during the summer months.

Business, leisure, and recreation facilities for the residents, together with the main entrance lobby are contained within a podium building designed to complement the unique character of the Rocks' streetscape and to offer an elegant, secure environment with vistas of the Rocks and Sydney Harbour.

The historic St Patrick's Church Hall and School adjacent to the residents' podium have been restored to accommodate complimentary commercial services such as a restaurant, fine food provisions, or cafés.

Car parking is located below ground level, together with building services, including loading and waste recycling and removal. The carpark is controlled by electronic access shutters and grilles. Car parking spaces are located near secured lift lobbies providing lift service directly to each apartment floor.

Espirito Santo Plaza

147 m/483 ft
36 stories
Offices, hotel, residential
2003

Miami, Florida, USA

Kohn Pedersen Fox Associates, PC;
Plunkett & Associates

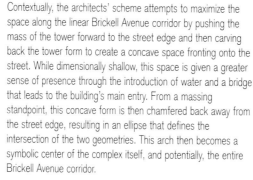

The design of the Espirito Santo Plaza attempts to reconcile the varying demands and requirements of diverse program elements within a simple sculptural, monolithic form.

Contextually, the architects' scheme attempts to maximize the space along the linear Brickell Avenue corridor by pushing the mass of the tower forward to the street edge and then carving back the tower form to create a concave space fronting onto the street. While dimensionally shallow, this space is given a greater sense of presence through the introduction of water and a bridge that leads to the building's main entry. From a massing standpoint, this concave form is then chamfered back away from the street edge, resulting in an ellipse that defines the intersection of the two geometries. This arch then becomes a symbolic center of the complex itself, and potentially, the entire Brickell Avenue corridor.

While the office and hotel floors are planned around a central services core, the condominium floors at the top of the building have been configured around an 11-story atrium facing east. This space above has been created as a sky-lobby for the hotel and residential elements, and also allows for the building's focus to be reoriented toward Biscayne Bay. A covered courtyard with a linear, glass bottom reflecting pool sits one story above the outside grade and at the level of the office elevator lobby.

Four Seasons Hotel & Tower

238 m/780 ft
64 stories
Residential, hotel, offices, retail
2003

Miami, Florida, USA

Gary Edward Handel + Associates;
Bermello Ajamil & Partners

Situated one block from Biscayne Bay, the Four Seasons Hotel & Tower will be one of the tallest structures in the southeastern United States and Miami's first true mixed-use urban residential building. Integrating a Four Seasons Hotel with luxury residential condominiums, timeshare units, a state-of-the-art fitness facility, and class A office space, the Four Seasons Hotel & Tower will offer a new model of urban living for Miami.

Clad entirely in a glass and metal skin, the tower is intended to capture the ample light native to the region, creating a striking new addition to the Miami skyline. Bordering both the financial district and Coral Gables, program uses will be vertically organized into a cohesive architectural statement occupying the entire block of Brickell Avenue between 14th Lane and 14th Terrace. The intermediate scale of the buildings along Brickell Avenue is reflected in the 16-story podium of the tower. A masonry base for the entire project will act as an elevated ground plane, with retail uses enlivening the surrounding streets. Amenities will be further enhanced by a 6038-square-meter/64,993-square-foot roof terrace including a pool and sundeck designed in collaboration with renowned landscape architect Dan Kiley.

renderings   The 7th Art

Gallery Park Place

152 m/499 ft
46 stories
Residential
2003

Chicago, Illinois, USA
DeStefano and Partners, Ltd.

The Neighborhood Rejuvenation Partnership LP is redeveloping the Michigan-Roosevelt Wabash Property located on Michigan Avenue and Roosevelt Road. DeStefano and Partners will provide full master planning, architectural, interior design, planning, and zoning services for the residential portions of the floors and retail base. The interior design services include interior partitions, ceilings, doors, light fixtures, floor and wall finishes, and cabinets. The project consists of building a 46-story condominium tower on the Michigan Avenue parcel area and restoring the existing Wabash Avenue building into an art gallery complex.

The Michigan Avenue building is a brick and masonry structure with a symmetrical plan reflecting the high-rise buildings along Michigan Avenue. The building will have setback terraces and balconies with extensive landscaping and a roof garden on top of the eight-story base. A peaked roof highlights the pinnacle of the building, a common architectural style in the Michigan Avenue Streetwall. The building plan will permit 225 residential units. With this configuration, 57 percent of the units will be family-sized two and three bedrooms. The building offers over 929 square meters/10,000 square feet of retail space on the first floor. The ground floor of the tower will continue the high-quality art gallery tenancy projected for the Wabash building, providing unbroken display window opportunities from Michigan to Wabash along Roosevelt Road.

Rendering   ImageFiction

The HarbourSide

242 m/794 ft
74 stories
Residential
2003

Hong Kong SAR, People's Republic of China
P&T Architects and Engineers Ltd.

Kowloon Station Package 4 is a prestigious residential development situated on top of the Airport Railway Kowloon Station. The development consists of three towers of 67 residential floors over a seven-story carpark podium. The total gross floor area is around 130,000 square meters/1,399,320 square feet, with a total of 1134 units. Unit sizes range from 74 square meters/800 square feet to 111 square meters/1200 square feet.

In order to create visual interest facing the harbor, several large openings are punched within the curvilinear elevation as sky gardens for the residents.

The tower is clad in pearl-white aluminum panels together with blue-green tinted glass and matching spandrel panels, and exterior-facing tiles to create a glazed-tower look.

Kingsbury on the Park

89 m/291.1 ft
25 stories
Residential, retail
2003

Chicago, Illinois, USA

Lucien Lagrange Architects

220

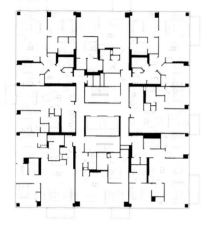

This bold, contemporary design complements the creative, cutting-edge design on the opposite corner. Both buildings were designed by Lucien Lagrange for the same client. The design of the buildings reflects the young, dynamic culture of the new residential neighborhood rapidly developing along the Chicago River in a former manufacturing area.

Floor-to-ceiling windows provide expansive views of the city, river, and park. The building has 18 floors to house 130 condominium units. Most of these are one- and two-bedroom units and all feature balconies. Three-bedroom units are located on the top two floors of the building as well as on the seventh floor, which is the first residential floor. Cutbacks on the top four floors and the seventh floor provide terraces for the three-bedroom units.

Parking is located on the second through sixth floors. The ground floor has a two-story lobby and a 372-square-meter/4000-square-foot retail space. A fitness center is located on the seventh floor.

Kuzuha Tower City

136.8 m/449 ft
41 stories
Residential, retail
2003

Hirakata City, Osaka Prefecture, Japan

Takenaka Corporation

The project site is located in a "bedroom community" 30 minutes by express train from central Osaka and Kyoto. The project has a total of five towers, including a 41-floor superhigh-rise residential tower and fitness club facilities.

Privacy is ensured for all residents, and all the units face south. By using the overall design system, vacant land with public access has been provided, most of the parking area has been built underground, and rooftop greening has been used to ensure plenty of open space, and different areas for pedestrian and car traffic. The project has been base-isolated to give buildings high safety features during an earthquake, and the skeleton infill system has been used to give flexibility for renewal and other work.

photography   Courtesy Keihan Construction Co., Ltd.

Las Olas Riverhouse

127.4 m/418.2 ft
43 stories
Residential
2003

Fort Lauderdale, Florida, USA

The Sieger Suarez Architectural Partnership

Riverhouse is a luxury condominium project between southeast First and Second avenues, which will be situated along the New River. This signature building has been designed to take full advantage of the wonderful urban amenities offered in downtown Fort Lauderdale.

The building has been folded in the middle, stepping away from the New River to provide a public plaza adjacent to and part of the Fort Lauderdale Riverwalk.

The plaza, raised 61 centimeters/2 feet above the Riverwalk is accessed via a broad section of stairs and has as its centerpiece a large plaza fountain. Computer-controlled jets will spray up from openings in the plaza surface allowing people to interact directly with the fountain. Seating, planting, and potted plants will complete the atmosphere to create a lively new public amenity compatible with the Riverwalk.

Located at the southeast corner of the building, available to the public and condo owners, will be a small café with terraced seating opening up to the Riverwalk and adjacent to the water plaza. At the north end of the building, a four-story health spa, sheathed in floor-to-ceiling glass, allows panoramic views to the Riverwalk. At the same time, the public can walk along the Riverwalk and view the activities of the spa.

All proposed design elements will be fully coordinated with the existing paving, benches, lighting, and so on, of the Riverwalk. No construction will take place south of the Riverwalk pedestrian path and only minimal construction as required to integrate the two areas on the north side of the path will take place. Several trees will be relocated into other areas along the walkway to open the plaza to the Riverwalk.

From its initial concept, the design between the public Riverwalk and proposed plaza and the private area of the building has been of the utmost importance as to the integration of the existing Riverwalk and the building. The creation of this public area provides the building with an active, lively backyard and provides an exciting new space for Fort Lauderdale and its residents.

rendering   Art Associates

Lincoln Square

Hotel/Residential tower: 137 m/450 ft;
office tower: 126 m/412 ft
42/28 stories
Hotel, residential offices, commercial,
retail, cinema, health club
2003

Bellevue, Washington, USA

James KM Cheng Architects Inc.; Mithun Partners

Lincoln Square in Bellevue, Washington, USA is located at "ground zero" of the town center. It is directly across the street from the most successful shopping center in Washington, and on the busiest street intersection of the city. It is also at a point in the city where views of Lake Washington and the skyline of Seattle are possible from three floors up.

The concept of this 148,640 square-meter/1.6 million-square-foot mixed-use project is to elevate the residential units as high as possible and integrate them with as much amenities and technology as possible. As a result, the project program is rich in diversity, consisting of a 126-meter/412-foot-high office tower; a retail podium of 23,225 square meters/250,000 square feet with a 12 screen cinema on top, a 137-meter/450-foot-high hotel/condominium tower (One Lincoln Tower) and a 6038-square-meter/65,000-square-foot sports club.

In order to maximize the view, the residential units are stacked on top of the 303-room hotel below. Being the highest tower in the city at 137 meters/450 feet (the other towers are at 91 meters/300 feet), the residential units laterally start where others end.

Due to the unusual nature of the land parcel, the resultant residential/hotel tower is long and narrow, thus making it a much-compromised shape in seismic design. To counter this deficiency, the structural core was split into two and placed apart so that the long rectangular building became in concept, square buildings. This is more effective in countering seismic forces. These cores also serve as separate vertical circulation cores for the hotel and residential.

Being the tallest building in Bellevue, penthouses are designed with double-height living rooms to take advantage of an unobstructed panoramic view in all directions.

Multifunctional Residential Complex

Moscow, Russia

George Mailov & Archizdrav's Partners

135 m/423 ft
25/35/40 stories
Residential, public, commercial, offices
2003

222

This residential complex was designed within the "Development Program of the New Ring" under the auspices of the Moscow government.

It includes 369 residential apartments, all necessary public facilities, offices, and a sports complex, all of which are situated in the two-story podium. All the offices have separate entries, which provide an opportunity for independent use.

The complex has various dwelling types, with areas between a minimum of 90 square meters/969 square feet and a maximum of 180 square meters/1937 square feet.

It includes two-story underground parking area for 400 cars and guest parking for 88 cars outside.

The overall great scope of the building has been articulated as a configuration of three towers with various heights, so the external appearance resembles the form of a high cliff. The architects are sensitive to the nuances of place and precedent, and approve of a holistic approach, which integrates interior design details and site-related improvements as integral parts of the architectural solution; and maintains a harmonious balance between heaven, earth, and people.

One Central Park at AOL Time Warner Center

New York, New York, USA

Skidmore, Owings and Merrill LLP

228 m/750 ft
52 stories
Offices, hotel, residential
2003

The design of AOL Time Warner Center is motivated by programmatic requirements as well as the unique context of its surroundings. The design alludes to twin residential towers lining Central Park West—the Century, the Majestic, the San Remo, and the El Dorado. The AOL Time Warner Center consists of several distinct forms that moderate the scale of the project and allow light and air to filter through the building, reaching the streets and park below. The building rises from a stone and glass base containing the retail and studio components. Two glass trapezoidal towers set atop the podium rise to a height of 750 feet/ 228 meters and culminate in luminous glass and steel crowns. The towers house the headquarters of AOL Time Warner in the lower floors, a Mandarin Oriental Hotel, and One Central Park luxury condominiums, located on the 18th to the 52nd floors.

digital image   Archimation/SOM

The design is formed by the overlap of three of Manhattan's most significant urban constituents: the city grid, Broadway, and Central Park. The Manhattan grid, or more specifically 59th Street, is reflected in the project on two levels. First, it is recreated within a 26-meter/85-foot-wide and 46-meter/150-foot-high transparent glass cable net wall with a retail street at the base of the project and Jazz @ Lincoln Center performance lobby situated above. Second, the line of 59th Street is re-articulated as a "window" between the towers, extending the view corridor west of Central Park.

While the re-inscription of the city grid is the primary organization and massing strategy, its transformation and articulation is suggested by the diagonal passing of Broadway and resonating geometries of the circle. The sweeping base continues the pedestrian scale of Broadway and curves along Columbus Circle juxtaposed to the grid. As the glass and stone wall transforms to facets of glass at office floors' levels, the outward spread of the circle contrasts the angular faces of the towers aligned with Broadway below. The presence of Central Park further defines the design as the towers' angles reinforce the diagonal relationship between site and park, presenting a new face to the park.

The North Apartments

55 m/180 ft
15 stories
Residential, commercial, retail
2003

Sydney, New South Wales, Australia
Harry Seidler & Associates

This 15-story city center apartment building is different compared to the mostly bland and characterless high-rise residential blocks that have gone up in recent times facing narrow streets.

Oriented with its single façade to the north, facing the width of Goulburn Street, the design breaks away from the usual box-like structures.

Every one of the 48 apartments has a wave-shaped balcony, so as to accommodate outdoor furniture, at its widened part. The balconies are arranged in a vertically staggered pattern so as to maximize the spatial feeling.

Color is introduced into the façade by the use of integrally permanent colored toughened glass on the balconies' end rails and dividing screens. They are a mixture of primary- and neutral-colored accents all over the façade creating a scintillating effect when seeing them as one walks past the building.

The apartments are designed following a split-level planning system, which results in a ceiling height of 2850 millimeters/ 112 inches over the living area and 2700 millimeters/106 inches in the raised bedrooms.

There are 22 one-bedroom (55 square meters/592 square feet), 20 two-bedroom (81 square meters/872 square feet), and six three-bedroom (137 square meters/1745 square feet) apartments. On the second floor is a 12.5-meter/41-foot-long indoor swimming pool, saunas, and gym on two floors exclusively for the occupants. There is a street-fronting retail area and a commercial-use first floor.

The underground carpark, accessible by car elevator, accommodates 24 cars.

Branksome Tower III

168 m/551 ft
44 stories
Residential
2004

Hong Kong SAR, People's Republic of China
P&T Architects and Engineers Ltd.

Branksome Tower is located on 3 Tregunter Path, mid-levels of Hong Kong Island.

It comprises a 39-story residential tower block sitting on a five-story carpark podium. The total height is 168 meters/551 feet with a total gross floor area of 13,277 square meters/142,913 square feet. Each floor consists of two residential units with major rooms facing the magnificent Victoria Harbour. Each typical unit will have the same area of 186 square meters/2000 square feet.

Other than the typical unit layout, special garden duplexes and top floor duplexes have been designed to cater for various unit-size market requirements. Each duplex will have its own pool and open deck with areas ranging from 418 square meters/ 4500 square feet to 557 square meters/6000 square feet.

The exterior will be finished in a combination of beige Italian granite and exterior ceramic tiles together with fluorocarbon-coated aluminum panels and blue-green tinted glass panels.

LDC Kennedy Town Development

Hong Kong SAR, People's Republic of China

Ronald Lu & Partners (HK) Ltd.

178 m/584 ft, 170 m/558 ft,
165 m/541 ft

42–45 stories

Residential

2004

224

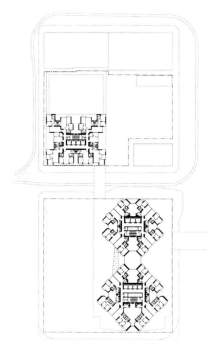

This urban renewal project consists of two separate sites in the old built-up area of the Western District, with three residential towers of 42 to 45 stories above a five-story podium. A series of local open spaces are provided at ground level, with a public passageway connecting the pedestrian link to other comprehensive developments and the future MTR Station.

The tower layouts are designed in order to maximize sea views. Private recreational facilities and a clubhouse are provided for each site.

Prinsenhof
(Tower and Hotel)

The Hague, The Netherlands

atelier PRO architekten (hotel, offices); Kraaijvanger Urbis (tower); Architectengroep (apartments)

Tower: 109 m/358 ft; hotel: 70 m/230 ft

26/23 stories

Offices, hotel, residential

2004

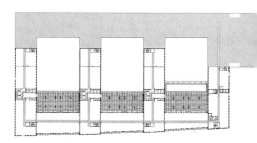

The municipality of The Hague has commenced with the redevelopment of the Beatrixkwartier (Beatrix district), which includes the Prinsenhof. The urban design plan was created by Juan Busquets. The focus of his design is to create cohesion in the Beatrixkwartier. Atelier PRO was responsible for creating the design for the hotel and around 51,000 square meters/548,964 square feet of office space as well as the parking garage below it with room for at least 1000 cars. The 200 apartment dwellings were designed by the Architectengroep from Amsterdam and the offices (around 26,000 square meters/279,864 square feet) on the corner of the Schenkkade are the design of Kraaijvanger Urbis from Rotterdam. This particular plan embraces high density and a blending of functions. It is characterized by a tightly controlled rhythm of high-rise and medium-height construction and fits well with the existing structures.

On the south side, along the Prinses Beatrixlaan, the building height averages 50 meters/164 feet. On the north side, in the second zone, buildings reach 70 meters/230 feet culminating in a height accent of 109 meters/358 feet on the corner. A similar cohesion exists among the buildings at ground level to that which has been achieved up above. In between the buildings, space has been kept open at street level for what will be one of the distinguishing features of the construction: the Corporate Gardens; these three partially covered outdoor areas are important quality indicators for the plan. They can be reached from the Prinses Beatrixlaan and are linked to each other. The parking garage can be accessed from this area and from the area that is not covered over some of the apartments can just be seen.

The cohesion between the various functions is also emphasized with the use of dark red brick around the outside of the entire complex (the "skin") and a light-colored brick around the open inner spaces (the "lining").

Riparian Plaza

200 m/656 ft
53 stories
Residential, commercial, retail
2004

Brisbane, Queensland, Australia

Harry Seidler & Associates

This composite-usage building accommodating both office and residential vertical sectors is unique in this country, especially for Brisbane.

Placed in the adjacent waterfront site on the river to the 10-year-old "Riverside Centre," it is more extensive in that it continues the promenade along the river, but it adds more facilities for the public, restaurants, plazas, and covered seating right on the water's edge.

The shape of the tower has been carefully formed to maximize the outlook for occupants up and down the river. The base sector houses cars, the mid-segment is column-free offices, and the reshaped top consists of the greatest apartments the architect has ever built. Each of the luxurious penthouses has large curvilinear-shaped projecting terraces facing the water, shaped so as to accommodate furniture grouping comfortably. A swimming pool, gymnasium, and other communal facilities are in a recessed upper floor. The dramatic top "sky houses" even have their own spa pools on huge private terraces.

Riparian Plaza extends the indestructible quality of materials used in many of the architect's tall buildings, which maintain their "as-new" look for many decades. Granite exterior cladding complements the stainless steel balcony facings and sunshades, which do not only ensure longevity, but conserve energy in that they save on air-conditioning and power-running costs.

The regular repetitive system structure is of reinforced concrete with a "gathering" of columns at the main approach entries, which collects columns to create a huge two-story-high entrance portico covered with a projecting glass canopy.

The Pinnacle

163 m/535 ft
50 stories
Residential
2004

Chicago, Illinois, USA

Lucien Lagrange Architects

This 50-story tower is located immediately west of Chicago's Magnificent Mile, the City's premiere upscale shopping street. The gothic design evolves from the neighboring cathedral district with several significant buildings. The natural stone base soars into a rhythmic integration of articulated concrete ribs and glass.

Each of the 230 luxury condominium units will have an exceptional floor plan and an expansive view of the city. At least one balcony is provided for every unit and some of the units feature terraces, created as the building steps back as it rises.

The four largest penthouses will each feature 5000 square feet of space and standard units will have 102 to 260 square meters/1100 to 2800 square feet. Eight penthouses in all are featured on the top stories of the building. Retail space at the ground floor will open onto the three street exposures. Five levels of parking will rise above the ground level. Building amenities, including a health club, technology center, and entertainment facilities, will separate the parking component of the building from the residential floors.

Tsuen Wan
Serviced Apartments

Tsuen Wan, Hong Kong SAR, People's Republic of China

Dennis Lau & Ng Chun Man
Architects & Engineers (H.K.) Ltd

210 m/689 ft

43/56 stories

Residential

2004

This development comprises two serviced apartment towers built above four-story podia containing car parking and central housekeeping facilities.

The buildings are situated on a brownfield site, formerly occupied by a bottling plant, on the border between a zone of high-rise factories and the Tsuen Wan town centre and residential areas. The buildings act as a buffer between the two contrasting land uses.

Air-conditioning equipment for each building is centralized in the plantroom penthouses.

The communal recreational facilities comprising restaurant, gymnasium, and indoor pool are located on the fifth and sixth floors, where they enjoy views of the tennis courts and landscaped garden located on the podium roofs.

Freshwater Place

Melbourne, Victoria, Australia

Bates Smart Pty Ltd

First residential tower: 220 m/722 ft;
second residential tower: 200 m/656 ft;
commercial tower: 165 m/541 ft;
strata commercial: 53 m/174 ft

69/64/40/14 stories

Retail, residential, commercial

2005

Freshwater Place is the last remaining riverfront site in central Melbourne. Bates Smart was commissioned by Australand for the high-profile development after winning a limited design competition.

The project will create important linkages along the riverfront and complete the redevelopment of the south side of the Yarra River. The residential tower podium forms the principal façade of Melbourne's new Queensbridge Square, linking Southgate, the Crown, and Melbourne Exhibition Centre.

Freshwater Place is a new urban neighborhood for Melbourne, combining residential, office, neighborhood retail, and hospitality in a single

coherent precinct focused on a new urban space—Freshwater Place. From this new space, a network of arcades and small open spaces will link to the surrounding residential and office precinct.

The towers have been designed as crystalline forms clad largely in glass. The glazed forms will be sculptural and elegant with as much transparency as possible. Environmental objectives will be achieved through high-performance low-e glazing combined with internal screening devices.

Bates Smart will be working closely with the client to develop Freshwater Place as a dynamic living and working destination for the Southbank area.

photography   Gollings & Pidgeon

Herzl Tower

143.6 m/471 ft
46 stories
Residential
2005

Ramat Gan, Israel
Eli Attia Architects

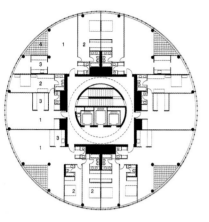

Located in an area largely covered by three- to five-story walkups in the second-largest town within metropolitan Tel Aviv, the tower addresses the need for greater urban densities along major arteries within Tel Aviv's growing metropolitan area.

The design opts for as small a footprint as possible so that much of the large site area will remain open for the enjoyment of its residents and pedestrians at street level.

Since the tower will rise high above the buildings in the surrounding areas and will be seen from great distances, a round cylindrical form was chosen so that the tower will radiate equally to all parts of town.

The building's height relative to surrounding structures makes it a reference point throughout the city.

To accentuate the tower's height and its 360-degree citywide orientation, its balconies are arranged in four vertical combined spirals that guide the viewer's eyes upward.

King's Park Residential Development

108 m/354 ft
29 stories
Residential
2005

Kowloon, Hong Kong SAR, People's Republic of China

Dennis Lau & Ng Chun Man
Architects & Engineers (H.K.) Ltd

The apartment complex at King's Park departs from conventional Hong Kong practice in a number of innovative ways. The project benefits from a site that permits the eight plots to be fused at their gable ends to form a single crescent-shaped building and from recent changes in the local statutory controls that have rendered the provision of sky gardens at high level realistic.

The continuous and linear form of the complex ensures that there is no inter-block overlooking, which is a common problem on larger housing projects in the territory. The terracing of the blocks also offers significant structural and construction economies. The provision of a sky garden shall increase both the extent and variety of open spaces available to residents.

The blocks are elevated high above the landscaped podium deck on pilotis creating a permeable and open environment that contrasts with the fragmented and residual garden spaces that occur when separate blocks occupy the ground level.

Orient City Garden

79.8 m/261.8 ft
27 stories
Residential
2005

Pudong District, Shanghai, People's Republic of China

East China Architectural Design & Research Institute Co., Ltd. (ECADI)

The Oriental City Garden is a model residential housing project of the state. It is situated in the Pudong New Area; Pujian Road runs to its north, Longyang Road runs to its south, Dongfang Road runs to its east, and on the west runs Linyi Road, and it is adjacent to the Sino-American Children's Medical Center and Shanghai Renji Hospital Pudong Branch. There are 1575 households in this residential quarter, which is made up of high-rises, mid-rises, multistory housings, office buildings, meeting halls, nurseries, and kindergartens.

The road system in this residential area is of a 'one axis and two circles' pearl chain structure. The whole area is covered with spots, belts, and stretches of green, and a river system runs through this area. Taking functions as pointers, roads as the framework, a Shanghai-style residential area characterized by 'water' and 'green' is formed.

Pe'at Yam Tower

131.3 m/431 ft
41 stories
Residential, hotel
2005

Herzlia, Israel

Eli Attia Architects

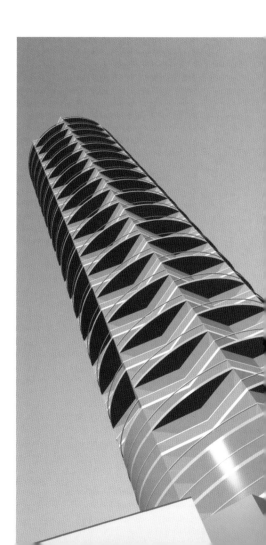

Located on a cliff that separates a beautiful low-rise community from the Mediterranean Sea, Pe'at Yam Tower seeks to minimize the adverse effects of several large, wide buildings that already exist in the area. These buildings block much of the city from the refreshing sea breezes and majestic sunsets that are the primary benefits of living by the sea.

Pe'at Yam Tower utilizes the smallest footprint possible so that the building will allow the greatest openness between land and sea, allowing for greater freedom of air movements and more open views.

It features a cylindrical tower base, so that it will prevent air turbulence at street level associated with square-corner buildings under similar circumstances.

Above the cylindrical base the tower's plan changes gradually from circular to a star-octagon shape with staggered balconies that maintain the circular form. In addition to providing private outdoor access for tower residents, these balconies prevent the disturbing cumulative downdrafts at pedestrian level that are associated with tall buildings. This is a particularly important issue with this project because primary public access to the beach is alongside the tower.

These balconies are able to achieve twice the height of traditional ones because they alternate every other floor. Their forms, nesting within the star-shaped enclosure, also provides residents with the luxury of total privacy with respect to the building's other balconies.

Willem Ruys – Müller Pier

72.2 m/237 ft
23 stories
Residential
2005

Rotterdam, The Netherlands

de Architekten Cie.-Amsterdam; Frits van Dongen

The Müller Pier is a wedge of land jutting into the River Maas near the Euromast. Standing at the border between the city centre and Rotterdam West, it is largely defined by the surrounding harbor basins and by being hemmed in on three sides by water.

The masterplan for the Müller Pier specifies some 600 apartments and ground-based housing units in 13 distinct housing blocks. The differing dimensions of the blocks drive home the contrast between the intimacy of the peninsular and the vast expanse of the water. Each building enjoys a great degree of autonomy as regards size, height, and housing typology—an autonomy further consolidated by their architecture. Some are

rotated strategically to engage their surroundings. All activity is concentrated on the ground floors, including the eventuality of studios and live–work units.

At the head of the Müller Pier stands block 12, a tapering kinked building with a three-story base. The approximately 72-meter/ 237-foot-tall tower contains 58 apartments, three to a level below the kink and two above. The base houses services and seven grounded live–work units with a parking garage below. The apartments in the tower make the connection with the river, the harbor basins and the city, while the grounded dwellings in the base stand the building in good stead with its immediate surroundings. Its salient position at the head of the pier prompted its sculptural form, with the kink articulating the relationship with the Maas. The dark slate cladding of all its façades and roofs adds to the sculptural effect.

7 South Dearborn

472 m/1550 ft
108 stories
Residential, office, retail

Chicago, Illinois, USA

Skidmore, Owings & Merrill LLP

7 South Dearborn will be a 108-story, 472-meter/1550-foot tower, which would be the world's tallest building if eventually built. 8417 square meters/90,600 square feet on the top 13 floors will be dedicated to communications facilities. Three to five primary antennae will support digital television, analog television, and other communication functions. 7 South Dearborn will achieve a total height of 610 meters/2000 feet. The mixed-use complex will include commercial office, residential, retail, and parking.

The 176,510-square-meter/1.9 million-square-foot building will also include 360 residential units on 40 floors, 71,068 square meters/765,000 square feet of office space on 32 floors, and 800 parking spaces. The 6967 square meters/75,000 square feet of retail will include restaurants, shops, and amenities such as food delivery service, a private fitness club, laundry/cleaner, and drugstore. The tower will continue the successful

transformation of Chicago's Central Business District into a community enlivened by a full range of residential, retail, and commercial activity 24 hours a day, seven days a week.

The stainless steel and aluminum exterior façade will be accented by light green, lightly tinted low-e-coated double glazing. Six distinct groups of floors will be visible. The lower two groupings will be separated by standard setbacks, while the upper four groupings will be divided by distinctive notches that underscore the building's role as a transmission tower and reveal the cantilevered character of its construction.

7 South Dearborn represents a major advancement in the engineering of tall buildings. Although taller than the Sears Tower, the building's floor plates are substantially smaller. This is a result of its stayed mast structural system, formed from a series of spaces that evolve from a reinforced concrete core. A limited number of widely spaced columns dot the perimeter of the office component, and the interior is column-free. The cantilevering of the upper 57 residential floors from a concrete core makes columns unnecessary on the exterior walls and provides 3.3-meter/11-foot uninterrupted views in all directions.

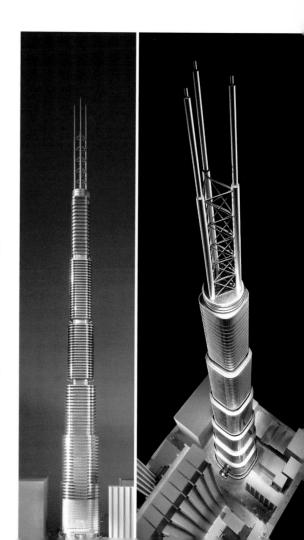

Boylston Square

198 m/675 ft
59 stories
Residential, hotel, retail

Boston, Massachusetts, USA

Gary Edward Handel + Associates;
CBT/Childs Bertman Tseckares, Inc.

Boylston Square is a 59-story, two-building mixed-use residential entertainment complex situated in Back Bay Boston near the historic Fenway. Located on two air-rights parcels over the Massachusetts Turnpike in a mixed residential and commercial district, the western site is comprised of retail, hotel, residential, and fitness club functions with a roof garden on the low-rise portion. Hotel rooms and condominiums comprise the 198-meter/675-foot-high tower. The eastern parcel contains ground level retail, a new MBTA subway entry, and a 14-screen movie theater.

The two buildings re-establish the street wall along Boylston Street and Massachusetts Avenue that has remained an ill-defined part of the city grid since the construction of the original 19th century railroad right-of-way. The complex also enhances the relationship between the Boston Common and the Fenway gardens while the tower marks the western edge of Back Bay along the high-rise "spine." The podium is composed of masonry walls and large glass openings while the tower is conceived as a more jewel-like glass and metal spire.

photography   David Desroches; rendering: Vladislav Yeliseyev

Cityfront Center Plaza

215 m/704 ft
59 stories
Hotel, residential

Chicago, Illinois, USA

Lohan Caprile Goettsch architects

The Cityfront Center Plaza Hotel and Residential Tower will rise 215 meters/704 feet from its site on the Chicago River's edge. The project includes 36 condominium floors, 18 hotel floors, plus ancillary spaces. To optimize the value of the unique site, which offers spectacular views in all directions, Lohan Associates generated a unique architectural and structural solution.

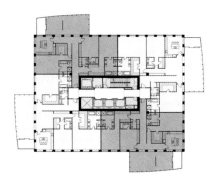

The solution utilizes an economical and efficient structural tube in concert with a system of shallow, post-tensioned concrete beams to provide soaring 5-meter/16-feet-deep by 14-meter/46-foot-wide cantilevered living/dining rooms. These cantilevered rooms offer dramatic views in three directions completely unimpeded by any structure.

This system of cantilevers is employed for all residential floors, and to a limited extent on the hotel floors. The majority of the hotel rooms are contained within the basic tube, while a single cantilever on the riverside of the building contains the hotel suites.

The base of the building contains the hotel ancillary functions and rooftop terrace. The riverfront level houses a restaurant with outdoor seating and public promenade.

The primary function of the tower is residential. The units are luxury condominiums and the building has been designed to provide an extremely flexible unit mix: the typical floorplate can be subdivided into a multitude of unit types and styles.

Elephant & Castle Eco-towers

138 m/453 ft
35/12 stories
Residential, retail, hotel, offices

London, United Kingdom
T. R. Hamzah & Yeang Sdn. Bhd.

The massive regeneration project for the Elephant & Castle Eco-towers includes three towers by T. R. Hamzah & Yeang to the east, a central railway interchange, and a project by Foster and Partners to the west, surrounding a major plaza. The overall project also incorporates housing intended for private ownership, which will be financed by revenue from the towers. As well as a huge shopping and leisure facility and other communal provisions, the development will also have three major parks.

The three buildings by T. R. Hamzah & Yeang, known as the Garden Towers, represent the firm's first competition success in London that may form a built proposition. In most major respects these towers, which vary in height between 12 and 35 stories, repeat much of the concept of Bishopsgate Towers, as a precedent. This is to say that the building configuration, orientation, façade design, and landscaping policy directly reflect the earlier model. However, in this instance, the lifts and staircores are brought together in a more compact arrangement, but again within a centralized, landscaped, access-gallery atrium. The typical floor plan, for instance, of Eco-tower 1, is again a two-sided arrangement, which offers a variety of unit-orientation and outward views. To the overall form, in addition to the skycourts and apartment balconies, Yeang has added generous "sky-pod" volumes for communal facilities and the summit incorporates a major winter garden, which outwardly signals the building's ecological presence.

Migdal Zedek

164 m/538 ft
33 stories
Residential

Tel Aviv, Israel
Gabai Architects Inc.

A luxury residential tower in the romantic neighborhood of Neve Zedek, this building features a lower section with a variety of duplex apartments. Large luxurious apartments form the upper section in a modular fashion. In between the two there are a health spa and swimming pool. The most upper floor houses three penthouse apartments with private swimming pools on outdoor decks.

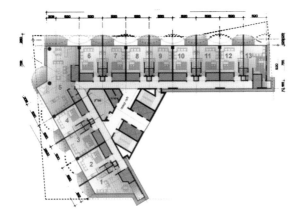

Centre International Rogier
(also known as Tour Martini)
Location Brussels, Belgium
Completion date 1961 (demolished in 2001)
Height 110 m/361ft
Stories 30 + 1 underground
Area Site: 4167 m²/44,854ft²; total floor: 58,800 m²/632,923 ft²; typical floor: 1496 m²/16,103 ft²; offices: 26,750 m²/287,937 ft²; apartment units: 14,200 m²/152,849 ft²; retail shops: 4850 m²/52,205 ft²; theaters: 13,000 m²/139,932 ft²
Structure Concrete (top three levels: steel)
Materials Glazed aluminum façades
Use Offices, residential, theaters, retail, penthouse Martini Club
Architect Jacques Cuisinier
Structural engineer J. Mauquoy
Services engineers H. Marcq
Electricity adviser A. Lazarus
Isolation engineer Grunenwaldt
Developer/General contractor Lotimo s.a.

Astor Tower
Location Chicago, Illinois, USA
Completion date 1962 (original building)/October 1996 (renovation)
Height 91 m/300 ft
Stories 28
Area Site: 1672 m²/18,000 ft²; building: 9290 m²/100,000 ft²
Structure Original: all concrete frame; renovation: steel and glass frame
Materials Exterior: steel and glass
Use Residential
Cost US$2.35 M
Architect Bertrand Goldberg Associates (original building 1962); DeStefano and Partners, Ltd. (renovation 1966)
Associate architect Donald Lee Sickler Associates (1996)
Structural engineer Tylk, Gustafson and Associates
Client Astor Tower Condominium Association
Contractor Chicago Ornamental Iron, Inc.

University Plaza
Location New York, New York, USA
Completion date October 1966
Height 84 m/275.5 ft
Stories 30 + 1 below grade
Area Site: 19,762 m²/212,728 ft²; gross floor: 69,399 m²/747,000 ft² (including 12,542 m²/135,000 ft² underground parking)
Structure Reinforced cast-in-place concrete
Materials Interior: lobby: concrete flooring and exposed architectural concrete or glass walls with gypsum wallboard partitions; suspended ceilings: painted cement plaster; co-op lobby: flooring: terrazzo; walls: brick or glass; suspended ceiling: painted gypsum wallboard; floors of the university apartments: vinyl asbestos tile covers; co-op apartments: asphalt tile or wood; walls in each building: painted gypsum wallboard;

suspended ceilings: painted simulated textured cement
Use Residential (university graduate student/faculty and middle-income co-op apartment complex)
Cost Total: US$11,333,000
Architect I. M. Pei & Partners Architects and Planners
Structural engineer Farkas and Barron
Mechanical engineer Caretsky and Associates
Contractor Tishman Construction Corporation
Client Dormitory Authority of the State of New York; Washington Square Southeast Apartments, Inc.

John Hancock Center
Location Chicago, Illinois, USA
Completion date 1970
Height 344 m/1127 ft
Stories/Levels 100
Area 260,000 m²/2.8 million ft²
Structure Steel exterior columns and spandrel beams create a structural tube that is reinforced by clearly articulated diagonal steel members and structural floors that meet those diagonals and corner columns
Materials Clad in black aluminum with bronze glare-reducing glass, bronze-colored aluminum window frames; public spaces: travertine marble and dark granite
Use Retail, offices, residential, observatory
Architect Skidmore, Owings & Merrill LLP
Structural/Mechanical/Electrical engineer Skidmore, Owings & Merrill LLP
Client John Hancock Mutual Life Company (current owner: Shorenstein Company)

Galleria
Location New York, New York, USA
Completion date November 1974
Height 155 m/510 ft
Stories 55
Area Site: 1579 m²/17,000 ft²; building: 39,947 m²/430,000 ft²
Structure Reinforced concrete
Materials Brick, granite, concrete, structural steel
Use Residential, offices, retail, health clubs, restaurants, public space
Cost US$50 M (1972–3)
Architect David Kenneth Specter
Architect for typical apartment floor plan Office of Philip Birnbaum
Structural engineer Office of Irwin Cantor
Mechanical/Electrical engineer Sidney Barbanel
Client Madison Equities
Contractor HRH Construction

Four Leaf Towers
Location Houston, Texas, USA
Completion date June 1982
Height 134 m/439 ft
Stories 40
Area Site: 3.8 hectares/9.3 acres; gross: 92,900 m²/100,000 ft²

Structure Flat-slab, reinforced concrete
Materials Curtain wall: tinted vision glass with three colors of ceramic glass supported by a fixed fluoropolymer painted aluminum frame
Use Residential
Cost Project: US$66 M; construction: US$100 M
Architect Cesar Pelli & Associates Inc.
Architect for construction Melton Henry/Architects; Albert C. Martin & Associates
Structural engineer CBM Engineers
MEP engineer Cook & Holle
Civil engineer Lockwood, Andrews & Newman
Client Interfin Corporation
Contractor Henry C. Beck & Company

The Atlantis
Location Miami, Florida, USA
Completion date January 1982
Height 53.94 m/177 ft
Stories 20
Area 17,651 m²/190,000 ft²
Structure Reinforced concrete, post-tension, curtain wall
Use Residential
Design architect Arquitectonica
Structural/Mechanical engineer John Ross & Associates
Electrical engineer/Contractor Cohen-Ager, Inc.
Client Sol Group Corp.

Kanchanjunga Apartments
Location Bombay, Maharashtra, India
Completion date 1983
Height 84 m/276 ft
Stories 27
Area Site: 5120 m²/55,112 ft²; building: 19,960 m²/214,849 ft²
Structure Cast-in-situ reinforced cement concrete structure with brick infill walls
Materials Exterior: paint on reinforced cement concrete
Use Residential
Architect Charles Correa Architects/Planners
Associate architect Pravina Mehta
Structural engineer Shirish Patel
Electrical engineer Babubhai Shah
Client Parmanand Patel
Contractor ECC Limited

Trump Tower
Location New York, New York, USA
Completion date October 1983
Height 202 m/664 ft
Stories 58
Area Site: 3265 m²/35,145 ft²; building: 70,453 m²/758,376 ft²
Structure Reinforced concrete
Materials Exterior: solar bronze glass, aluminum curtain wall; interior: marble, drywall

Use Retail: six levels; commercial offices: 13 levels; residential: 38 levels

Cost US$90 M

Architect of Record Swanke Hayden Connell Architects

Principal in charge of project Richard Seth Hayden, FAIA, RIBA

Partner in charge of architectural design Der Scutt

Structural engineer Office of Irwin G. Cantor, P.C.

Mechanical/Electrical engineer W.A. DiGiacomo Associates

Joint Developers The Trump Organization; The Equitalbe Life Assurance Society of the United States

Contractor HRH Construction Company

388 Market Street

Location San Francisco, California, USA

Completion date 1985

Height 114 m/375 ft

Stories 26

Area 46,450 m²/500,000 ft²

Structure Structural steel

Materials Red granite, glass, clear glazing, copper dome Mixed-use: residential, commercial offices, retail, parking

Cost US$52 million

Architect Skidmore, Owings & Merrill LLP

Structural engineer Skidmore, Owings & Merrill LLP

Client Honorway Investment Corporation

Contractor Swinerton & Walberg

Tung Wang Palace

Location Taipei, Taiwan

Completion date 1985

Height 65 m/213 ft

Stories 18/19 + 2 basement

Area Site: 5000 m²/53,820 ft²; building: 2940 m²/ 31,646 ft²; total floor: 57,183 m²/615,518 ft²

Structure Reinforced concrete

Materials Exterior: tile

Use Residential

Cost US$25 M

Architect C.Y. Lee & Partners

Client/Contactor Tuntex Group

100 United Nations Plaza Tower

Location New York, New York, USA

Completion date October 1986

Height 176 m/578 ft

Stories 55 + 1 basement level

Area Site: 3447 m²/37,108 ft²; building: 42,404 m²/ 456,444 ft²

Structure Reinforced concrete

Materials Exterior: brick, aluminum, and glass in frames; interior: marble, drywall

Use Services and parking: basement level; commercial and services: ground level; residential: 54 levels

Cost US$110 M

Design architect Der Scutt Architect

Architect of record (base building) Schuman, Lichtenstein, Claman & Efron

Structural engineer The Office of Irwin G. Cantor, P.C.

Mechanical/Electrical engineer I.M. Robbins, P.C.

Client United Nations Plaza Tower Associates; Albanese Development Corporation

Contractor DeMatteis Organization

Olympia Centre

Location Chicago, Illinois, USA

Completion date 1986

Height 219 m/728 ft

Stories 63

Area 132,000 m²/1,420,000 ft²

Structure Reinforced concrete

Materials Tai Vasallo dual-finished granite, bronze-tinted dual glazing glass, steel exterior

Use Residential, offices, retail

Architect Skidmore, Owings & Merrill LLP

Structural engineer Skidmore, Owings & Merrill LLP

Mechanical/Electrical engineer Jaros, Baum & Bolles

Client Chicago Superior Associates Development Corp.

Contractor Paschen Newberg Joint Venture

The Park Belvedere

Location New York, New York, USA

Completion date December 1986

Height 112.8 m/370 ft

Stories 35

Area Site: 1394 m²/15,005 ft²; building: 20,446 m²/ 220,081 ft²

Structure Reinforced concrete

Use Residential, shops at grade level

Cost US$45 M

Architect Frank Williams & Partners, Architects

Structural engineer Rosenwasser Grossman

Mechanical engineer I.M. Robbins, P.C.

Owner/Developer The Zeckendorf Company; World Wide Holdings

Contractor H.R.H. Construction Company

279 Central Park West

Location New York, New York, USA

Completion date 1988

Height 71.5 m/235 ft

Stories 23 + cellar and sub-cellar

Area 13,200 m²/142,085 ft²

Structure Structure/foundation walls: reinforced concrete supported on concrete footing or on brick arch foundation walls

Materials Structure/foundation: reinforced concrete; exterior walls: masonry cavity-wall with brick exterior, limestone, in-swing casement window construction

Use Mixed-use residential/community facility including school

Architect Costas Kondylis & Partners LLP (formerly Costas Kondylis & Associates PC)

Client Sutton East Associates

The Corinthian

Location New York, New York, USA

Completion date July 1988

Height 166 m/546 ft

Stories 55 + 1 basement level

Area Site: 7541 m²/81,172 ft²; building: 90,485 m²/ 974,000 ft²

Structure Reinforced concrete

Materials Exterior: black aluminum frames, bronze glass; interior: marble, wood floors, drywall

Use Recreation/health club: one level; commercial offices: three levels; residential: 53 levels

Cost US$90.6 M

Design architect Der Scutt Architect

Production architect Michael Schimenti, P.C.

Structural engineer Alvin Fischer & Robert D. Redlein, P.C.

Mechanical/Electrical engineer Irving Keinan & Associates, P.C.

Client Bernard Spitzer, P.E. with Kriti Properties

Contractor Kreisler Borg Florman

CitySpire

Location New York, New York, USA

Completion date 1989

Height 248 m/814 ft

Stories 72

Area 78,222 m²/842,000 ft²

Structure Reinforced concrete

Materials High-strength poured-in-place concrete, tinted vision glass, vertical and horizontal granite panels, painted aluminum mullions, painted steel plate ribs, aluminum fins at the dome

Use Residential, offices, retail

Architect Murphy/Jahn, Inc. Architects

Structural engineer Robert Rosenwasser Associates

Mechanical/Electrical engineer Cosentini Associates

Construction manager Tishman Construction Corp.

Client West 56th Street Associates

Contractor

Wonderland Villa

Location Kwai Chung, Hong Kong SAR, People's Republic of China

Completion date 1989

Height 103 m/338 ft

Stories 35

Area Site: 65,129 m²/701,048 ft²; domestic gross floor: 151,136 m²/1,626,828 ft²

Structure In-situ reinforced concrete on end-bearing piles

Materials Exterior: vitreous mosaic tiles, conventional windows with bronze-anodized aluminum frames, reconstituted and natural granite paving; interior: hardwood parquet floors, plaster wall finishes (to apartments)

Use Residential, with neighborhood commercial facilities

Architect Dennis Lau & Ng Chun Man Architects & Engineers (H.K.) Ltd (formerly Ng Chun Man & Associates Architects & Engineers (H.K.) Ltd)

The Wilshire

Location Los Angeles, California, USA
Completion date 1990
Height 104 m/340 ft
Stories 27
Area 32,236 m²/347,000 ft²
Materials Exterior: copper roof and balconies with ornate copper and other metal work, highly detailed granite and marble facade, French cobblestone-paved court, marble and polished granite lobby with mahogany paneling; interior: lobby floor: honed, pale cream limestone surrounding an elaborately inlaid rosette of pink and gold marble; lower levels: glass-enclosed conservatories
Use Residential
Cost US$48 M
Architect KMD
Associate architect Richard Magee Associates
Structural engineer Robert Englekirk, Consulting Structural Engineers, Inc.
Mechanical engineer Robert M. Young and Associates
Electrical engineer Frederic Russell Brown & Associates
Client The Wilshire, Bill Schwarz
Contractor HCB Contractors

Trump Palace

Location New York, New York, USA
Completion date January 1990
Height 190 m/623 ft
Stories 55
Area Site: 4089 m²/44,014 ft²; building: 47,955 m²/ 516,188 ft²
Structure Reinforced concrete
Use Residential, retail, parking
Cost US$98 M
Architect Frank Williams & Partners, Architects
Structural engineer Rosenwasser Grossman
Mechanical engineer I.M. Robbins, P.C.
Interior designer Zaniz and Jakobowski
Owner/Developer The Trump Organization
Contractor H.R.H. Construction Company

Weena Apartment Tower

Location Rotterdam, The Netherlands
Completion date June 1990
Height 103 m/338 ft
Stories 34
Area Gross floor: 17,749 m²/191,050 ft²
Structure Concrete structure with load-bearing walls made in-situ
Materials Exterior: clad with concrete panels with a top layer of grated stone/stone chippings (black, except for a section of south and west elevations, where there are strips in black, mid-gray, and virtual white), white aluminum window frames; central slab: white aluminum

Use Residential
Cost NLG 15 M (including installations)
Architect Hoogstad Architecten
Associate architect Bureau voor Bouwkunde
Structural advisor Aronsohn Raadgevende Ingenieurs b.v.
Installations advisor TM Verhoeven Raadgevende Ingenieurs
Environmental control advisor Adviesbureau Peutz & Associes
Contractor Bouwcombinatie Boele van Eesteren

Weenatoren (The Weena Tower)

Location Rotterdam, The Netherlands
Completion date October 1990
Height 106 m/348 ft
Stories 34
Area Site: 1200 m²/12,917 ft²; building: 26,023 m²/ 280,111 ft²
Structure Reinforced concrete central core
Materials Interior: ground floor: natural stone, white Carrara marble; walls: black veined Marasquino; ceilings: metal ceiling panel; floors offices: carpet; exterior: façade: aluminum curtain wall (silver), low-reflection transparent solar glass, natural Norwegian marble cladding; window-frame: black aluminum
Use Entrance: level 0; office: levels 1–13; residential: levels 14–33
Cost Dfl.35,169,458 (excluding taxes)
Architect Klunder Architecten
Structural engineer Ingenieursbureau Zonneveld
Mechanical/Electrical engineer Hiensch Engineering
Client Vesteda Management B.V./Kantoren Fonds Nederland
Contractor IBC Van Hoorn

La Tour

Location Westwood, Los Angeles, California, USA
Completion date 1991
Height 87 m/285 ft
Stories 24
Area 19,044.5 m²/205,000 ft²
Structure Steel superstructure
Use Residential
Cost US$160/ft²
Design architect Starkman Vidal Christensen
Executive architect Sheperd Nelson & Wheeler
Structural engineer John A. Martin & Associates
Mechanical/Electrical engineer Frederick Russell Brown & Associates
Client Pacific Triangle Corporation (initial stages); Daiwa House Corporation

Pacific View

Location Hong Kong SAR, People's Republic of China
Completion date January 1991
Height 135 m/443 ft
Stories 39
Area Site: 8554 m²/92,075 ft²; building: 67,738 m²/ 729,132 ft²
Structure Reinforced concrete
Materials Interior: granite; exterior: ceramic mosaic tile, granite
Use Residential: 39 levels; carpark: seven levels
Cost HK$450 M
Architect P&T Architects and Engineers Ltd.
Structural engineer H.K. Cheng
Mechanical/Electrical engineer P&T (M&E) Ltd.
Client Sun Hung Kai Properties Ltd.
Contractor Shun Fai Construction Co., Ltd.

Queen's Garden

Location Hong Kong SAR, People's Republic of China
Completion date August 1991
Height 167 m/548 ft
Stories 35
Area Site: 5818 m²/62,625 ft²; building: 39,845 m²/ 428,892 ft²
Structure Reinforced concrete
Materials Interior: granite; exterior: ceramic mosaic tile
Use Residential: 35 levels; sky gardens: four levels; carpark: three levels; clubhouse: one level
Cost HK$340 M
Architect P&T Architects and Engineers Ltd.
Structural engineer Ove Arup & Partners Hong Kong Ltd.
Mechanical/Electrical engineer P&T (M&E) Ltd.
Client Eton Properties Ltd.
Contractor Paul Y. Construction Co., Ltd.

Le Mondrian

Location New York, New York, USA
Completion date January 1992
Height 90 m/295 ft
Stories 42
Area 22,296 m²/240,000 ft²
Structure Flatslab concrete
Materials Stone base, steel and glass curtain wall, drywall partitions, wood floors
Use Residential
Cost US$140/ft²
Architect Fox & Fowle Architects PC
Structural engineer Robert Rosenwasser Associates
Mechanical/Electrical engineer Cosentini Associates
Client Beneson Capital Corp./Loews Corporation
Contractor HRH

Marine Prospect Housing

Location Tanshui, Taipei County, Taiwan
Completion date 1992
Height 90 m/295 ft
Stories 23
Area Site: 10,073 m²/108,426 ft²; building: 3365 m²/36,221 ft²; total floor: 73,231 m²/788,258 ft²
Structure Reinforced concrete
Materials Granite base, tiles
Use Residential
Cost US$44 M
Architect C.Y. Lee & Partners
Structural engineer T.Y. Lin Structural Engineering
Mechanical/Electrical engineer Wang Chiang Yi
Client Ruentex & Tuntex Group

Permanent Mission of India to the United Nations

Location New York, New York, USA
Completion date 1992
Height 82.3 m/270 ft
Stories 26
Area Site: 620 m²/6674 ft²; building: 6145 m²/66,145 ft²
Structure Reinforced cement concrete
Materials Exterior finish: metal panels, granite stone
Use Office: levels 1–4; mechanical services: levels 5–6; residential: levels 7–26
Cost US$22,420,000
Architect Charles Correa Architects/Planners
Associate architect Bond Ryder and Associates
Structural engineer Tor and Partners
Mechanical engineer George Langer Associates
Client Ministry of External Affairs, Government of India
Construction management Morse Diesel

Sceneway Garden

Location Kowloon, Hong Kong SAR, People's Republic of China
Completion date 1992
Height 100 m/328 ft
Stories 17 towers of 29–35 stories over multistory commercial and public transport interchange
Area Site: 47,000 m²/505,908 ft²; gross floor: 306,369 m²/3,297,756 ft²
Structure In-situ reinforced concrete on end-bearing piles
Materials Exterior: vitreous mosaic tiles, conventional windows with clear-anodized aluminum frames, reconstituted granite paving; interior: hardwood parquet floors, plaster wall finishes (to apartments)
Use Residential, with neighborhood commercial facilities and public transport interchange

Architect Dennis Lau & Ng Chun Man Architects & Engineers (H.K.) Ltd (formerly Ng Chun Man & Associates Architects & Engineers (H.K.) Ltd)
Structural engineer ACER Freeman Fox; Dennis Lau & Ng Chun Man Architects & Engineers (H.K.) Ltd
Mechanical engineer Associated Consulting Engineers Ltd
Client Cheung Hong (Holdings) Ltd
Contractor Kumagai Hong Kong Ltd

The Alexandria

Location New York, New York, USA
Completion date January 1992
Height 79.3 m/260 ft
Stories 28
Area Site: 1162 m²/12,508 ft²; building: 16,728 m²/180,060 ft²
Structure Reinforced concrete
Use Residential, shops at grade and cellar levels
Cost US$36 M
Architect Frank Williams & Partners, Architects
Consultant Skidmore, Owings & Merrill LLP
Structural engineer Rosenwasser & Grossman
Mechanical engineer IM Robbins
Owner Zeckendorf Company; Wein, Malkin & Bettex
Contractor Leher, McGovern Bovis Construction Co.

888 Beach Avenue

Location Vancouver, British Columbia, Canada
Completion date May 1993
Height Northwest tower: 88 m/290 ft; southeast tower: 54 m/176 ft
Stories Northwest tower: 31; southeast tower: 18
Area Site: 5593 m²/60,200 ft²; building: 33,212 m²/357,500 ft²
Structure Reinforced concrete structure consisting of central core elements with column/flat slab floor assembly
Materials Brick veneer by Pacific Masonry; pre-cast concrete features by Pacific Precast; Aluccobond Architectural Panels by Keith Panels; window wall by N.A.P.; millwork by Seagul Millwork; marble by Bridgeport; passenger elevator by Dover; plumbing fixtures and fittings by Kohler
Use Residential, retail
Cost CAN$43.7 M
Architect James KM Cheng Architects Inc.
Project architect Terry Mott
Structural engineer Jones Kwong Kishi
Mechanical engineer Yoneda & Associates Ltd.
Electrical engineer Arnold Nemetz & Associates Ltd.
Client Park Georgia Development Ltd.
Contractor Keith Construction Ltd.

MBf Tower

Location Penang, Malaysia
Completion date 1993
Height 111 m/365 ft
Stories 31
Area Site: 7482 m²/80,540 ft²; total built-up: 17,538 m²/188,779 ft²
Structure Reinforced concrete
Materials Granite, marble, ceramic tiles, spray tile finishes
Use Residential, offices
Architect T. R. Hamzah & Yeang Sdn. Bhd.
Civil and structural engineer Reka Perunding LC Sdn Bhd
Client MBf Holdings Berhad
Contractor Bina MBf Sdn Bhd

The Indigo

Location Toronto, Ontario, Canada
Completion date March 1993
Height 74 m/243 ft
Stories 27 + 3 below grade
Area Residential: 14,864 m²/159,996 ft²; commercial: 3530 m²/38,000 ft²
Structure Reinforced concrete
Materials Exterior: precast concrete, glass
Use Residential: levels 4–26; retail/commercial/common: levels 1–3; parking: three sub-levels
Cost CAN$20.5 M
Architect Architects Alliance (formerly Wallman Clewes Bergman Architects)
Structural engineer Halsall and Associates
Mechanical/Electrical engineer Bayes Yates McMillan
Client Lombard Tower Development Ltd.
Contractor Mollenhauer

Villa Athena

Location Hong Kong SAR, People's Republic of China
Completion date September 1994
Height 94.85 m/311 ft
Stories Tower: 27–28; podium/basement: 4–5 (10 blocks)
Area Site: 32,220 m²/346,816 ft²; building: 100,228 m²/1,078,854 ft²
Structure Reinforced concrete
Materials Towers: ceramic tiles; podium: granite slab, sprayed granite, ceramic tiles
Use Carpark and clubhouse: levels 1–5; residential flats: levels 1–28
Cost HK$850 M
Architect Ronald Lu & Partners (HK) Ltd.
Structural engineer HK Cheng & Partners Ltd.
Mechanical/Electrical engineer Sun Hung Kai Engineering Co. Ltd.
Client Sun Hung Kai Properties Ltd.
Contractor Manfield Building Contractors Ltd.

SkyCity Tower

Location Chung Ho, Taipei County, Taiwan
Completion date November 1995
Height 130 m/427 ft
Stories 34
Area Site: 6082.13 m²/65,468 ft²; total floor: 83,944.29 m²/903,576 ft²
Structure Mixed-use office/Commercial (levels B1–4) and residential towers (levels 5–29): steel reinforced concrete; office/suite tower (levels 1–34): structural steel
Materials Stone, glass, aluminum panels
Use Parking: levels B2–B4; department store podium: levels B1–4F; office building: 34 levels above grade; two residential buildings: 29 levels above grade
Architect KRIS YAO / Artech Inc. Architects & Designers
Structural engineer Evergreen Consulting Engineering Inc.
Mechanical/Electrical engineer Chung-Hsiao M & E Engineering Co., Ltd.
Client Synpac Development Inc.
Contractor Pacific Construction Co., Ltd.

Golfhill Terraces

Location Jakarta, Indonesia
Completion date April 1996
Height 64 m/210 ft
Stories 18 + 2 levels of parking
Area Site: 16,966 m²/182,622 ft²; building: 42,037 m²/452,486 ft²
Structure Reinforced concrete
Materials Interior: stone, timber; exterior: stucco, clay roof tiles
Use Residential
Architect Development Design Group, Inc.
Client Brasali Realty

Le Park Tower

Location Buenos Aires, Argentina
Completion date September 1996
Height 160 m/525 ft
Stories 50
Area Site: 10,040 m²/108,070 ft²; building: 57,000 m²/613,548 ft²
Structure Exposed and reinforced concrete
Materials Exterior: exposed concrete; bathroom: marble; kitchen: pulled-in marble; bedrooms: wood floors
Use Parking, ballroom, two squash courts, and services: two basement levels; access, guest parking, and swimming pool: ground floor; two apartments per floor: levels 1–44; apartments in duplex typology: levels 45–48; double-height machine area and heliport: level 49
Architect Mario Roberto Alvarez y Asociados, Alvarez-Kopiloff-Alvarez-Rivanera-Bernabó

Structural engineer Eng. Sciamarella-Canela
Mechanical engineer Eng. Mario P. Hernandez
Electrical engineer Eng. Israel Grispun
Client R.A.G.H.S.A

Libertador 4444

Location Buenos Aires, Argentina
Completion date 1996
Height Two lateral buildings: 50 m/164 ft; central tower: 130 m/427 ft
Stories Two lateral buildings: 15; central tower: 40
Area Site: 6130 m²/65,983 ft²; building: 37,184 m²/400,249 ft²
Structure Exposed and reinforced concrete
Materials Exterior: exposed concrete, ceramic bricks; interior: bathroom: marmol; kitchen: floors and pulled-in marmol; bedrooms: wood floors
Use Lateral buildings: machine area: basement; principle access, service access, doorman's flat, one principle elevator, and one service elevator: ground floor; one flat per floor, with balcony and terrace: levels 1–13; duplex with similar characters to the typical apartments, swimming pool, gym, and playroom: levels 14–15; central tower: one apartment per floor with balcony and terrace: levels 1–40; machine area: second basement level; parking, laundry, squash site: first basement level; triple-height principal access and two service elevators: ground floor
Architect Mario Roberto Alvarez y Asociados, Alvarez-Kopiloff-Alvarez-Rivanera-Bernabó
Structural engineer Eng. Sciamarella-Canela
Mechanical engineer Eng. Mario P. Hernandez
Electrical engineer Eng. Israel Grispun
Client Kineret S.A.

Nexus Momochi Residential Tower

Location Fukuoka, Japan
Completion date May 1996
Height 87 m/285 ft
Stories 27 above ground
Area 25,580 m²/275,343 ft² (approximately)
Structure Steel, reinforced concrete
Materials Precast concrete, glass curtain wall
Use Residential
Cost ¥3,650,400,009
Architect Michael Graves & Associates
Associate architect Maeda Construction Company, Ltd Architectural Division
Structural/Mechanical/Electrical engineer Maeda Construction Company, Ltd Architectural Division
Client Fukuoka Jisho Co., Ltd.
Contractor Maeda Construction Company, Ltd Architectural Division

Palisades

Location Vancouver, British Columbia, Canada
Completion date August 1996
Height East tower: 91 m/300 ft; west tower 67 m/219.8 ft
Stories East tower: 33; west tower: 24
Area Site: 6531 m²/60,610 ft²; Building: 23,421 m²/252,115 ft²
Structure Reinforced concrete structure consisting of central core elements with a column/flat slab floor assembly
Materials Zinc and Aluccobond Architectural Panels by Keith Panels; window wall by Allan Windows; marble by Star Tile; Limestone by Cerco Industries; millwork by Seagull Woodworking; passenger elevator by Fujitec; plumbing fixtures and fittings by Kohler
Use Residential
Cost CAN$34.85 M
Architect James KM Cheng Architects Inc.
Project architect Terry Mott
Structural engineer Jones Kwong Kishi
Mechanical engineer Vel Engineering
Electrical engineer Falcon Engineering Ltd.
Client Pacific Palisades Hotels Ltd.; Westbank Projects Corporation
Contractor Ledcor Industries

Schielandtoren

Location Rotterdam, The Netherlands
Completion date 1996
Height 102 m/335 ft
Stories 32 above ground + 1 below
Area Floor: 18,300 m²/196,981 ft²
Structure Reinforced concrete
Materials Red brick and metal
Use Residential, retail
Cost EUR11.400.000
Architect de Architekten Cie. (Prof. Ir. Pi de Bruijn)
Design team Syb van Breda
Structural engineer Ingenieursbureau Zonneveld, Rotterdam
Mechanical/Electrical engineer Techniplan, Rotterdam
Client Multivastgoed, Gouda
Contractor HBM, Rijswijk + Volker bouwmaatschappij, Rotterdam

Searea Odaiba Tower-4

Location Tokyo, Japan
Completion date March 1996
Height 105.10 m/344.8 ft (without antenna)
Stories 33 + 2 basement
Area Site: 5699 m²/61,344 ft²; building footprint: 1731 m²/18,632 ft²; total floor: 34,057.02 m²/366,590 ft²
Structure Reinforced concrete

Materials Interior: entrance lobby: floor: granite; wall: ceramic tile; ceiling: rock wool acoustical tile; residential unit: floor: composite wood flooring; wall: vinyl wall covering; ceiling: vinyl wall covering; exterior: wall: ceramic tile, acrylic coating; openings: aluminum sash anodized finish
Use Residential
Architect KAJIMA DESIGN
Associate architect Urban Development Corporation
Structural/Mechanical/Electrical engineer KAJIMA DESIGN
Client Urban Development Corporation
Contractor JV of KAJIMA and Haseko Corporation

Horizon Apartments

Location Sydney, New South Wales, Australia
Completion 1997
Height 139 m/456 ft
Stories 43
Area 32,000 m²/344,448 ft²
Structure Prestressed concrete
Materials Concrete façade
Use Residential
Architect Harry Seidler & Associates
Structural engineer Bruechle Gilchrist & Evans
Mechanical engineer Addicoat Hogarth Wilson
Client Elarosa Investments
Contractor Grocon

Portofino Tower

Location Miami Beach, Florida, USA
Completion date June 1997
Height 136.25 m/447 ft
Stories 42 + 3-level garage with pool deck on top
Area 64,103 m²/690,000 m²
Structure Reinforced concrete shell
Materials Exterior walls: combination of concrete block walls with stucco finish and floor-to-ceiling colored glass; pool deck and trim: keystone; exterior balcony and exterior rails: glass, aluminum frames; interior finishes: marble and exotic woods in the lobby and spa areas
Use Residential
Cost US$150 M
Architect The Sieger Suarez Architectural Partnership
Structural engineer Gopman Consulting Engineers
Mechanical/Electrical engineer Florida Engineering Service
Client Marquessa Group
Contractor Morse Diesel

The Floridian

Location Quarry Bay, Hong Kong SAR, People's Republic of China
Completion date 1997
Height 81 m/266 ft

Stories Block 1: 26; block 2: 22
Area Site: 2755 m²/29,655 ft²; domestic gross floor: 20,665 m²/222,438 ft²
Structure In-situ reinforced concrete on end-bearing piles
Materials Exterior: tiles, conventional windows with green painted aluminum frames, reconstituted granite paving, painted aluminum feature louvers; interior: Canadian maple-strip floors, plaster wall finishes (to apartments)
Use Residential
Architect Dennis Lau & Ng Chun Man Architects & Engineers (H.K.) Ltd
Structural engineer Dennis Lau & Ng Chun Man Architects & Engineers (H.K.) Ltd
Mechanical engineer Kennedy and Donkin International
Client Swire Properties Ltd
Contractor Square Construction Company Ltd

Watertower Entrepôt

Location Amsterdam, The Netherlands
Completion date 1997
Height 60 m/197 ft
Stories 22
Area 8000 m²/86,112 ft²
Structure Reinforced concrete
Materials Bright white plaster and tiles
Use Residential
Architect atelier PRO architekten
Structural engineer Bouwadviesbureau v/h J. L. Stackee
Client Muwi Vastgoed Ontwikkeling BV
Contractor Muwi van Gent's Bouwbedrijf BV

Baan Piya Sathorn

Location Bangkok, Thailand
Completion date April 1998
Height 102 m/335 ft (without antenna); 127 m/417 ft (with antenna)
Stories 34
Area Site: 3344 m²/35,995 ft²; building: 30,000 m²/322,920 ft²
Structure Reinforced concrete
Materials Interior: granite, marble; exterior: ceramic tile, granite at base
Use Residential: levels 8–34; lobby, carpark, and recreation facility: levels 1–7
Cost Baht 500 M
Architect Palmer & Turner (Thailand) Ltd.
Associate architect Concept International Design
Structural engineer Palmer and Turner (Thailand) Ltd.; Civil Technology Consultant Co., Ltd.
Mechanical/Electrical engineer Palmer and Turner (Thailand) Ltd.; Unique EM Co., Ltd.
Client Sansiri Group PCL.
Contractor Christiani and Nielsen (Thai) PCL.

Del Bosque

Location Mexico City, Mexico
Completion date 1998
Height 110 m/361 ft
Stories Office tower: 13; residential towers: 31
Area Office tower: 14,642 m²/157,611 ft²; residential towers: 29,623 m²/318,871 ft² each tower
Materials Office tower: clad in Brazilian green granite, semi-reflective insulated glass, polyfluorimer-painted aluminum curtain wall; residential towers: clad in alternating bands of butt-glazed and red precast terrazzo spandrels with accents of glazed Mexican tiles
Use Offices, residential
Cost US$110 M
Architect Cesar Pelli & Associates Inc.
Associate architect Diseño y Arquitectura Urbe; Kendall Heaton Associates
Landscape design Balmori Associates
Curtain wall consultant Peter M. Muller
Precast subcontractor Fapresa Company
Client Metropolis-Hines
Developer Hines Interests Limited Partnership in conjunction with Promociones Metropolis
Contractor Constructora Ideurban, S.A. de C.V.

Elsa Tower 55

Location Kawaguchi City, Saitama Prefecture, Japan
Completion date July 1998
Height 185.8 m/610 ft
Stories 55 above ground + 2 penthouse levels + 1 underground
Area Site: 18,551.72 m²/199,691 ft²; building: 6269.08 m²/67,480 ft²; total floor: 75,820.95 m²/816,137 ft²
Structure Concrete-filled steel tube
Materials Exterior: roof: sheet waterproofing; walls: border tiles, PCA panel (tiles, fluoropolymer painting), extrusion cement boards (AE painting, EP painting), aluminum spandrels, marble; openings: aluminum sashes; atrium interior: floor: granite; walls: marble and granite; ceiling: rock wool sound-absorbing boards with ribs; central part roof: space truss, aluminum sash, glass
Use Residential: levels 3–55; entrance lobby: level 1
Cost ¥20 B
Architect Takenaka Corporation
Structural/Mechanical/Electrical engineer Takenaka Corporation
Client Daikyo Incorporate
Contractor Takenaka Corporation

Lotus Village

Location Hsichih, Taipei County, Taiwan
Completion date 1998
Height 95 m/312 ft
Stories 23–28

Area Site: 100,000 m^2/1,076,400 ft^2; floor: 318,346 m^2/3,426,676 ft^2

Structure Reinforced concrete

Materials Tile

Use Residential

Cost US$182 M

Architect C.Y. Lee & Partners

Structural engineer Join Engineering Consultants

Mechanical/Electrical engineer Sine & Associates

Client Koos Property Development Group

Quayside Marina Neighborhood

Location Vancouver, British Columbia, Canada

Completion date Aquarius: 1998; Marinaside: 2001; Quay West: 2002

Height Aquarius (4 towers): 95 m/312 ft, 89 m/292 ft, 43 m/141 ft, & 40 m/130 ft; Marinaside (3 towers): 88 m/289 ft, 67.3 m/221 ft, & 38.5 m/126 ft; Quay West (2 towers): 69 m/227.7 ft & 95 m/312.3 ft

Stories Aquarius (4 towers): 33, 30, 14, & 12; Marinaside (3 towers): 32, 22, & 12; Quay West (2 towers): 24 & 34

Area Residential: 48013.5 m^2/516,830 ft^2; commercial: 7357.6 m^2/79,200 ft^2

Structure Poured-in-place concrete

Materials Pre-finished metal panel, window wall glazing

Use Residential, commercial, office, retail

Cost CAN$80 M

Architect James KM Cheng Architects Inc.

Project architect Jones Lee

Structural engineer Glotman Simpson

Mechanical engineer Yoneda and Associates

Electrical engineer Arnold Nemetz & Associates

Client Concord Pacific Developments Corporation

Contractor Centreville Construction Ltd.

Residences on Georgia

Location Vancouver, British Columbia, Canada

Completion date 1998

Height West tower: 100 m/330 ft; east tower: 98 m/322 ft

Stories 36 with three-story townhouses

Area Site: 5630 m^2/60,603 ft^2; building: 36,933 m^2/397,556 ft^2

Structure Reinforced concrete structure consisting of central core elements with a column/flat slab floor assembly

Materials Window wall by Allan Windows; granite by Granicor; curtain wall by Kawneer; zinc and Aluccobond Architectural Panels by Keith Panels; passenger elevators by Fujitec; plumbing fittings and fixtures by Kohler

Use Residential

Cost CAN$50,026,370

Architect James KM Cheng Architects Inc.

Project architect Terry Mott

Structural engineer Jones Kwong Kishi

Mechanical engineer Vel Engineering

Electrical engineer Arnold Nemetz & Associates

Client Pacific Palisades Hotels Ltd.; Westbank Projects Corporation

Contractor Ledcor Industries

SEG Apartment Tower

Location Vienna, Austria

Completion date 1998

Height 60 m/197 ft

Stories 25

Area Site: 1660 m^2/17,868 ft^2; floor: 7100 m^2/76,424 ft^2

Use Residential, offices

Cost 120 Mio. ATS

Architect COOP HIMMELB(L)AU

Structural engineer Projektierungsbüro für Industrie-, Hoch- und Tiefbauten AG

Mechanical/Electrical engineer Vienna Öko Systems

Client SEG Stadterneuerungs- und Eigentumswohnungsgesellschaft m.b.H.

Terminal City Club Tower

Location Vancouver, British Columbia, Canada

Completion date 1998

Height 91 m/300 ft

Stories Parkade: four levels underground; podium: street level; club facilities: street to level 3; tower: strata office units: levels 2–7; strata hotel units: levels 8–12; strata residential units: levels 14–30

Area 3284 m^2/35,349 ft^2

Materials Metal cladding by Keith Panel Systems; windows by Allan Windows Systems; cabinetry by Benson Industries Ltd.; countertops and tile by C+S Ceramic Tile; fireplaces by Fireplaces Unlimited; plumbing fixtures and Trim by Western Supplies; washroom accessories by Shanahan's Ltd.; hardware by Shanahan's Ltd.; light fixtures by Nedco; interior doors by McGregor Thompson; suite entry doors by Lambton doors; duite entry door frames by Candor; appliances by GPM Distributing; carpeting by Jordan's

Use Residential, hotel, offices, retail, parking

Cost CAN$35 M (excluding $7 M club fitout) ($142/Built FSR square foot)

Architect James KM Cheng Architects Inc.; Musson Cattell Mackay Architects

Project architect Gerry Ruehle

Structural engineer Jones Kwong Kishi

Mechanical engineer Keen Engineering Ltd.

Electrical engineer Sokulski Engineering Ltd.

Client Terminal City Project Limited Partnership

Contractor PCL Constructors Canada Inc.

Three Sails Tower

Location Abu Dhabi, United Arab Emirates (UAE)

Completion date February 1998

Height 70 m/230 ft (top of building); 85 m/279 ft (top of sails)

Stories 24

Area 26,985 m^2/290,466 ft^2

Structure Reinforced concrete, reinforced concrete floor slabs, columns steel superstructure, shear walls

Materials Interior: marble lobby; exterior: glass curtain wall, metal panels

Use Retail: ground floor; residential: levels 20–40; restaurant: level 23

Architect WZMH Architects (Webb Zerafa Menkès Housden Partnership Architects)

Associate architect A.E.C. (Architectural & Engineering Consultants)

Structural engineer A.E.C. (Architectural & Engineering Consultants)

Mechanical/Electrical engineer Ian Banham & Associate

Contractor Dhabi Contracting, UAE

TriBeCa Pointe

Location New York, New York, USA

Completion date 1998

Height 122 m/400 ft

Stories 42

Area 31,035 m^2/333,967 ft^2

Structure Concrete, flat plate

Materials Brick, limestone, aluminum, glass

Use Residential

Architect Gruzen Samton Architects Planners & Interior Designers LLP

Structural engineer Ysrael Seinuk, PC

Mechanical/Electrical engineer Cosentini Associates

Developer Rockrose Development Corporation

Contractor HRH Construction Corporation

Canal Town West Housing–7

Location Kobe, Hyogo Prefecture, Japan

Completion date July 1999

Height 118.55 m/389 ft (without antenna)

Stories 37 + 1 basement

Area Site: 4543.41 m^2/48,905 ft^2; project site: 26,623.3 m^2/286,573 ft^2; building footprint: 1168.23 m^2/12,575 ft^2; total floor: 27,064.46 m^2/291,322 ft^2

Structure Reinforced concrete (70 percent precast concrete)

Materials Interior: entrance lobby: floor: ceramic tile; wall: stoneware tile, partially granite, gypsum board paint finish; ceiling: aluminum spandrel baked enamel finish; residential unit: floor: composite wood flooring; wall and ceiling: vinyl wall covering; exterior: wall: stoneware tile, acrylic coating; openings: aluminum sash anodized finish

Use Residential

Cost ¥4.9 B

Architect KAJIMA DESIGN KANSAI

Associate architect Urban Development Corporation

Structural/Mechanical/Electrical engineer
KAJIMA DESIGN KANSAI
Client Urban Development Corporation
Contractor JV of KAJIMA; Hihon-Kokudo; Asanuma Corporation

Eurotheum

Location Frankfurt, Germany
Completion date 1999
Height 110 m/361 ft
Stories 32 (including ground floor) + 3 basements (including parking)
Area Site: 3900 m²/41,980 ft²; building: 34,500 m²/371,358 ft²
Structure Reinforced concrete
Materials Glass, aluminum
Use Shops and restaurant: ground floor; offices: levels 1–21; 74 residential units and services: levels 22–29
Architect Novotny Mähner Assoziierte
Associate architect Krafft Design (apartment interiors)
Structural engineer Grebner GmbH
Mechanical engineer Canzler Ingenieure
Client CGI Commerz Grundbesitz Investmentgesellschaft mbH
Contractor Philipp Holzmann AG

Highland Park

Location Hong Kong SAR, People's Republic of China
Completion date March 1999
Height Blocks 1 and 2: 96 m/315 ft; blocks 3–6: 101 m/331 ft
Stories 28–30 (6 blocks)
Area Site: 18,900 m²/203,440 ft²; building: 94,500 m²/1,017,198 ft²
Structure Reinforced concrete
Materials Exterior: tile and spray painting
Use Residential
Cost HK$880 M
Architect Ronald Lu & Partners (HK) Ltd.
Structural engineer HK Cheng & Partners Ltd.
Mechanical/Electrical engineer Mott MacDonald (HK) Ltd.
Client Hong Kong Housing Society
Contractor Hip Hing Construction Co. Ltd.

Hollywood Terrace

Location Hong Kong SAR, People's Republic of China
Completion date 1999
Height 128 m/420 ft
Stories 35 + 5-level podium
Area Gross floor: 40,780 m²/438,956 ft²
Structure Reinforced concrete
Materials Ceramic glazed external wall tiles
Use Residential
Cost HK$573 M

Architect Rocco Design Ltd
Structural engineer/Geotechnical consultant
Ove Arup & Partners
Electrical/Mechanical consultant Parsons Brinckerhoff (Asia) Ltd.
Client Hong Kong Housing Society
Contractor Gammon Construction Ltd

Republic Tower

Location Melbourne, Victoria, Australia
Completion date April 1999
Height 110 m/361 ft
Stories 36
Area 25,000 m²/269,100 ft²
Structure Reinforced concrete
Materials Concrete, stainless steel, glass, bluestone
Use Restaurant: two levels; apartments: 30 levels; pool: one level; carpark: three levels
Architect Nation Fender Katsalidis Pty Ltd
Structural engineer Barry Gale Engineers & Partners
Mechanical/Electrical Engineer Simpson Kotzman
Client Republic Tower Pty Ltd
Contractor Multiplex

Riverside Boulevard at Trump Place

Location New York, New York, USA
Completion date A: 2003; B: 2002; C: 1999; D: 1999; E: 2001
Height A: 102 m/336 ft; B: 180 m/591 ft; C: 165 m/540 ft; D: 132 m/432 ft; E: 109 m/359 ft
Stories A: 31 + 4 cellars; B: 48 + 4 cellars; C: 46 + 3 cellars; D: 40 + 3 cellars; E: 33 + 3 cellars
Area A: 38,750 m²/417,105 ft²; B: 74,400 m²/800,842 ft²; C: 60,000 m²/645,840 ft²; D: 53,950 m²/580,718 ft²; E: 51,520 m²/554,561 ft²
Structure Reinforced concrete
Materials A: precast; B and E: masonry and precast; C: masonary
Use Residential
Cost B: US$169 M; C: US$97 M; D: US$86 M; E: US$99 M
Architect Costas Kondylis & Associates PC; Philip Johnson/Alan Ritchie Architects for 200 Riverside Blvd (C), 180 Riverside Blvd (D), 160 Riverside Blvd (E); Costas Kondylis & Partners LLP for 240 Riverside Blvd (A), 220 Riverside Blvd (B)
Structural engineer A and B: Rosenwasser/Grossman Consulting Engineers, PC; C and D: Ysrael Seinuk
Mechanical engineer I.M. Robbins, P.C.
Client Trump New World Management Ltd/Hudson Waterfront Associates, LP
Contractor Bovis Lend Lease

Royal Pavilion

Location Shanghai, People's Republic of China
Completion date 1999
Height 129 m/423 ft
Stories 39
Area Site: 8798 m²/94,702 ft²; domestic gross floor: 31,573 m²/339,858 ft²
Structure In-situ reinforced concrete on end-bearing piles
Materials Exterior: glazed ceramic tiles, conventional windows with bronze-anodized aluminum frames, granite paving; interior: hardwood parquet floors, plaster wall finishes (to apartments)
Use Residential
Architect Dennis Lau & Ng Chun Man Architects & Engineers (H.K.) Ltd
Structural engineer Maunsell Structural Consultants Ltd
Mechanical engineer Parsons Brinckerhoff (Asia) Ltd
Client CITIC (China International Trust and Investment Corporation)
Contractor Heng Tat Construction Co. Ltd

The Bristol

Location Chicago, Illinois, USA
Completion date December 1999
Height 149 m/488 ft
Stories 42
Area Site: 1691 m²/18,200 ft²; building: 47,379 m²/510,000 ft²
Structure Reinforced concrete
Materials Exterior: painted articulated concrete, glass
Use Residential, retail
Cost US$42 M
Architect Solomon Cordwell Buenz & Associates Inc. (SCB)
Structural engineer Chris P. Stefanos Associates, Inc.
Mechanical engineer Environmental Systems Design, Inc.
Client Golub & Company
Contractor Power Contracting

The Golden Bay Garden

Location Futian, Shenzhen, People's Republic of China
Completion date Phase I: 1999; Phase II: 2001
Height 100 m/328 ft
Stories 25–31
Area Site: 42,500 m²/457,470 ft²; total gross floor: 123,500 m²/1,329,354 ft²
Structure Reinforced concrete
Materials Ceramic tiles and granite
Use Residential: levels 25–31; parking: two levels; covered playground: one level
Cost RMB$12 B (superstructure)
Architect Wong & Tung International Limited

Structural/Mechanical/Electrical engineer
Zhong Tian Wong Tung International Engineering Design
Consultants Co. Ltd.
Client Goldfield Industries Inc.
Contractor Futian Construction

Wohnpark Neue Donau Tower

Location Vienna, Austria
Completion date March 1999
Height 100 m/328 ft
Stories 33
Area Site: 47,500 m²/511,290 ft²; building: 87,000 m²/
936,468 ft²
Structure Concrete
Materials Exterior: insulated façade cladding system over
concrete; interior: terrazzo floors, plasterboard lined walls,
finished concrete ceilings
Use Residential
Architect Harry Seidler & Associates
Structural engineer Vasko + Partner
Mechanical/Electrical Engineer Freudensprung
Engineering
Client Arwag Holding Aktiengesellschaft
Contractor Universale Bau Aktiengesellschaft

300 Park Avenue

Location Atlanta, Georgia, USA
Completion date July 2000
Height 152 m/500 ft
Stories 44
Area Site: 9104 m²/98,000 ft²; building: 67,445 m²/
726,000 ft²; public open space: 8082 m²/87,000 ft²
Structure Pre-stressed concrete
Materials Glass, marble, bronze, hardwood
Use Residential
Cost US$72 M
Architect Burt Hill Kosar Rittelmann Associates
Structural engineer Uzun & Case Engineers
Interior design Jack Adams
Landscape architect Hughes Good O'Leary & Ryan
MEP engineer Burt Hill Kosar Rittelmann Associates
Client Brickstone Properties
Contractor Gilbane Building Company

515 Park Avenue

Location New York, New York, USA
Completion date January 2000
Height 157.3 m/516 ft
Stories 43
Area Site: 1672 m²/17,997 ft²; building: 20,446 m²/
220,081 ft²
Structure Reinforced concrete
Use Residential

Cost US$36 M
Architect Frank Williams & Partners, Architects
Structural engineer Cantor Seinuk Group, Inc.
Mechanical engineer Jaros Baum & Bolles
Owner/Developer Zeckendorf Realty; Goldman Saks
Contractor Jones J.M.O. Construction Company

Edgewater Apartments

Location West Vancouver, British Columbia, Canada
Completion date 2000
Height 59 m/194.6 ft
Stories 15 above grade + 2 levels underground parking
Area Site: 2615 m²/28,153 ft²; building: 5049 m²/
54,353 ft²
Structure Reinforced concrete
Materials First three floors: limestone; upper floors: precast
aggregate stone panel system; roof: lead-coated copper;
sills: stone; window frames: painted metal; trellises: fire-
resistant treated wood
Use Residential
Design architect Robert A.M. Stern Architects
Architect of record Lawrence Doyle Architect, Inc. (LDA)
Structural engineer Glotman Simpson Group
Mechanical engineer Sterling Cooper Associates
Electrical engineer Arnold Nemetz Associates
Client Millennium Development Corporation

Florencia

Location St. Petersburg, Florida, USA
Completion date July 2000
Height 75 m/246 ft
Stories 23
Area Building: 25,548 m²/274,999 ft²
Structure Poured-in-place, reinforced concrete
Materials Walls: EIFS exterior insulation finish; roof: clay tile
Use Retail and parking: two levels; entrance and amenities:
one level; residential: 20 levels
Architect Sydness Architects, P.C.
Associate architect Gillett Associates, Inc.
Structural engineer O.E. Olson and Associates
Mechanical engineer Cosentini Associates
Client JMC Associates

Glorietta 4/The Oakwood

Location Makati City, Philippines
Completion date December 2000
Height 116 m/380 ft
Stories 26 in each tower
Area Site: 13,000 m²/139,932 ft²; building 102,000 m²/
1,097,928 ft²
Structure Concrete moment frame

Materials Exterior: stone base (Dragon White) granite,
green tinted glass, painted concrete; interior: natural wood
trim and marble
Use Residential, retail, restaurants, cinemas
Architect Architecture International Ltd. (John P. Sheehy,
FAIA, RIBA; William J. Higgins, AIA; Sherry Caplan, IIDA)
Associate architect GF & Partners
Structural engineer E.H. Sison
Mechanical/Electrical engineer DCCD Engineers
Visual consultant R.M.D.A.
Client Ayala Land, Inc.; Ayala Hotels, Inc.
Contractor D.M. Consunji, Inc.

Miranova

Location Columbus, Ohio, USA
Completion date 2000
Height 86.9 m/285 ft
Stories 27
Area 56,669 m²/610,000 ft²
Structure Reinforced concrete, post-tension and glass
curtain wall
Use Residential
Design architect Arquitectonica (design principals:
Bernardo Fort Brescia, FAIA and Laurinda Spear, FAIA)
Architect of record HKS Inc.
Structural engineer Thornton – Tomasetti Engineers
Mechanical/Electrical engineer Flack + Kurtz Consulting
Engineers, LLP
Client Pizzuti Development, Inc.
Contractor Turner Construction

Monte Vista

Location Hong Kong SAR, People's Republic of China
Completion date March 2000
Height 116.94 m/384 ft
Stories 30 (12 blocks)
Area 25,825 m²/277,980 ft²
Structure Reinforced concrete
Materials Exterior finishes of podium: spray granite and
natural granite; exterior finishes of residential towers:
ceramic tiles
Use Residential
Cost HK$1499 M
Architect Ronald Lu & Partners (HK) Ltd.
Structural engineer JMK Consulting Engineers
Building Service Engineer Parsons Brinckeroff (Asia) Ltd.
Client Wonder Pacific Investment Ltd.
Contractor B.F. Construction Co. Ltd.

Olympic City

Location Hong Kong SAR, People's Republic of China
Completion date July 2000
Height 120 m/394 ft

Stories 35–39 (nine blocks)

Area Site: 66,204 m²/712,620 ft²; building: 169,950 m²/829,342 ft²

Structure Reinforced concrete

Materials Interior: natural stone; exterior: curtain wall

Use Residential; carpark: three levels

Cost HK$3200 M

Architect P&T Architects and Engineers Ltd.

Structural engineer Maunsell Consultants Asia Ltd.

Mechanical/Electrical engineer Parsons Brinckerhoff (Asia) Ltd.

Client MTRC / Harvest Sun Ltd.

Contractor Hongkong Construction (Holding) Ltd.

Park Tower

Location Chicago, Illinois, USA

Completion date June 2000

Height 251 m/825 ft

Stories 67 + 1 basement + 3 mechanical levels

Area Site: 2601 m²/28,000 ft²; building: 78,036 m²/840,000 ft²

Structure Reinforced concrete

Materials Precast concrete and natural stone cladding, aluminum windows

Use Residential: 45 levels; luxury hotel: 20 levels; retail

Cost US$94,665,000 plus residential interior construction

Architect Lucien Lagrange Architects (formerly Lucien Lagrange and Associates)

Associate architect HKS Inc.

Structural engineer Chris P. Stefanos Associates

Mechanical/Electrical engineer Environmental Systems Design, Inc.

Client Hyatt Development Corporation

Contractor James McHugh Construction Company

Tavistock II, Aigburth, and Valverde

Location Hong Kong SAR, People's Republic of China

Completion date 1999/2000

Height Tavistock II: 166 m/545 ft; Aigburth: 183 m/600 ft; Valverde: 119 m/390 ft

Stories Tavistock II: 46; Aigburth: 47; Valverde: 36

Area Building: 60,000 m²/645,840 ft²; site: 8495 m²/91,440 ft²

Structure Reinforced concrete

Materials Ceramic tiles, granite, glass curtain wall

Use Residential and parking

Cost HK$800 M

Architect Wong Tung & Partners Limited.

Structural engineer Ove Arup & Partners Hong Kong Ltd.

Mechanical/Electrical engineer Meinhardt (M & E) Ltd.

Client Kerry Properties Ltd.

Contractor Shimizu Corporation

The Chatham

Location New York, New York, USA

Completion date July 2000

Height 122 m/399.5 ft

Stories 32 above grade + 3 below grade

Area Site: 1866 m²/20,084 ft²; building: 23,767 m²/255,838 ft²

Structure Concrete frame (20-centimeter/8-inch typical poured concrete slab)

Materials Levels one and two: limestone veneer; upper floors: brick veneer with precast accents; window sills: precast stone; bay windows, casement windows, and handrails: painted aluminum; roof: copper

Use Retail: ground level; gym: basement; residential: levels 2–32

Design architect Robert A.M. Stern Architects

Architect of record Ismael Leyva Architects, P.C.

Structural engineer DeSimone Consulting Engineers, P.L.L.C.

Mechanical/Electrical engineer Cosentini Associates, P.C.

Client The Related Companies, L.P.

Contractor HRH Construction Corporation

Trinity Place

Location Boston, Massachusetts, USA

Completion date May 2000

Height 79 m/260 ft

Stories 18

Area Site: 2415 m²/26,000 ft²; building: 22,296 m²/240,000 ft²; street-level retail and restaurant: 836 m²/9000 ft²

Structure Steel frame with composite-action reinforced concrete slab floor decks

Materials Exterior: precast concrete panel system with aluminum-framed operable windows with insulating high-e glass; interior: painted and papered gypsum wall board on steel studs, solid core doors, carpeted public corridors, hardwood floors in living rooms, kitchens, and bedrooms, marble floor and walls in bathrooms, crown molding and coffered ceilings in principal residential spaces

Use Residential: 18 levels; underground parking: three levels; world class restaurant: street level; retail

Cost US$63 M

Architect CBT/Childs Bertman Tseckares, Inc.

Structural engineer McNamara/Salvia, Inc.

Mechanical/Electrical engineer Abbood/Hallorn Associates, Inc.

Civil engineer Cullinan Engineering Company, Inc.

Geotechnical engineer Haley & Aldrich

Developer Raymond Property Company

Contractor Turner Construction

COSCO Brilliant City

Location Shanghai, People's Republic of China

Completion date First phase: 2001; to last phase (estimated): 2004

Height 48–100 m/157–328 ft

Stories 15–34

Area Land: 50 hectares/123.5 acres; floor: 1,600,000 m²/17,222,400 ft²

Structure Frame supported shear wall

Materials Granite, aluminum window, paint

Use Residential, commercial, school, kindergarten

Architect East China Architectural Design & Research Institute Co., Ltd. (ECADI)

Developer COSCO Real Estate Purchasing Development Co., Ltd.

Elit Residence

Location Sisli, Istanbul, Turkey

Completion date June 2001

Height 132.5 m/435 ft (from upper external ground level to top of building) + 17.5 m/57 ft below (partly below ground due to sloping site); total: 150 m/492 ft

Stories 39

Area Site: 4700 m²/50,591 ft²; building 30,800 m²/331,531 ft²

Structure Reinforced concrete

Materials Exterior: tower cladding: curtain wall glazing system with insulated aluminum panels and double glazing; tower: vertical core special render system on insulation; lower floors: external walls partly clad in stone (granite) panels, partly with special rendering on insulation; swimming pool roof: sliding glazed roof with steel structure

Use Residential: levels 2–18; mechanical plant rooms: levels 1 and 19; restaurant, shops, roof terrace with tennis court: ground; main entrance hall, shops, health club (upper level), and administration offices: basement 1; health club, lower level with swimming pool, gymnasium, saunas and squash courts, laundry, and staff areas: basement 2; car parking, mechanical/electrical plant rooms and storage/service areas: basements 3–5

Cost US$28 M

Architect BSB Architects, London

Interior design Sinan Kafadar Arch. Design

Structural engineer Balkar

Mechanical engineer Cilingiroglu

Electrical engineer HB Teknik

Client Al-Huda Construction Ltd; Koray Holding; Yapi kredi koray (investment partners)

Contractor Koray Construction

Hoge Erasmus

Location Rotterdam, The Netherlands
Completion date July 2001
Height 90 m/295 ft
Stories 29
Area Site: 3800 m²/40,903 ft²; building: 26,750 m²/ 287,937 ft²
Structure Poured reinforced concrete superstructure
Materials Interior: floors/walls, ground floor: natural stone, white and gray; apartment ceilings: wood panels (beech); exterior: walls, levels 1–4: black granite; walls, parking: transparent hollow glass blocks; walls, other floors: brick, black sand stone and "Gronings" red; window frames: black aluminium; glass: low-reflection transparent solar glass
Use Offices: levels 1–4; residential: levels 5–28
Architect Klunder Architecten/Ir. B.J. Sybesma
Structural engineer IMD Raadgevende Ingenieurs
Mechanical engineer Spindler Installatietechniek
Electrical engineer Burgers Verwarming + Airconditioning
Client William Properties/ING Vastgoed
Contractor Ballast Nedam

Leninsky Prospekt

Location Moscow, Russia
Completion date 116-1: November 1998; 128-1: March 2001
Height 116-1: 114.6 m/376 ft (with "crown"); 128–1: 106.7 m/350 ft (with "crown")
Stories 116–1: 30 + 3 underground; 128–1: 30 + 2 underground
Area 116-1: site: 3500 m²/37,674 ft²; total floor: 35,548 m²/382,639 ft²; living: 20,980 m²/225,829 ft²; 128-1: site: 7300 m²/78,577 ft²; floor: 41,791 m² /449,838 ft²; living: 24,374 m²/262,362 ft²
Structure Reinforced concrete
Materials Exterior: brick, reflective glass, aluminum curtain walls; windows: wood and aluminum; balconies: precast concrete panels with plaster finish; interior: ceramic granite; ceiling panels (lobby): "Ecophon"
Use Residential
Cost Approximately US$27 M per building
Architect George Mailov & Partners of Architectural-Planning-Artistic Firm Archizrav Ltd
Structural/Mechanical/Electrical engineer Architectural-Planning-Artistic Firm Archizrav Ltd
Client JSC Kvartal 32-33
Contractor 116-1: JSC Kvartal 32-33; 128-1: JSC Kvartal 32-33; Yugo-Union Co.

Millennium Place

Location Boston, Massachusetts, USA
Completion date October 2001
Height North building: 114 m/375 ft; south building: 122 m/400 ft
Stories 33/37
Area Site: 13,517 m²/145,497 ft²; building: 167,220 m² /1,799,956 ft²
Materials Exterior: unitized curtain wall, metal panel, granite
Use Residential: south tower, levels 9–31 and north tower, levels 9-36; extended stay: north tower, levels 2–8; hotel: south tower, levels 5–8; retail: south and north towers, ground level; theaters: south tower, third level; sports club: south tower, fourth level; parking: south tower, levels b1–b5
Cost US$350 M
Design Architect Gary Edward Handel + Associates
Executive architect CBT/Childs Bertman Tseckares, Inc.
Structural engineer DeSimone Consulting Engineers
Mechanical engineer Cosentini Associates
Client Millennium Partners / MDA Associates
Contractor Bovis Lend Lease

Neguri Gane

Location Benidorm, Alicante, Spain
Completion date 2001
Height 150 m/492 ft (without antenna); 160 m/525 ft (with antenna)
Stories 41
Area Site: 5804.6 m²/62,481 ft²; building: 236.65 m²/ 2547 ft² in a projection plot of 5804.6 m²/62,480.70 ft²
Structure Outward reinforced concrete
Materials Interior: floor: beige marble; doors and wardrobes: cherry wood; kitchen and bathrooms: high-quality stoneware; exterior: outward reinforced concrete, scraped brick in straw color; carpentry: dark red lacquered aluminum, double glazing
Use Residential
Cost EUR8.000.000
Architect Peréz-Guerras Arquitectos & Ingenieros
Associate architect Urbano Igaralde Telletxea
Design co-ordinator Consuelo Arana Higalgo
Structural engineer Cype Ingenieros
Mechanical/Electrical engineer Peréz-Guerras Arquitectos & Ingenieros
Client D. Jose Ignacio de la Serna, Negur 2000 Promociones, S.A. (Grupo Arcentales) General Director
Construction company ECISA

Ocean Pointe

Location Hong Kong SAR, People's Republic of China
Completion date January 2001
Height 172 m/564 ft
Stories 52 (three towers)
Area Site: 9132 m²/98,297 ft²; domestic gross floor: 45,660 m²/491,484 ft²
Structure In-situ reinforced concrete with end-bearing large-diameter bored piles to residential towers and driven H-piles to carpark
Materials Exterior: glazed ceramic tiles and conventional windows with bronze-anodized aluminum window frames to superstructures and natural granite in combination with sprayed reconstituted granite to podium; interior: German origin hardwood strip floors and plaster wall finishes (to apartments)
Use Residential
Architect Dennis Lau & Ng Chun Man Architects & Engineers (H.K.) Ltd
Structural engineer W.S.P Ltd
Mechanical engineer Consolidated Consulting Engineers Ltd
Client Kerry Properties Ltd
Contractor Win House Industries Ltd

One Wall Centre

Location Vancouver, British Columbia, Canada
Completion date 2001
Height 146 m/480 ft (with light pipe); 137 m/450 ft (without light pipe)
Stories 46 above grade; 5 below grade
Area Site: 4088 m²/44,000 ft²; building: 41,805 m²/ 450,000 ft²
Structure Reinforced concrete
Materials Exterior: four-sided structural silicone curtain wall
Use Residential: levels 31–48; hotel: ground–level 30
Cost CAN$80,000+ (construction cost only, does not include furnishings/equipment)
Architect Busby + Associates Architects
Structural engineer Glotman • Simpson
Mechanical engineer Keen Engineering
Electrical engineer Arnold Nemetz & Assoc.
Client Wall Financial Corporation
Contractor Siemens Development

Orchard Scotts

Location Singapore
Completion date 2001
Height 20-story towers: 64 m/ 210 ft; 18-story tower: 58 m/190 ft
Stories Two towers: 20; one tower: 18
Area 68,396 m²/865,182 m²
Structure Reinforced concrete, steel, glass
Materials Reflective cladding
Use Residential
Architect Arquitectonica
Associate architect Ong & Ong Architects Pte. Ltd.
Structural engineer KTP Consultants Pte Ltd
Mechanical/Electrical engineer United Project Consultants Pte Ltd
Client Far East Organization
Contractor Golden Development Pte Ltd (subsidiary of Far East Organization)

Pacific Plaza Towers

Location Makati City, Philippines
Completion date February 2001
Height 170.8 m/560.4 ft
Stories 52 (each tower) + 4 levels parking
Area 102,770 m²/1,300,000 ft²
Structure Reinforced concrete, steel, and glass
Materials Interior: bedrooms, living room, dining room, foyer, and den: American hardwood planks; bathroom floor, walls, and countertops: Italian stone, imported fixtures with chrome fittings and brass trimmings, imported wood doors and trims fitted with imported hardware, European kitchen countertops; exterior: aqua blue/green reflective glass curtain wall; simulated white textured stone finish, aluminum cover, fascia and frame, clear, frameless, full-height glass at lobby level
Use Residential
Architect Arquitectonica
Associate architect Recio + Casas
Structural engineer Skilling Ward Magnusson Barkshire; Aromin & Sy + Associates
Mechanical engineer Flack + Kurtz; R.J. Calpo & Partners; NBF Water & Waste Water Services (Philippines)
Electrical engineer Flack + Kurtz; R.A. Mojica & Partners
Client Metro Pacific Corporation
Contractor SAEI-EEI Construction Corporation\

Régence Royale

Location Mid-levels Hong Kong SAR, People's Republic of China
Completion date 2001
Height 133 m/437 ft
Stories Tower 1: 38; tower 2: 39
Area Site: 4505 m²/48,492 ft²; domestic gross floor: 22,525 m²/242,459 ft²
Structure In-situ reinforced concrete on end-bearing piles
Materials Exterior: combination of curtain wall and structural glazing with aluminum spandrel panels and glazed ceramic tiles; interior: timber strip floors and plaster wall finishes (to apartments)
Use Residential
Architect Dennis Lau & Ng Chun Man Architects & Engineers (H.K.) Ltd
Structural engineer Stephen Cheng Consulting Engineers Ltd
Mechanical engineer MECS Consulting Engineers
Client Henderson Land Development Company Ltd
Contractor Heng Tat Construction Company Ltd

Roxas Triangle Towers

Location Makati City, Philippines
Completion date 2001
Height 175 m/574 ft
Stories 50

Area 69,400 m²/747,021 ft²
Structure Reinforced concrete
Materials Aluminum panels, window wall
Use High-end residential with parking
Architect Skidmore, Owings & Merrill LLP
Associate architect Pimentel Rodriguez Simbulan and Partners
Structural engineer Skilling Ward Magnusson Barkshire, Inc.; Aromin & Sy + Associates
Mechanical/Electrical engineer Flack + Kurtz Consulting Engineers; DCCD Engineering Corporation
Client Ayala Land, Inc.; Hongkong Land
General contractor D.M. Consunji, Inc. (DMCI)

The Melburnian

Location Melbourne, Victoria, Australia
Completion date October 2001
Height 73.65 m/242 ft (with lift overrun); 65.85 m/216 ft (without lift overrun)
Stories 29
Area Site: 9702 m²/104,432 ft²
Structure Reinforced concrete
Materials Precast concrete external panels, glass curtain wall, glass balustrades and balcony edges, natural bluestone, stainless steel
Use Residential: 25 levels; car parking: three levels; mixed use (restaurants, offices, retail): one level
Architect Bates Smart Pty Ltd
Associate architect HPA Architects Pty Ltd
Structural engineer Bonacci Winward Pty Ltd
Client Mirvac Group
Contractor Grocon Pty Limited

The Ritz-Carlton New York, Battery Park (Millennium Point)

Location New York, New York, USA
Completion date October 2001
Height 131 m/430 ft
Stories 42
Area Site: 3910 m²/42,087 ft²; building: 55,740 m²/599,985 ft²
Materials Exterior: brick and curtain wall
Use Residential: levels 14–39; guestrooms: levels 3–12; lobbies, restaurant, skyscraper museum: ground floor; ballrooms, meeting rooms: level two; roof deck and fitness center: level 13
Cost US$175 M
Architect Gary Edward Handel + Associates; The Polshek Partnership Architects
Landscape architect Hargreaves Associates
Structural engineer DeSimone Consulting Engineers
Mechanical engineer IM Robbins, Inc
Client Millennium Partners
Contractor Bovis Lend Lease

The Sterling

Location Chicago, Illinois, USA
Completion date October 2001
Height 142 m/466 ft
Stories 48
Area Site: 3772 m²/40,600 ft²; building: 66,609 m²/717,000 ft²
Structure Reinforced concrete
Materials Exterior: painted articulated concrete, glass
Use Residential, retail
Cost US$60 M
Architect Solomon Cordwell Buenz & Associates Inc. (SCB)
Structural engineer Chris P. Stefanos Associates, Inc.
Mechanical engineer Khatib & Associates
Client Kinzie, Peabody, Sterling L.L.C.
Contractor Walsh Construction Company

The Waverly

Location Miami Beach, Florida, USA
Completion date August 2001
Height 108.2 m/355 ft
Stories 35
Area 81,355 m²/875,706 ft²
Structure Post-tension concrete column
Materials Exterior: concrete block, stucco
Use Residential
Design architect Arquitectonica
Structural engineer CHM Consulting Engineers
Mechanical/Electrical engineer Florida Engineering Services
Client ZOM Development
Contractor CG Chase Construction

Trump World Tower

Location New York, New York, USA
Completion date 2001
Height 262 m/860 ft
Stories 72 plus sub-cellar, cellar, and mechanical penthouse
Area 80,450 m²/865,964 ft²
Structure High-strength concrete, two shearwalls with a column perimeter
Materials Glass and aluminum structure, glazed curtain wall; interior finishes: bronze, marble, wood
Use Residential
Cost US$181,159,000
Architect Costas Kondylis & Partners LLP
Structural engineer Cantor Seinuk Group, Inc.
Mechanical/Electrical engineer I.M. Robbins, P.C.
Landscape architect Abel, Bainnson & Butz
Client The Trump Organization; Daewoo
Contractor Bovis Lend Lease

Harbourfront Landmark

Location Kowloon, Hong Kong SAR, People's Republic of China
Completion date 2002
Height 230 m/755 ft
Stories 68
Area Site: 7402 m²/79,675 ft²; gross floor area: 55,505 m²/597,456 ft² (domestic); 6957 m²/74,885 ft² (commerical)
Structure In-situ reinforced concrete on end-bearing piles
Materials Exterior: combination of blue-tinted curtain wall, conventional windows with blue-painted aluminum frame, deep blue glazed ceramic tiles; interior: hardwood parquet floors, plaster wall finishes (to apartments)
Use Commercial: levels 1–6; clubhouse: level 7; residential: levels 8–68
Architect Dennis Lau & Ng Chun Man Architects & Engineers (H.K.) Ltd
Structural engineer Maunsell Structural Consultants Ltd
Mechanical engineer Meinhardt (Hong Kong) Ltd
Developers Cheung Kong Holdings Ltd & Hutchison Whampoa Ltd
Contractor Paul Y – ITC Construction Ltd

Les Saisons

Location Shau Kei Wan, Hong Kong SAR, People's Republic of China
Completion date 2002
Height 139 m/456 ft–160 m/525 ft
Stories 44–50
Area Site: 7056 m²/75,951 ft²; building: 68,948 m²/742,156 ft²
Structure Reinforced concrete
Materials Ceramic tiles, granite
Use Residential: levels 40–48; parking: two levels; mechanical: one level; clubhouse: one level
Cost HK$1000 M
Architect Wong Tung & Partners Limited
Structural engineer Ove Arup & Partners Hong Kong Ltd.
Mechanical/Electrical engineer J. Roger Preston Ltd.
Contractor Dragages et Travaux Publics (HK) Ltd.
Developer Swire Properties; Sun Hung Kai Properties; China Motor Bus

Residences at RiverBend

Location Chicago, Illinois, USA
Completion date April 2002
Height 137 m/450 ft
Stories 37
Area 51,559 m²/555,000 ft²; site: 3688 m²/39,700 ft²
Structure Concrete frame, aluminum, glass and exposed skin
Materials Exterior: limestone, precast concrete, painted concrete; interior: two styles of units, a loft-style with exposed concrete ceilings and a traditional-style with dry wall ceilings and crown moldings; gypsum board walls, generally hardwood floors, owner's choices; lobbies: marble, wood, fabric and aluminum paneled walls
Use Residential tower of a mixed-use development
Cost US$68.5 M
Architect DeStefano and Partners, Ltd.
Structural engineer Halvorsen and Kaye Structural Engineers
Mechanical/Electrical engineer WMA Consulting Engineers, Ltd.
Client Bejco Development Corporation
Contractor Power Construction

River East Center Residential Tower

Location Chicago, Illinois, USA
Completion date 2002
Height 189 m/620 ft
Stories 58
Area Site: 11,362 m²/122,303 ft² or 1.13 hectares/2.81 acres; building: 74,612 m²/803,142 ft²;
Structure Poured-in-place concrete frame, masonry skin
Materials Exterior: limestone color precast and metal wall panel system; interior: lobbies: millwork wall panels, terrazzo floor paving; typical floor: wall coverings, painted wood trim, custom-designed carpeting, owner's choice
Use Residential
Cost US$210 M (whole project)
Architect DeStefano and Partners, Ltd.
Structural engineer Chris P. Stefanos and Associates
Mechanical/Electrical engineer WMA Consulting Engineers, Ltd.
Client River East LLC
Contractor AMEC

The Essex on Lake Merritt

Location Oakland, California, USA
Completion date May 2002
Height 69.2 m/227 ft
Stories 20
Area 31,574 m²/339,873 ft² (gross)
Structure Post-tensioned concrete
Materials Stone, EIFS, green tinted glass, double glazed
Use Residential
Architect Architecture International Ltd. (John P. Sheehy, FAIA, RIBA; William J. Higgins, AIA; Sherry Caplan, IIDA)
Consulting architect Philip Banta and Associates
Interior design Architecture International, Ltd.
Structural engineer The Watry Design Group
Owner Essex Property Trust, Inc.
Development manager Lakeshore Partners LLC
General contractor Swinerton Builders

The Summit

Location Mount Nicholson, Hong Kong SAR, People's Republic of China
Completion date 2002
Height 207 m/679 ft
Stories 69
Area Site: 3045 m²/32,776 ft²; domestic gross floor: 15,225 m²/163,882 ft²
Structure In-situ reinforced concrete on bored end-bearing piles
Materials Exterior: structurally glazed unitized curtain wall spandrels in combination with conventional windows with painted aluminum frames, aluminum feature sills; interior: timber strip floors, plaster wall finishes (to apartments)
Use Residential
Architect Dennis Lau & Ng Chun Man Architects & Engineers (H.K.) Ltd
Structural engineer Skilling Ward Magnusson Barshire Inc; Maunsell Structural Consultants Ltd (Registered Engineer)
Mechanical engineer Associated Consulting Engineers Ltd
Client Hang Lung Development Company Ltd
Contractor Hong Kong Construction Co. Ltd

510 West Erie

Location Chicago, Illinois, USA
Completion date 2002
Height 86 m/280.7 ft
Stories 24
Area Site: 2831 m²/30,470 f²; building: 26,941 m²/290,000 f²
Structure Steel super-structure
Materials Exterior: steel, aluminum, glass windows and rails; interior lobbies: stone floors, wood, glass, concrete
Use Residential condominiums: 23 levels; lobby: ground floor
Cost US$27 M
Architect Lucien Lagrange Architects
Structural engineer Thornton Tomasetti Engineers
Mechanical engineer Advance Mechanical Systems, Inc.
Electrical engineer Innovative Building Concepts
Client Smithfield Properties
Contractor Wooton Construction Ltd

1322 Roxas Boulevard

Location Manila, Philippines
Scheduled for completion December 2002
Height 190 m; 203 m with spire
Stories 57
Area 111,000 m²
Structure Concrete moment frame
Materials Exterior: granite base with green tinted glass and painted concrete; interior: marble and natural wood with bronze features
Use Condominiums with amenities and retail
Architect Architecture International Ltd. (John P. Sheehy, FAIA, RIBA; William J. Higgins, AIA; Sherry Caplan, IIDA)
Associate architect GF & Partners
Structural engineer Aromin & Sy Associates; Ove Arup & Partners
Mechanical engineer RJ Calpo & Partners
Client Moldex Land, Inc.
Contractor D.M. Consunji, Inc.

Embassy House

Location Beijing, People's Republic of China
Completion date 2002
Height 100 m/328 ft
Stories 32 above grade + 3 basement
Area Site: 4778 m²/51,430 ft²; building: above grade: 40,689 m²/437,976 ft²; below grade: 13,238 m²/142,494 ft²
Structure Reinforced concrete
Materials Exterior: double-glazed curtain wall and metal panels; interior: high-end residential finishes including, stone, timber floors, dry-wall
Use Residential

Architect Hellmuth, Obata + Kassabaum (HOK)
Architect of record China Architecture Design & Research Group
Structural/Mechanical/Electrical engineer WSP
Client Hines Beijing
Contractor China State Construction Engineering Company Limited. (CSCBC)

Highcliff

Location Hong Kong SAR, People's Republic of China
Completion date Mid-2002
Height 252.3 m/828 ft
Stories 73
Area Site: 4366 m²/46,996 ft²; domestic gross floor: 34,931 m²/ 375,997 ft²
Structure In-situ reinforced concrete on end-bearing piles
Materials Exterior: structurally glazed unitized curtain wall with single leaf of reflecting blue tinted glass in combination with aluminum features and granite cladding at low level
Use Residential
Architect Dennis Lau & Ng Chun Man Architects & Engineers (H.K.) Ltd
Structural engineer Skilling Ward Magnusson Barshire Inc.; Canwest Consultants International Ltd (Structural Engineer)
Mechanical engineer Associated Consulting Engineers Ltd
Client Highcliff Investment Ltd
Contractor Hip Hing Construction Co. Ltd

Multifunctional Business Center with Residential Apartments

Location Moscow, Russia
Completion date 2002
Height 130.3 m/427 ft (with antenna); 118.5 m/389 ft (without antenna)
Stories 32 + 2 underground
Area Site: 4600 m²/49,514 ft²; total floor: 7000 m²/75,348 ft²
Structure Reinforced concrete
Materials Exterior: walls: ceramic granite; windows: wood and aluminum double-glazed system
Use Residential: levels 23–28; offices, commercial
Cost US$36 M
Architect George Mailov & Partners of Architectural-Planning-Artistic Firm Archizdrav Ltd
Structural/Mechanical/Electrical engineer Architectural-Planning-Artistic Firm Archizdrav Ltd
Client/Contractor BAMO Building Materials Ltd

Regent Tower

Location New York, New York, USA
Completion date January 2002

Height 158.5 m/520 ft
Stories 45
Area Site: 3966 m²/42,690 ft²; building: 40,457 m²/435,479 ft²
Structure Reinforced concrete
Use Retail: level 1; parking: levels 2–5; residential: levels 6–45; mechanical: cellar level
Cost US$72 M
Architect Frank Williams & Partners, Architects
Structural engineer Rosenwasser Grossman
Mechanical engineer IM Robbins
Owner The Moinian Group
Contractor Pavarini Construction Co.

Skybridge

Location Chicago, Illinois, USA
Completion date 2002
Height 128 m/420 ft
Stories 39
Area Site (gross): 10,752 m²/115,734 ft²; project (gross): 74,758 m²/804,695 ft²; residential: 39,458 m²/424,726 ft² parking: 15,379 m²/165,540 ft²; retail: 3716 m²/39,999 ft²
Structure and materials Cast concrete structure and exterior wall, glazing for windows, paint for the concrete
Use Four-story base: retail space and parking; ground level floor: commercial/retail space with first sublevel for customer parking facilities; four additional levels of parking facilities; residential (condominium) and retail
Cost US$95 M
Architect Perkins & Will
Structural engineer Samartano & Company
Construction manager MHC Construction LLC
MEP and fire protection WMA Consulting Engineers
Client/Owner Dearborn Development Corporation, LLC
Contractor Walsh Construction

St. Regis Museum Tower

Location San Francisco, California, USA
Completion date 2002
Height 146 m/479 ft
Stories 40
Area 51,588 m²/555,304 ft²
Structure Cast-in-place concrete
Materials Limestone, glass, precast concrete
Use Mixed-use: hotel, residential, 1858 m²/20,000 ft² African-American Cultural Center
Architect Skidmore, Owings & Merrill LLP
Associate architect Powell & Partners Architects
Structural engineer Skidmore, Owings & Merrill LLP
Mechanical/Electrical engineer Flack + Kurtz, Inc. in association with NBA Engineering, Inc.
Client St. Regis Museum Tower LLC
Contractor Webcor Builders

Students Accommodation in Laakhaven

Location The Hague, The Netherlands
Completion date May 2002
Height 62 m/203 ft
Stories 21
Area 1530 m²/16,469 ft²
Structure Concrete
Materials Brick, plaster
Use Residential
Cost F28 M/EUR12.705.846
Architect atelier PRO architekten
Structural engineer Van Eck
Mechanical engineer Deerns
Client DUWO Delft
Contractor Ballast NEDAM, Woningbouw Rotterdam

The Park Imperial at Random House

Location New York, New York, USA
Completion date 2002
Height 207.5 m/681 ft
Stories 50 (plus mechanical penthouse)
Area Building: 77,664 m²/836,000 ft²
Structure Combination steel and concrete (steel at the commercial floors—up to 27, and concrete at the residential floors—28 through 49)
Materials Granite, glass
Use Residential, offices
Architect Skidmore, Owings & Merrill LLP
Structural engineer Thornton Tomaseti
Mechanical/Electrical engineer Cosentini Associates, LLP
Client The Related Companies
Contractor Plaza Construction Company

Two Towers

Location Almere, The Netherlands
Completion date Expected 2002
Height 60 m/197 ft
Stories 22 above ground + 2 below
Area Floor: 24,750 m²/266,409 ft²
Structure Reinforced concrete
Materials U-profiled glass planks
Use Luxury residential apartments, including swimming pool, sauna, gym, winter garden, and marina
Cost EUR20.500.000
Architect de Architekten Cie. (ir. Frits van Dongen)
Design team Roel ten Bras, Caspar Smeets, René Bos, René Konijn

Structural engineer Pieters bouwtechniek bv, Delft
Mechanical/Electrical engineer T&H, Nieuwegein
Client Eurowoningen, Rotterdam

West One

Location Vancouver, British Columbia, Canada
Completion date October 2002
Height 108.5 m/356 ft (to roof); 116 m/381 ft (to top of concrete)
Stories 41
Area Site: 5070 m²/54,573 ft²; building: 22,600 m²/243,266 ft²
Structure Reinforced concrete
Materials Exterior: metal panel, concrete, sandstone, and glass in metal frames; interior: concrete, gypsum board, wood, glass, tile, and carpet
Use Residential (with sports club at base)
Cost US$34 M
Architect Hancock Brückner Eng + Wright Architects
Structural engineer Glotman Simpson Consulting Engineers
Mechanical engineer Sterling Cooper and Associates
Electrical engineer Arnold Nemetz and Associates
Client Pacific Place Development Corporation
Contractor Intertech Construction Ltd.

60 West Erie

Location Chicago, Illinois, USA
Completion date January 2003
Height 74 m/242 ft
Stories 26
Area Site: 813 m²/8753 ft²; building: 9646 m²/103,831 ft²
Structure Reinforced architectural cast-in-place concrete
Materials Exterior: architectural cast-in-place concrete, cast stone cladding, aluminum windows/window wall, steel and glass canopies, concrete terrace pavers; interior: stone flooring, wood flooring, drywall/ceilings, wood paneling, granite countertops
Use Residential: 25 levels; lobby: ground floor
Cost US$17.1 M
Architect Lucien Lagrange Architects
Structural engineer Halvorsen & Kaye Structural Engineers, PC
Mechanical/Electrical engineer WMA Consulting Engineers, Ltd
Client 60 West Erie, LLC
Contractor Bovis Lend Lease, Inc

235 West 51st Street

Location New York, New York, USA
Completion date June 2003
Height 178.2 m/584.6 ft
Stories 52
Area 30,935 m²/333,000 ft²

Structure Concrete
Materials Masonry exterior, drywall partitions, wood floors
Use Residential, offices
Architect Fox & Fowle Architects PC
Structural engineer Cantor Seinuk Group PC
Mechanical/Electrical engineer I.M. Robbins, P.C.
Client The Clarett Group
Contractor Bovis Lend Lease

250 East Pearson (The Pearson)

Location Chicago, Illinois, USA
Completion date 2003
Height 120 m/395 ft
Stories 36
Area Site: 1688 m²/18,170 ft²; building: 49,980 m²/538,000 ft²
Structure Cast-in-place concrete frame, painted concrete and glass skin
Materials Exterior: granite at base of building, precast concrete for first six floors, painted concrete aluminum glass wall; interior: unit: exposed concrete ceilings, painted gypsum board walls, hardwood floors; lobby: terrazzo floor, African cedar veneer paneled walls, granite
Use Residential
Cost US$62 M
Architect DeStefano and Partners, Ltd.
Structural engineer Chris P. Stefanos and Associates
Mechanical engineer Cosentini Associates; Midwesco Mechanical and Energy
Electrical engineer Cosentini Associates; Gurtz Electric Company
Client LR Development
Contractor McHugh Construction

425 Fifth Avenue

Location New York, New York, USA
Completion date June 2003
Height 188 m/617.1 ft
Stories 67
Area 30,193 m²/325,000 ft²
Materials Lobby: Madrona burl wood pilasters, with inset panels of Italian Cipollino marble; floor: two varieties of Cipollino stone, Crème Tirreno with a darker Classico accent; lighting: Baldinger pendant and sconce fixtures designed by Michael Graves; custom seating and reception desk: ebonized Santos rosewood; elevator cabs: ebonized Santos rosewood and burled woods, with Cipollino stone flooring; residential hallways: custom carpet, custom light fixtures, and wood-paneled entrance doors; kitchens: fruitwood cabinetry and granite countertops; bathrooms: Baldinger light fixtures, Dornbracht accessories, and Carrara marble floors; flooring for other rooms: Italian "Cosmo" black cherry or beech longstrip wood, with black slatelike Italian tile for the kitchens

Use Mechanical: level 9; "Fifth Avenue Club": levels 10–26; residential: 27–54
Design architect/Interior designer Michael Graves & Associates
Architect of record H. Thomas O'Hara, Architect, PLLC
Structural engineer DeSimone Consulting Engineers
Mechanical/Electrical/Plumbing (MEP) Cosentini Associates
Client RFR Davis & Partners, LP
Owner Davis & Partners, LP
General contractor/Construction manager Davis Construction Company, Inc.

840 North Lake Shore Drive

Location Chicago, Illinois, USA
Completion date June 2003
Height 99 m/325 ft
Stories 26 + 2 basements + 1 mechanical floor
Area Building: 34,187 m²/368,000 ft²
Structure Concrete
Materials Precast concrete and French limestone wall cladding, painted aluminum windows, wood and stone floors
Use Residential
Cost US$37 M (not including residential interior construction)
Architect Lucien Lagrange Architects
Structural engineer Thornton Tomasetti Engineers
Mechanical/Electrical engineer Environmental Systems Design, Inc.
Client Lakeshore LLC
Contractor James McHugh Construction Company

Al Hitmi Residential/ Office Complex

Location Doha, Qatar
Completion date 2003
Height 101 m/331 ft
Stories 26 above grade
Area Site: 7130 m²/76,747 ft²; building: 64,000 m²/ 688,896 ft²
Structure Reinforced concrete
Materials Limestone cladding in combination with clear anodized aluminum mullions and spandrels, blue tinted glass.
Use Residential: 22 levels; office: three levels; health club: level four
Cost $US52 M
Architect NORR Group Consultants International Limited
Structural/Mechanical/Electrical engineer NORR Group Consultants International Limited
Client Ali Bin Khalifa Al Hitmi & Co

Al Jaber Complex

Location Dubai, United Arab Emirates
Completion date February 2003 (estimated)
Height 199 m/653 ft
Stories 44 above grade + 2 below grade
Area Site: 9735 m²/104,788 ft²; building: 110,000 m²/ 1,184,040 ft²
Structure Reinforced concrete
Materials Granite cladding in combination with clear anodized aluminum mullions and spandrels, blue tinted glass
Use Residential: 16 levels; hotel: 24 levels; office: four levels
Cost $US85 M
Architect NORR Group Consultants International Limited
Structural/Mechanical/Mechanical engineer NORR Group Consultants International Limited
Client Al Jaber Investments
Contractor Al Habtoor/ Murray Robarts

Cove

Location Sydney, New South Wales, Australia
Completion date March 2003
Height 160 m/525 ft
Stories 45 above ground, 10 below ground
Area Building: 45,000 m²/484,380 ft²
Structure High-strength reinforced concrete
Materials Exterior: concrete, aluminum, stainless steel; interior: floors: carpets and stone; walls: concrete, plaster, plasterboard; ceilings: plasterboard
Use Residential
Architect Harry Seidler & Associates
Structural engineer Meinhardt (NSW) Pty Ltd
Mechanical/Electrical engineer AHW Engineering
Client Grocon International (Harrington Street) Pty Ltd
Contractor Grocon Constructors Pty Ltd

Espirito Santo Plaza

Location Miami, Florida, USA
Completion date 2003
Height 147 m/483 ft
Stories 36
Area Total: 111,480 m²/1,200,000 ft²
Structure Reinforced concrete, concrete beams
Materials Exterior: stainless steel, aluminum panels, insulating glass, museo blue stone, bleu de savoie stone; interior: stainless steel, laminated glass, Mount Airy stone, bleu de savoie stone, museo blue stone, calicata stone, English sycamore wood
Use Office: levels 2, 4–15; hotel: levels 3, 16–22; residential: levels 26–36; hotel back-of-house: 23–24; residential sky lobby and martini lounge: level 26; parking: 980 spaces
Cost US$160 M

Architect Kohn Pedersen Fox Associates, PC
Associate architect Plunkett & Associates
Structural engineer Leslie Robertson Associates R.L.L.P.
Mechanical/Electrical engineer Flack + Kurtz Consulting Engineers
Client Estoril, Inc.
Contractor Amec Construction Company

Four Seasons Hotel & Tower

Location Miami, Florida, USA
Completion date 2003
Height 54 m/780 ft
Stories 64 + rooftop mechanical floor
Area Building: 167,220 m²/1,799,956 ft²; pool deck: 6038 m²/64,993 ft²
Use Residential: levels 26–32, 35-64; hotel: levels 16–25; office: levels 8–14; retail: ground level
Cost US$350 M
Architect Gary Edward Handel + Associates; Bermello Ajamil & Partners
Structural engineer DeSimone Consulting Engineers
Mechanical engineer Hufsey Nicolaides Garcia Suarez
Landscape architect Office of Dan Kiley (pool deck)
Client Millennium Partners / Terremark
Contractor Bovis Lend Lease

Gallery Park Place

Location Chicago, Illinois, USA
Completion date 2003
Height 152 m/499 ft
Stories 46
Area Site: 1582 m²/17,030 ft²; building: 49,327 m²/ 530,000 ft²
Structure Concrete frame; masonry skin
Use Residential
Cost US$60 M
Architect DeStefano and Partners, Ltd.
Client Neighborhood Rejuvenation Partnership LP

The HarbourSide

Location Hong Kong SAR, People's Republic of China
Completion date August 2003
Height 242 m/794 ft
Stories 74 (three blocks)
Area Site: 13,386 m²/144,087 ft²; building: 128,845 m²/ 1,386,888 ft²
Structure Reinforced concrete
Materials Interior: natural stone; exterior: window wall system
Use Residential: 67 levels; clubhouse: two levels; carpark: five levels
Cost HK$2200 M
Architect P&T Architects and Engineers Ltd.

Structural engineer Ove Arup & Partners Hong Kong Ltd.

Mechanical/Electrical engineer Parsons Brinckerhoff (Asia) Ltd.

Client Hang Lung Properties Limited

Contractor Hip Hing Construction Co., Ltd.

Kingsbury on the Park

Location Chicago, Illinois, USA

Completion date 2003

Height 89 m/291.11 ft

Stories 25

Area Site: 2717 m²/29,250 ft²; building: 24,340 m²/262,000 ft²

Structure Steel super-structure on cast-in-place concrete

Materials Exterior: precast concrete, aluminum, glass windows

Use Residential condominiums: 18 levels; lobby: ground floor; retail

Cost US$27 M

Architect Lucien Lagrange Architects

Structural engineer Thornton Tomasetti Engineers

Mechanical engineer Advance Mechanical Systems, Inc.

Electrical engineer Innovative Building Concepts

Client Smithfield Properties

Contractor Wooton Construction Ltd

Kuzuha Tower City

Location Hirakata City, Osaka Prefecture, Japan

Completion date November 2003

Height 136.8 m/449 ft

Stories 41 + 1 below ground

Area Site: 14,402.08 m²/155,024 ft²; building: 7103.81 m²/76,465 ft²

Structure Reinforced concrete; fitness club: steel-framed reinforced concrete and steel

Materials Exterior: roof: asphalt exposed, heat-insulated, waterproofed method (flat roof); walls: lower part: granite-texture finish spray; upper part: porcelain mosaic tiles; openings: aluminum sash; interior: dwellings: floors: long PVC sheets (piping areas), marble (entrance); walls and ceilings: PVC cloth; entrances: floors and walls: marble; ceilings: emulsion paint; common-use corridors: floors: long PVC sheets; ceilings: sprayed tiles; balconies: floors: long PVC sheets; ceilings: lithing spray

Use Residential: levels 2–41; shops and fitness club: levels 1-4

Architect Takenaka Corporation

Structural/Mechanical/Electrical engineer Takenaka Corporation

Client Keihan Electric Railway Co., Ltd.

Contractor Takenaka Corporation; Keihan Construction Co., Ltd

Las Olas Riverhouse

Location Fort Lauderdale, Florida, USA

Completion date December 2003

Height 127.46 m/418.2 ft (main roof); 136.53 m/447.11 ft (highest point)

Stories 43 + service level + 5-level garage

Area Site: 7,689.03 m²/82,764 ft²; building: 113,063 m²/1,217,000 ft²

Structure Reinforced concrete shell

Materials Exterior walls: combination of concrete block walls with stucco finish and floor-to-ceiling colored glass; exterior: balcony exterior rails: glass, aluminum frames; canopies at the ground level: combination of aluminum, painted steel, perforated aluminum, and translucent panels; paving: combination of natural stone and concrete interlocking pavers; interior walls: combination of concrete block, and metal studs with drywall; floors: concrete, with wood/slate/marble in the common areas

Use Residential

Cost US$300 M

Architect The Sieger Suarez Architectural Partnership

Structural engineer Gopman Consulting Engineers

Mechanical/Electrical engineer Florida Engineering Service

Client Richard D. Zipes

Contractor Suffolk Construction

Lincoln Square

Location Bellevue, Washington, USA

Completion date 2003

Height Hotel/Residential tower: 137 m/450 ft; office tower: 126 m/412 ft; commercial podium structure: 24 m/80 ft

Stories Hotel/Residential tower: 42; residential: 23; hotel suites: 14; office tower 28; commercial podium structure: 5

Area Hotel/Residential tower: residential: 26,755 m²/288,000 ft²; hotel: 24,897 m²/268,000 ft²; office tower: 52,581 m²/566,000 ft²; commercial podium structure: 37,531 m²/404,000 ft²; total: 222,495 m²/2,395,000 ft²

Structure Office tower: structural steel floor frame with a reinforced concrete coupled core; hotel/residential: post-tensioned concrete flat floor with two reinforced concrete coupled cores; podium: structural steel beams and girders with braced steel frames; parking: reinforced concrete slab and slab bands with long span bands post-tensioned

Use Hotel, residential offices, commercial, retail, cinema, health club

Cost US$200 M

Design architect James KM Cheng Architects Inc.

Architect of record Mithun Partners

Project architect Terry Mott

Structural engineer Jones Kwong Kishi

Mechanical engineer Glumac International

Electrical engineer Arnold Nemetz & Associates

Client Westbank Investments (USA) Inc.

Contractor Bellvue Master LLC; Bovis – CM & D

Multifunctional Residential Complex

Location Moscow, Russia

Completion date 2003

Height 145 m/476 ft (with antenna); 135 m/423 ft (without antenna)

Stories 2; 4; 25; 35; 40 + 2 underground

Area Site: 20,000 m²/215,280 ft²; total floor: 108,500 m²/1,167,894 ft²; living: 52,158 m²/561,429 ft²

Structure Reinforced concrete

Materials Exterior: tile finishing with aluminum construction; windows: wood and aluminum double-glazed system

Use Residential, public, commercial, offices

Cost US$54 M

Architect George Mailov & Partners of Architectural-Planning-Artistic Firm Archizrav Ltd

Structural/Mechanical/Electrical engineer Architectural-Planning-Artistic Firm Archizdrav

Client/ Contractor JSC Konty Corporation

One Central Park at AOL Time Warner Center

Location New York, New York, USA

Completion date 2003

Height 228 m/750 ft

Stories 52

Area Building: 195,090 m²/2.1 million ft²; site: 14,306 m²/154,000 ft²

Structure Mixed: Steel and Reinforced Concrete

Materials Granite, metal, glass

Use Offices, hotel, residential, retail

Architect Skidmore, Owings & Merrill LLP

Residential architect Ismael Leyva Associates

AOL/TWI architect Perkins & Will

Hotel architect Brennan Beer Gorman/Architects

Jazz at Lincoln Center architect Rafael Viñoly Architects

Retail architect Elkus Manfredi Architects, Ltd.

Structural engineer Cantor Seinuk Group P.C.

Mechanical/Electrical engineer Cosentini Associates, LLP

Client The Related Companies

Contractor Bovis Lend Lease

The North Apartments

Location Sydney, New South Wales, Australia

Completion date 2003

Height 55 m/180 ft

Stories 15

Area Site: 403 m²/4338 ft²; gross: 8000 m²/86,112 ft²

Structure Concrete frame

Materials Exterior: precast concrete

Use Residential, commercial, retail

Architect Harry Seidler & Associates

Structural engineer Birzulis Associates Pty Ltd
Mechanical/Electrical engineer Norman Disney & Young
Client Goulburn J.V. Pty Ltd; Gregmal Corporation Pty Ltd
Contractor Lateral Developments

Branksome Tower III

Location Hong Kong SAR, People's Republic of China
Completion date 2004
Height 168 m/551 ft
Stories 44
Area Site: 7320 m²/78,792 ft²; building: 13,277 m²/142,914 ft²
Structure Reinforced concrete
Use Residential: 39 levels; clubhouse: two levels; carpark: five levels
Cost HK$240 M
Architect P&T Architects and Engineers Ltd.
Structural engineer WSP Hong Kong Ltd.
Mechanical/Electrical engineer Far East Consulting Engineers Ltd.
Client Kerry Properties (HK) Ltd.

LDC Kennedy Town Development

Location Hong Kong SAR, People's Republic of China
Completion date November 2004
Height 178 m/584 ft, 170 m/558 ft, 165 m/541 ft
Stories 42–45 + 5-story podium
Area Site: 3744 m²/40,300 ft², 2331 m²/25,090.8 ft²; building: 42,033 m²/452,443 ft², 23,066 m²/248,282 ft²
Structure Reinforced concrete
Materials Exterior: mainly ceramic tiles; interior: tiles, timber, granite, paint
Use Residential
Cost HK$970 M
Architect Ronald Lu & Partners (HK) Ltd.
Structural/Mechanical/Electrical engineer WSP Hong Kong Ltd.
Client New World Development Ltd.
Contractor Hip Hing Construction Co. Ltd.

Prinsenhof (Tower and Hotel)

Location The Hague, The Netherlands
Completion date 2004
Height Tower: 109 m/358 ft; hotel: 70 m/230 ft
Stories Tower: 26; hotel: 23
Area Tower: 32,900 m²/354,135 ft²; hotel: 14,738 m²/158,640 ft²
Structure Reinforced concrete
Materials Tower: brick tiles in steel frames; hotel: interior: glass, steel, natural stone and wood; exterior: brickwork (two colors)

Use Offices, hotel
Cost F92 M/EUR41.747.779
Architect atelier PRO architekten (offices, hotel); Kraaijvanger Urbis (tower); Architectengroep (apartments)
Structural engineer Arcadis
Mechanical/Electrical engineer Deerns (tower); Valstar Simonis, Rijswijk (hotel)
Client SFB Vastgoed Amsterdam
Contractor BAM / NBM Bouw, Bunnik

Riparian Plaza

Location Brisbane, Queensland, Australia
Completion date February 2004
Height 200 m/656 ft
Stories 53
Area Site: 6723 m²/72,366 ft²; building: 70,000 m²/753,480 ft²
Structure Concrete
Materials Polished granite, tinted glass, painted concrete
Use Residential, commercial, retail
Architect Harry Seidler & Associates
Structural engineer Robert Bird
Mechanical/Electrical engineer Norman Disney & Young, Brisbane
Client Riverside Development Pty Ltd
Contractor Multiplex Constructions (Qld) Pty Ltd

The Pinnacle

Location Chicago, Illinois, USA
Completion date January 2004
Height 163 m/535 ft
Stories 48 + 1 basement + 2 mechanical penthouse
Area Building: 61,035 m²/657,000 ft²
Structure Reinforced concrete
Materials Limestone and precast concrete at base, tinted glass and aluminum window wall at tower
Use Residential
Cost US$110 M (estimated)
Architect Lucien Lagrange Architects
Structural engineer Halvorsen & Kaye Structural Engineers, PC
Mechanical/Electrical engineer Environmental Systems Design, Inc.
Client The Fordham Company
Contractor AMEC

Tsuen Wan Serviced Apartments

Location Tsuen Wan, Hong Kong SAR, People's Republic of China
Completion date 2004
Height 210 m/689 ft

Stories Block A: 43; Block B: 56
Area Site: 10,416 m²/112,118 ft²; domestic gross floor: 103,404 m²/1,113,040 ft²
Structure In-situ reinforced concrete on end-bearing piles
Materials Exterior: conventional windows with painted aluminum frames in combination with glazed ceramic tiles; penthouse plantrooms with aluminum-feature fins; interior: polished granite to lobbies
Use Residential with associated recreational, catering, and back-of-house facilities
Architect Dennis Lau & Ng Chun Man Architects & Engineers (H.K.) Ltd
Structural engineer Ove Arup & Partners Hong Kong Ltd
Mechanical engineer J Roger Preston Ltd
Client Sun Hung Kai Real Estate Agency Ltd

Freshwater Place

Location Melbourne, Victoria, Australia
Completion date June 2005
Height First residential tower: 220 m/722 ft; second residential tower: 200 m/656 ft; commercial tower: 165 m/541 ft; strata commercial: 53 m/174 ft; retail: 3 m/10 ft (ground floor only)
Stories First residential tower: 69; second residential tower: 64; commercial tower: 40; strata commercial: 14; retail: 1
Area First residential tower: 105,000 m²/1,130,220 ft²; second residential tower: 92,000 m²/990,288 ft²; commercial tower: 65,000 m²/699,660 ft²; strata commercial: 40,000 m²/430,560 ft²; retail: 8000 m²/86,112 ft²; site: 17,750 m²/191,061 ft²
Use First residential tower: retail: ground level; car parking: levels 1–7; residential: levels 8–68; second residential tower: retail: ground level; car parking: levels 1–7; commercial: levels 8–12; residential: levels 13–63; commercial tower: retail: ground level; car parking: levels 1–7; commercial: 8–39; strata commercial: commercial: ground–level 14; retail: retail: ground
Cost A$750 M (approximately)
Architect Bates Smart Pty Ltd
Structural engineer Winward Structures
Mechanical/Electrical engineer Norman Disney & Young (residential); Simpson Kotzman (commercial)
Client Australand Holdings Ltd

Herzl Tower

Location Ramat Gan, Israel
Completion date 2005
Height 143.6 m/471 ft
Stories 46 floors above grade; 3 levels below grade
Area Above grade: 39,330 m²/423,348 ft²; below grade: 24,500 m²/263,718 ft²
Structure Reinforced concrete
Materials Exterior: glass, aluminum and stainless steel curtain wall; interior (public spaces): marble, wood paneling, carpet

Use Residential

Architect Eli Attia Architects

Structural engineer CBM Engineers, Inc

Client Ruben Development Co. Ltd.

King's Park Residential Development

Location Kowloon, Hong Kong SAR, People's Republic of China

Completion date 2005

Height 108 m/354 ft

Stories 29

Area Site: 36,006 m²/387,568 ft²; domestic gross floor: 84,000 m²/904,176 ft²

Structure In-situ reinforced concrete on friction piles

Materials Exterior: conventional windows with painted aluminum frames in combination with glazed ceramic tiles to apartment towers, curtain walling in combination with polished granite and glazed ceramic tiles to podium

Use Residential

Architect Dennis Lau & Ng Chun Man Architects & Engineers (H.K.) Ltd

Structural engineer Wong Pak Lam & Associates

Mechanical engineer Meinhardt Consulting Engineers

Client Grace Sign Co.

Contractor Vibro

Orient City Garden

Location Pudong District, Shanghai, People's Republic of China

Completion date First phase: 2000–2003; last phase (estimated): 2005

Height 79.8 m/261.8 ft

Stories 27

Area Approximately 270,621 m²/ft² will be completed in 2003

Structure Shear wall

Materials Exterior: wall tiles, granite and aluminum plate

Use Residential

Architect East China Architectural Design & Research Institute Co., Ltd. (ECADI)

Developer Oriental City Garden Co., Ltd.

Pe'at Yam Tower

Location Herzlia, Israel

Completion date 2005

Height 131.3 m/431 ft

Stories 41 above grade + 3 below grade

Area Above grade: 28,091 m²/302,371 ft²; below grade: 13,422 m²/144,474 ft²

Structure Reinforced concrete

Materials Exterior: glass, aluminum and stainless steel curtain wall; interior (public spaces): marble, granite, wood

paneling, carpet

Use Residential, hotel

Architect Eli Attia Architects

Structural engineer CBM Engineers, Inc

Client Haksharat Hayeshuv Kakshuri

Willem Ruys – Müller Pier

Location Rotterdam, The Netherlands

Completion date Scheduled 2005

Height 72.2 m/237 ft

Stories 23 above ground + 2 below

Area Floor: 16,360 m²/176,099 ft²

Structure Reinforced concrete

Materials Exterior: black slate; interior: wood, slate, and stucco

Use Luxury residential

Cost EUR14.000.000

Architect de Architekten Cie. (ir. Frits van Dongen)

Design team Adriaan Mout, René Bos

Structural engineer Van Ruitenburg - ABC, Rotterdam

Mechanical/Electrical engineer T&H, Nieuwegein

Client Eurowoningen, Rotterdam

7 South Dearborn

Location Chicago, Illinois, USA

Completion date To be determied

Height 472 m/1550 ft; 610 m/2000 ft with antennae

Stories 108

Area Residential: 176,510 m²/1.9 million ft²; office space: 71,068 m²/765,000 ft²; communications facilities: 8417 m²/90,600 ft²; retail: 6967 m²/75,000 ft²

Structure Reinforced concrete core

Materials Glass and steel exterior

Use Residential, office, retail

Architect Skidmore, Owings & Merrill LLP

Structural/Mechanical/Electrical engineer Skidmore, Owings & Merrill LLP

Boylston Square

Location Boston, Massachusetts, USA

Completion date To be determined

Height 198 m/675 ft

Stories 59

Area Building: 130,060 m²/1,399,966 ft²

Materials Brick and curtain wall

Use Residential: levels 27–59; extended stay: levels 14–26; hotel: levels 6–14; retail: ground level

Cost US$200 M

Architect Gary Edward Handel + Associates

Associate architect CBT/Childs Bertman Tseckares, Inc.

Client Millennium Partners / MDA Associates

Cityfront Center Plaza

Location Chicago, Illinois, USA

Completion date To be determined

Height 215 m/704 ft

Stories 59

Area Site: 6521 m²/70,192 ft²; building: 72,116 m²/776,257 ft²

Structure Reinforced concrete

Materials Aluminum and glass windows and curtain wall

Use Hotel: levels 1–21; residential: levels 23–59

Architect Lohan Caprile Goettsch architects

Structural engineer Skilling Ward Magnusson Barkshire

Mechanical engineer Cosentini Associates

Client Sunbelt Realty

Elephant & Castle Eco-towers

Location London, United Kingdom

Completion date To be determined

Height 138 m/453 ft

Stories Tower 1: 35; tower 2 and 3: 12

Area Site: 68.8 hectares/170 acres; tower 1: gross: 25,669 m2/276,304 ft²; net: 30,015 m²/323,095 ft²; plantation and circulation: 4107 m²/44,209 ft²; towers 2 and 3: gross: 8896 m²/95,765 ft²; net: 7384 m²/79,485 ft²; plantation and circulation: 1512 m²/16,280 ft²

Structure Reinforced concrete

Materials Metal panels, aluminum sunshades and louvers, glass, natural stone, photovoltaic panels, brickwork

Use Residential, retail, hotel, offices

Architect T. R. Hamzah & Yeang Sdn. Bhd.

Project engineer (structural/mechanical/electrical) Battle McCarthy

Migdal Zedek

Location Tel Aviv, Israel

Completion date To be determined

Height 164 m/538 ft

Stories 33

Area 48,000 m²/516,672 ft²

Use Residential

Architect Gabai Architects Inc.

Client Nehoshtan Properties, Almog Yam-Suf Construction

Index
Architects

Selected Bibliography

Books

Aillaud, Emile, *Chanteloup Les Vignes: Quartier "La Noé"*, Fayard, Paris, 1978.

Ali, Mir M., *Art of the Skyscraper: The Genius of Fazlur Khan*, Rizzoli, New York, 2001.

Alpern, Andrew, *Apartments for the Affluent: A Historical Survey of buildings in New York*, McGraw-Hill Book Company, New York, 1975.

Alpern, Andrew, *The New York Apartment Houses of Rosario Candela and James Carpenters*, Acanthus Press, New York, 2001.

Aregger, Hans & Glaus, Otto, *Highrise Building and Urban Design*, Frederick A. Praeger, New York/Washington, 1967.

Binder, Georges, ed., *Tall Buildings of Asia & Australia*, The Images Publishing Group, Melbourne, 2001.

Carter, Peter, *Mies van der Rohe at Work*, Praeger Publishers, New York/Washington, 1974.

Conway, Donald J., ed., *Human Response to Tall Buildings*, Dowden, Hutchinson & Ross, Stroudsburg, 1977.

Crosbie, Michael J., *The Architecture of Frank Williams*, Rockport Publishers, Rockport, 1997.

Dart, Susan, *Edward Dart Architect*, Evanston Publishing, Evanston, 1993.

Gaillard, Marc, *Andrault-Parat Architectes*, Dunod, Paris, 1978.

Glibota, Ante & Edelmann, *Goldberg: Chicago 150 Ans d'Architecture/Chicago 150 Years of Architecture: 1833–1983*, Paris Art Center/Musée-Galerie de la SEITA, Paris, 1983.

Glendinning, Miles & Muthesius, Stefan, *Tower Block: Modern Public Housing in England, Scotland, Wales and Northern Ireland*, Yale University Press, New Haven/London, 1994.

Hassenpflug, Gustav & Peters, Paulhaus, *Ecrans, tours et collines: L'habitat en hauteur aujourd'hui et demain*, Dunod, Paris, 1971.

Hornbeck, James S., Senior Editor, *Apartments and Dormitories*, McGraw-Hill Book Company, New York/Toronto/London, 1962.

Jones, Peter Blundell, *Hans Scharoun*, Fayard, London, Phaidon, 1995, reprinted in paperback 1997, 2000.

Lambert, Phyllis, ed., *Mies in America*, Canadian Centre for Architecture, Montreal/Whitney Museum of American Art, New York/Harry N. Abrams, New York, 2001.

Mario Roberto Alvarez y Asociados, *Arq. Mario Roberto Alvarez y Asociados-Obras 1937–1993*, Mario Roberto Alvarez y Asociados, Buenos Aires, 1993.

Mierop, Caroline in collaboration with Binder, Georges, *Skyscrapers – Higher and Higher*, Norma/Institut français d'Architecture, Paris, 1995.

Oosterman, Arjen, *Woningbouw in Nederland/Housing in the Netherlands/*, NAI Uitgevers, Rotterdam, 1996.

Paul, Samuel, *Apartments: Their Design and Developments*, Reinhold Publishing Corporation, New York/Amsterdam/London, 1967.

Polshek, James Stewart, *James Stewart Polshek: Context and Responsibility*, Rizzoli, New York, 1988.

Ragon, Michel, *Goldberg: Dans La Ville/On the City*, Paris Art Center, Paris, 1985.

Ragon, Michel, *La cité de l'an 2000*, Casterman, Tournai, 1968.

Rubin, Sy & Mandell, Johnathan, Sy, *Trump Tower*, Lyle Stuart, Secaucus, 1984.

Ruttenbaum, Steven, *Mansions in the Clouds: The Skyscrapers Palazzi of Emery Roth*, Balsam Press, New York, 1986.

Saliga, Pauline A., ed., *The Sky's the Limit: A Century of Chicago Skyscrapers*, Rizzoli, New York, 1990.

Stern, Robert A.M., Mellins, Thomas & Fishman, David, *New York 1960*, The Monacelli Press, Rotterdam, 1995.

Stoller, Ezra & Kahn, Yasmin Sabina, *The John Hancock Center*, Princeton Architectural Press, New York, 2000.

Trump, Donald J. & Schwartz, Tony, *The Art of the Deal*, Random House, New York, 1987.

Tuccille, Jerome, *Trump*, Donald I. Fine, New York, 1985, 1986.

Xiao, Erbin & Xu, Xiaofei, *Building Design Institute of Ministry of Construction*, Heilongjiang Science and Technology Press, Harbin, 1998.

Wiseman, Carter, *I.M. Pei: A Profile in American Architecture*, Harry N. Abrams, New York, 1990.

Zeckendorf, William with McCreary, Edward, *Zeckendorf*, Holt, Rinehart and Winston, New York/Chicago/San Francisco, 1970.

___. *Dennis Lau & Ng Chun Man: Selected and Current Works*, The Images Publishing Group, Melbourne, 2002.

___. *Harry Seidler: Selected and Current Works*, The Images Publishing Group, Melbourne, 1997.

___. *Hoogbouw in Nederland/High-rise in the Netherlands/: 1990–2000*, NAI Uitgevers, Rotterdam, 1997.

___. *Michael Graves: Selected and Current Works*, The Images Publishing Group, Melbourne, 1999.

___. *P&T Group: 130 Years Architecture in Asia*, Pace Publishing, Hong Kong SAR, 1998.

Periodicals and other material

"A Florentine touch". *Architectural Record*, New York, July 1983: pp. 96–7.

"Are building designs safe from plagiarism?". *Business Week*, New York, July 9, 1984: p. 34.

"Australians battle for tallest residences". *Architectural Record*, New York, July 2001: p. 30.

Braybrooke, Susan, "To old hands talk about housing". *Architectural Record*, New York, February 1988: pp. 122–35.

"Cool high-rise". *The Architectural Review*, London, September 1994: pp. 26–31.

Day, Norman, "Republic", *Architecture Australia*, Sydney, Port Melbourne, January/February 2000: pp. 36–43.

Doubilet, Susan, "Peeping into Pandora's box". *Progressive Architecture*, New York, July 1982: pp. 82–7.

Fisher, Ellen, *The Building of Metropolitan Tower*, Harry Macklowe Real Estate Company, New York, 1985.

Fisher, Thomas, "The New Urban Design". *Progressive Architecture*, New York, March 1988: pp. 79–92.

Futagawa, Yukio, *GA Document*, nr. 7, Global Architecture, ADA Edita Tokyo, Tokyo, August 1983.

Gandee, Charles K., "A 46-story apartment tower in Manhattan". *Architectural Record*, New York, December 1980: pp. 82–7.

Handel, Gary E., Middleton, Blake and Resclavo, Glenn, "Vertical urbanism", *Urban Land*, Washington, May 2002: pp. 64–70.

"Hong Kong Housing Authority-Housing Conference 24–25 November 1999: Better Homes in the Next Millennium". *Building Journal Hong Kong-China*, Hong Kong, October 1999: pp. 38–71.

"Lake Point Tower". *Architectural Record*, New York, October 1969.

Mengel, Robert, *Coops & Condos: Chicago's ultimate sourcebook*, Data Based Publishing, Chicago, 1992.

Metzger, Robert P., *Der Scutt Retrospective*, Reading Public Museum, Reading, 1996.

"Moving with the times: Ronald Lu & Partners 25th anniversary". *Building Journal Hong Kong-China*, Hong Kong, July 2001: pp. 36–57.

Millette, Daniel, "Reaching New Heights". *Canadian Architect*, Don Mills, November 2001: pp. 20–3.

"Mixed-use in a single building is still a relatively new idea; the Galleria in New York explores this route toward more productive buildings". *Architectural Record*, New York, December 1975.

Novgorodsky, L., "La Cité-Modèle du Heysel à Bruxelles". *La Technique des Travaux*, Liège, September-October 1966: pp. 258–74.

Novgorodsky, L., "Le Centre International Rogier à Bruxelles". *La Technique des Travaux*, Liège, July-August 1962: pp. 194–217.

"On High-Rise Residences", *Process: Architecture, nr. 64*, Process Architecture, Tokyo, January 1986.

"Once again, primary colors". *Architectural Record*, New York, July 1983: pp. 92–5.

Reuber, Paul, "Hong Kong: Culture of Density". *Canadian Architect*, Don Mills, August 1997: pp. 26–9.

Strickland, Roy, "At home in the city: Reviving the urban apartment house". *Architectural Record*, New York, June 1986: pp. 93–9.

Taylor III, Alex, "Smart moves for hard times". *Fortune International*, New York, December 8, 1986: pp. 25–30.

"The structural architecture of Chicago", *Process: Architecture, nr. 102*, Process Architecture, Tokyo, April 1992.

"Tregunter Tower: High in sky". *Building Journal Hong Kong-China*, Hong Kong, November 1993: pp. 62–4.

"Two buildings in Amsterdam and Harlingen". *Architecture + Detail*, nr. 15, Karl Krämer Verlag, Stuttgart, 2000: pp. 48–53.

"Urban Housing: Family of Four". *Canadian Architect*, Don Mills, August 1999: pp. 24–7.

Van Riel, Wijnand, "Residential building in China-No Open Kitchen". *Statement on real estate/over vastgoed*, ING Vastgoed, The Hague, Spring 2002: pp. 50–5.

Wiseman, Carter, "Good neighbor policy". *Architectural Record*, New York, July 1984: pp. 86–95.

___. *Donald Trump-Deal maker*, A&E Television Network-Biography, New York, 1995; (video tape).

___. *Hong Kong Housing Development 2000-Book 1*, China Trend Building Press, Hong Kong, November 1999.

___. *Hong Kong Housing Development 2000-Book 2*, China Trend Building Press, Hong Kong, December 1999.

___. *Hong Kong Housing Development 2001-Book 3*, China Trend Building Press, Hong Kong, 2000.

___. *Manhattan Condo Book 1998–99: The Complete Guide to Manhattan Condominiums*, Yale Robbins, New York, 1998.

___. *Manhattan Condominium*, West 61 Company, New York, 1994.